VIRTUALIZATION

ESSENTIALS

SECOND EDITION

VIRTUALIZATION

ESSENTIALS

SECOND EDITION

Matthew Portnoy

SYBEX®

A Wiley Brand

Executive Editor: Jody Lefevere
Development Editor: Kelly Talbot
Technical Editor: Van Van Noy
Production Editor: Barath Kumar Rajasekaran
Copy Editor: Kathy Grider-Carlyle
Editorial Manager: Mary Beth Wakefield
Production Manager: Kathleen Wisor
Proofreader: Nancy Bell
Indexer: Johnna VanHoose Dinse
Project Coordinator, Cover: Brent Savage
Cover Designer: Wiley
Cover Image: ©DrHitch/Shutterstock

Copyright © 2016 by John Wiley & Sons, Inc., Indianapolis, Indiana
Published simultaneously in Canada

ISBN: 978-1-119-26772-0
ISBN: 978-1-119-26774-4 (ebk.)
ISBN: 978-1-119-26773-7 (ebk.)

Manufactured in the United States of America

For general information on our other products and services or to obtain technical support, please contact our Customer Care Department within the U.S. at (877) 762-2974, outside the U.S. at (317) 572-3993 or fax (317) 572-4002.

Wiley publishes in a variety of print and electronic formats and by print-on-demand. Some material included with standard print versions of this book may not be included in e-books or in print-on-demand. If this book refers to media such as a CD or DVD that is not included in the version you purchased, you may download this material at http://booksupport.wiley.com. For more information about Wiley products, visit www.wiley.com.

Library of Congress Control Number: 2016944315

10 9 8 7 6 5 4 3 2 1

*To my friends
and family,
near and far.*

Acknowledgments

A project is rarely a solo affair, and this one depended on a large crew for it to arrive. I need to thank Scott Lowe for shoveling the path and aiming me at the correct door. My deepest gratitude goes to Mark Milow for helping me climb aboard this rocket, to Mike Szfranski for your always open book of knowledge, to Nick Gamache for the insights, and to Tony Damiano for keeping our vehicle in the fast lane.

My heartfelt thanks also go to the virtual team at Sybex: Kelly Talbot, Stephanie McComb, Van Van Noy, Kathy Grider-Carlyle, and Barath Kumar Rajasekaran for their steadfast support, forcing me to improve with each chapter and keeping it all neat and clean. Special thanks go to Agatha Kim for getting this whole adventure rolling.

I need to thank my family beginning with my parents, teachers both, who instilled me with a love of reading and writing and set me on a path that somehow led here. Thank you to my boys, Lucas and Noah, who fill our days with laughter and music. And finally, a huge hug to my wife, Elizabeth, who encouraged me even when she had no idea what I was writing about. I love you.

About the Author

 *Matthew Portnoy* has been an information technology professional for more than 30 years, working in organizations such as NCR, Sperry/Unisys, Stratus Computer, Oracle, and VMware. He has been in the center of many of the core technological trends during this period, including the birth of the PC, client-server computing, fault tolerance and availability, the rise of the Internet, and now virtualization, which is the foundation for cloud computing. As both a presales and post-sales analyst, he has worked with all of the disciplines computing offers, including innumerable programming languages, operating systems, application design and development, database operations, networking, security, availability, and virtualization. He has spoken at the industry's largest virtualization conference, VMworld, and is a frequent speaker at user group meetings. He also has been teaching virtualization and database classes as an adjunct professor at Wake Tech Community College in Raleigh, North Carolina, since 2007.

Contents at a Glance

Contents

CHAPTER 4   Creating a Virtual Machine   55

CHAPTER 5   Installing Windows on a Virtual Machine   81

CHAPTER 6   Installing Linux on a Virtual Machine   107

INTRODUCTION

We live in an exciting time. The information age is exploding around us, giving us access to dizzying amounts of data the instant it becomes available. Smart phones and tablets provide an untethered experience that offers streaming video, audio, and other media formats to just about any place on the planet. Even people who are not "computer literate" use Facebook to catch up with friends and family, use Google to research a new restaurant choice and print directions to get there, or Tweet their reactions once they have sampled the fare. The budding Internet-of-things will only catalyze this data eruption. The infrastructure supporting these services is also growing exponentially, and the technology that facilitates this rapid growth is virtualization.

On one hand, virtualization is nothing more than an increasingly efficient use of existing resources that delivers huge cost savings in a brief amount of time. On the other, virtualization also offers organizations new models of application deployment for greater uptime to meet user expectations, modular packages to provide new services in minutes instead of weeks, and advanced features that bring automatic load balancing, scalability without downtime, self-healing, self-service provisioning, and many other capabilities to support business-critical applications that improve on traditional architecture. Large companies have been using this technology for 10 to 15 years, while smaller and medium-sized businesses are just getting there now. Some of them might miss the movement altogether and jump directly to cloud computing, the next evolution of application deployment. Virtualization is the foundation for cloud computing as well.

This quantum change in our world echoes similar trends from our recent history as electrical power and telephony capabilities spread and then changed our day-to-day lives. During those periods, whole industries sprang up out of nothing, providing employment and opportunity to people who had the foresight and chutzpah to seize the moment. That same spirit and opportunity is available today as this area is still being defined and created right before our eyes. If not virtualization vendors, there are hardware partners who provide servers, networking vendors for connectivity, storage partners for data storage, and everyone provides services. Software vendors are designing and deploying new applications specifically for these new architectures. Third parties are creating tools to monitor and manage these applications and infrastructure areas. As cloud computing begins to become the de facto model for development, deployment, and maintaining application services, this area will expand even further.

The first generation of virtualization specialists acquired their knowledge out of necessity: They were server administrators who needed to understand the new infrastructure being deployed in their data centers. Along the way, they picked up some networking knowledge to manage the virtual networks, storage knowledge to connect to storage arrays, and application information to better interface with the application teams. Few people have experience in all of those areas. Whether you have some virtualization experience or none at all, this text will give you the foundation to understand what virtualization is, why it is a crucial portion of today's and tomorrow's information technology infrastructure, and the opportunity to explore and experience one of the most exciting and fastest growing topics in technology today.

Good reading and happy virtualizing!

Who Should Read This Book

This text is designed to provide the basics of virtualization technology to someone who has little or no prior knowledge of the subject. This book will be of interest to you if you are an IT student looking for information about virtualization or if you are an IT manager who needs a better understanding of virtualization fundamentals as part of your role. This book might also be of interest if you are an IT professional who specializes in a particular discipline (such as server administration, networking, or storage) and are looking for an introduction into virtualization or cloud computing as a way to advance inside your organization.

The expectation is that you have:

- ▶ Some basic PC experience
- ▶ An understanding of what an operating system is and does
- ▶ Conceptual knowledge of computing resources (CPU, memory, storage, and network)
- ▶ A high-level understanding of how programs use resources

This text would not be of interest if you are already a virtualization professional and you are looking for a guidebook or reference.

What You Need

The exercises and illustrations used in this text were created on a system with Windows 10 as the operating system. VMware Workstation Player version 12 is used as the virtualization platform. It is available as a free download from http://downloads.vmware.com/d/. It is recommended that you have at least 2 GB of memory, though more will be better. The installation requires 150 MB of disk storage. Also used is Oracle VirtualBox version 5. It is available as a free download from `http://www.virtualbox.org`. It is recommended that you have at least 2GB of memory. VirtualBox itself requires only about 30 MB of disk storage, but virtual machines will require more.

The examples demonstrate the creation and use of two virtual machines: one running Windows 10, the other running Ubuntu Linux. You will need the installation media for those as well. Each of the virtual machines requires about 30 GB of disk space.

What Is Covered in This Book

Here's a glance at what is in each chapter.

Chapter 1: Understanding Virtualization   Introduces the basic concepts of computer virtualization beginning with mainframes and continues with the computing trends that have led to current technologies.

Chapter 2: Understanding Hypervisors   Focuses on hypervisors, the software that provides the virtualization layer, and compares some of the current offerings in today's marketplace.

Chapter 3: Understanding Virtual Machines   Describes what a virtual machine is composed of, explains how it interacts with the hypervisor that supports its existence, and provides an overview of managing virtual machine resources.

Chapter 4: Creating a Virtual Machine   Begins with the topic of converting existing physical servers into virtual machines and provides a walkthrough of installing VMware Workstation Player and Oracle VirtualBox, the virtualization platforms used in this text, and a walkthrough of the creation of a virtual machine.

Chapter 5: Installing Windows on a Virtual Machine   Provides a guide for loading Microsoft Windows in the created virtual machine and then describes configuration and tuning options.

Chapter 6: Installing Linux on a Virtual Machine   Provides a guide for loading Ubuntu Linux in a virtual machine and then walks through a number of configuration and optimization options.

Chapter 7: Managing CPUs for a Virtual Machine   Discusses how CPU resources are virtualized and then describes various tuning options and optimizations. Included topics are hyper-threading and Intel versus AMD.

Chapter 8: Managing Memory for a Virtual Machine   Covers how memory is managed in a virtual environment and the configuration options available. It concludes with a discussion of various memory optimization technologies that are available and how they work.

Chapter 9: Managing Storage for a Virtual Machine   Examines how virtual machines access storage arrays and the different connection options they can utilize. Included are virtual machine storage options and storage optimization technologies such as deduplication.

Chapter 10: Managing Networking for a Virtual Machine   Begins with a discussion of virtual networking and how virtual machines use virtual switches to communicate with each other and the outside world. It concludes with virtual network configuration options and optimization practices.

Chapter 11: Copying a Virtual Machine   Discusses how virtual machines are backed up and provisioned through techniques such as cloning and using templates. It finishes with a powerful feature called snapshots that can preserve a virtual machine state.

Chapter 12: Managing Additional Devices in Virtual Machines   Begins by discussing virtual machine tools, vendor-provided application packages that optimize a virtual machine's performance, and concludes with individual discussions of virtual support for other peripheral devices like CD/DVD drives and USB devices.

Chapter 13: Understanding Availability   Positions the importance of availability in the virtual environment and then discusses various availability technologies that protect individual virtual machines, virtualization servers, and entire data centers from planned and unplanned downtime.

Chapter 14: Understanding Applications in a Virtual Machine   Focuses on the methodology and practices for deploying applications in a virtual environment. Topics include application performance, using resource pools, and deploying virtual appliances.

Appendix: Answers to Additional Exercises   Contains all of the answers to the additional exercises found at the end of every chapter.

Glossary   Lists the most commonly used terms throughout the book.

How to Contact the Author

I welcome feedback from you about this book or about books you'd like to see from me in the future. You can reach me by writing to mportnoyvm@gmail.com.

Sybex strives to keep you supplied with the latest tools and information you need for your work. Please check their website at www.wiley.com/go /virtualizationess2e, where we'll post additional content and updates that supplement this book if the need arises.

CHAPTER 1

Understanding Virtualization

We are in the midst of a substantial change in the way computing services are provided. As a consumer, you surf the Web on your cell phone, get directions from a GPS device, and stream movies and music from the cloud. At the heart of these services is *virtualization*—the ability to abstract a physical server into a virtual machine.

In this chapter, you will explore some of the basic concepts of virtualization, review how the need for virtualization came about, and learn why virtualization is a key building block to the future of computing.

▶ **Describing virtualization**

▶ **Understanding the importance of virtualization**

▶ **Understanding virtualization software operation**

Describing Virtualization

Over the last 50 years, certain key trends created fundamental changes in how computing services are provided. Mainframe processing drove the sixties and seventies. Personal computers, the digitization of the physical desktop, and client/server technology headlined the eighties and nineties. The Internet, boom and bubble, spanned the last and current centuries and continues today. We are, though, in the midst of another of those model-changing trends: virtualization.

Virtualization is a disruptive technology, shattering the status quo of how physical computers are handled, services are delivered, and budgets are allocated. To understand why virtualization has had such a profound effect on today's computing environment, you need to have a better understanding of what has gone on in the past.

The word *virtual* has undergone a change in recent years. Not the word itself, of course, but its usage has been expanded in conjunction with the expansion of computing, especially with the widespread use of the Internet and smart phones. Online applications have allowed us to shop in virtual stores, examine potential vacation spots through virtual tours, and even keep our virtual books in virtual libraries. Many people invest considerable time and actual dollars as they explore and adventure through entire worlds that exist only in someone's imagination and on a gaming server.

Virtualization in computing often refers to the abstraction of some physical component into a logical object. By virtualizing an object, you can obtain some greater measure of utility from the resource the object provides. For example, virtual LANs (local area networks), or VLANs, provide greater network performance and improved manageability by being separated from the physical hardware. Likewise, storage area networks (SANs) provide greater flexibility, improved availability, and more efficient use of storage resources by abstracting the physical devices into logical objects that can be quickly and easily manipulated. Our focus, however, will be on the virtualization of entire computers.

Some examples of virtual reality in popular culture are the file retrieval interface in Michael Crichton's *Disclosure, The Matrix, Tron,* and *Star Trek: The Next Generation's* holodeck.

If you are not yet familiar with the idea of computer virtualization, your initial thoughts might be along the lines of *virtual reality*—the technology that, through the use of sophisticated visual projection and sensory feedback, can give a person the experience of actually being in that created environment. At a fundamental level, this is exactly what computer virtualization is all about: it is how a computer application experiences its created environment.

The first mainstream virtualization was done on IBM mainframes in the 1960s, but Gerald J. Popek and Robert P. Goldberg codified the framework that describes the requirements for a computer system to support virtualization. Their 1974 article "Formal Requirements for Virtualizable Third Generation Architectures" describes the roles and properties of virtual machines and virtual machine monitors that we still use today. The article is available for purchase or rent at http://dl.acm.org/citation.cfm?doid=361011.361073. By their definition, a virtual machine (VM) can virtualize all of the hardware resources, including processors, memory, storage, and network connectivity. A virtual machine monitor (VMM), which today is commonly called a *hypervisor*, is the software that provides the environment in which the VMs operate. Figure 1.1 shows a simple illustration of a VMM.

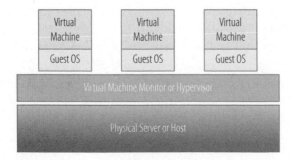

FIGURE 1.1   A basic virtual machine monitor (VMM)

According to Popek and Goldberg, a VMM needs to exhibit three properties in order to correctly satisfy their definition:

Fidelity   The environment it creates for the VM is essentially identical to the original (hardware) physical machine.

Isolation or Safety   The VMM must have complete control of the system resources.

Performance   There should be little or no difference in performance between the VM and a physical equivalent.

Because most VMMs have the first two properties, VMMs that also meet the final criterion are considered *efficient* VMMs. We will go into these properties in much more depth as we examine hypervisors in Chapter 2, "Understanding Hypervisors," and virtual machines in Chapter 3, "Understanding Virtual Machines."

Let's go back to the virtual reality analogy. Why would you want to give a computer program a virtual world to work in, anyway? It turns out that it was very necessary. To help explain that necessity, let's review a little history. It would be outside the scope of this text to cover all the details about how server-based computing evolved, but for our purposes, we can compress it to a number of key occurrences.

Between the late 1970s and mid-1980s, there were more than 70 different personal computer operating systems.

Microsoft Windows Drives Server Growth

Microsoft Windows was developed during the 1980s primarily as a personal computer operating system. Others existed, CP/M and OS/2 for example, but as you know Windows eventually dominated the market and today it is still the primary operating system deployed on PCs. During that same time frame, businesses were depending more and more on computers for their operations. Companies moved from paper-based records to running their accounting, human resources, and many other industry-specific and custom-built applications on mainframes or minicomputers. These computers usually ran vendor-specific operating systems, making it difficult, if not impossible, for companies and IT professionals to easily transfer information among incompatible systems. This led to the need for *standards,* agreed upon methods for exchanging information, but also the idea that the same, or similar, operating systems and programs should be able to run on many different vendors' hardware. The first of these was Bell Laboratories' commercially available UNIX operating systems.

Companies had both Windows-based PCs and other operating systems in-house, managed and maintained by their IT staffs, but it wasn't cost effective to train IT staffs on multiple platforms. With increasing amounts of memory, faster processors, and larger and faster storage subsystems, the hardware that Windows could run on became capable of hosting more powerful applications that had in the past primarily run on minicomputers and mainframes. These applications were being migrated to, or being designed to run on, Windows servers. This worked well for companies because they already had Windows expertise in house and no longer required multiple teams to support their IT infrastructure. This move, however, also led to a number of challenges. Because Windows was originally designed to be a single-user operating system, a single application on a single Windows server ran fine, but often when a second program was introduced, the requirements of each program caused various types of resource contention and even out and out operating system failures. This behavior drove many companies, application designers, developers, IT professionals, and vendors to adopt a "one server, one application" best practice; so for every application that was deployed, one or more servers needed to be acquired, provisioned, and managed.

> Current versions of Microsoft Windows run concurrent applications much more efficiently than their predecessors.

Another factor that drove the growing server population was corporate politics. The various organizations within a single company did not want any common infrastructure. Human Resource and Payroll departments declared their data was too sensitive to allow the potential of another group using their systems. Marketing, Finance, and Sales all believed the same thing to protect their fiscal information. Research and Development also had dedicated servers to ensure the safety of their corporate intellectual property. Sometimes companies had redundant applications, four or more email systems, maybe from different vendors, due to this proprietary ownership attitude. By demanding solitary control of their application infrastructure, departments felt that they could control their data, but this type of control also increased their capital costs.

Aiding the effects of these politics was the fact that business demand, competition, Moore's Law, and improvements in server and storage technologies all drastically drove down the cost of hardware. This made the entry point for a department to build and manage its own IT infrastructure much more affordable. The processing power and storage that in the past had cost hundreds of thousands of dollars could be had for a fraction of that cost in the form of even more Windows servers.

Business computers initially had specialized rooms in which to operate. These computer rooms were anything from oversized closets to specially constructed areas for housing a company's technology infrastructure. They typically had raised floors under which the cables and sometimes air conditioning conduits were run. They held the computers, network equipment, and often telecomm equipment. They needed to be outfitted with enough power to service all of that equipment. Because all of those electronics in a contained space generated considerable heat, commensurate cooling through huge air-conditioning handlers was mandatory as well. Cables to interconnect all of these devices, fire-suppression systems in case of emergency, and separate security systems to protect the room itself, all added to the considerable and ever-rising costs of doing business in a modern corporation. As companies depended more and more on technology to drive their business, they added many more servers to support that need. Eventually, this expansion created data centers. A *data center* could be anything from a larger computer room, to an entire floor in a building, to a separate building constructed and dedicated to the health and well-being of a company's computing infrastructure. Entire buildings existed solely to support servers, and then at the end of twentieth century, the Internet blossomed into existence.

"E-business or out of business" was the cry that went up as businesses tried to stake out their territories in this new online world. To keep up with their competition, existing companies deployed even more servers as they web-enabled old applications to be more customer facing and customer serving. Innovative companies, such as Amazon and Google, appeared from nowhere, creating disruptive business models that depended on large farms of servers to rapidly deliver millions of web pages populated with petabytes of information (see Table 1.1). IT infrastructure was mushrooming at an alarming rate, and it was only going to get worse. New consumer-based services were delivered not just through traditional online channels, but newer devices such as mobile phones compounded data centers' growth. Between 2000 and 2006, the Environmental Protection Agency (EPA) reported that energy use by United States data centers doubled, and that over the next five years they expected it to double again. Not only that, but servers were consuming about 2 percent of the total electricity produced in the country, and the energy used to cool them consumed about the same amount. Recent studies show that energy use by data centers continues to increase with no sign of decreasing any time soon.

TABLE 1.1 Byte Sizes

Name	Abbreviation	Size
Byte	B	8-bits (a single character)
Kilobyte	KB	1,024 B
Megabyte	MB	1,024 KB
Gigabyte	GB	1,024 MB
Terabyte	TB	1,024 GB
Petabyte	PB	1,024 TB
Exabyte	EB	1,024 PB
Zettabyte	ZB	1,024 EB
Yottabyte	YB	1,024 ZB

Let's take a closer look at these data centers. Many were reaching their physical limits on many levels. They were running out of actual square footage for the servers they needed to contain, and companies were searching for alternatives. Often the building that housed a data center could not get more electrical power or additional cooling capacity. Building larger or additional data centers was and still is an expensive proposition. In addition to running out of room, the data centers often had grown faster than the people managing them could maintain them. It was common to hear tales of lost servers. (A *lost server* is a server that is running, but no one actually knows which line of business owns it or what it is doing.) These lost servers couldn't be interrupted for fear of inadvertently disrupting some crucial part of the business. In some data centers, cabling was so thick and intertwined that when nonfunctioning cables needed to be replaced, or old cables were no longer needed, it was easier to just leave them where they were, rather than try to unthread them from the mass. Of course, these are the more extreme examples, but most data centers had challenges to some degree in one or more of these areas.

Explaining Moore's Law

So far you have seen how a combination of events—the rise of Windows, corporations increasing their reliance on server technology, and the appearance and mushrooming of the Internet and other content-driven channels—all contributed to accelerated growth of the worldwide server population. One 2006 study estimated that the 16 million servers in use in 2000 had grown to almost 30 million by 2005. This trend continues today. Companies like Microsoft, Amazon, and Google each have hundreds of thousands of servers to run their businesses. Think about all of the many ways you can pull information from the world around you; computers, mobile devices, gaming platforms, and television set tops are only some of the methods, and new ones appear every day. Each of them has a wide and deep infrastructure to support those services, but this is only part of the story. The other piece of the tale has to do with how efficient those computers were becoming.

If you are reading an electronic copy of this text on a traditional computer, or maybe on a smart phone or even a tablet, you probably have already gone through the process of replacing that device at least once. Phone companies typically give their customers the ability to swap out older smart phones every couple of years for newer, more up-to-date models, assuming you opt for another contract extension. A computer that you bought in 2010 has probably been supplanted by one you purchased in the last three to five years, and if it is closer to five years, you are probably thinking about replacing that one as well. This has little to do with obsolescence, although electronic devices today are rarely engineered to outlive their useful lifespan. It has more to do with the incredible advances that technology constantly makes, packing more and more capability into faster, smaller, and newer packages. For example, digital cameras first captured images at less than 1 megapixel resolution and now routinely provide more than 12 megapixel resolutions. PCs, and now smart phones, initially offered memory (RAM) measured in kilobytes; today the standard is gigabytes, an increase of two orders of magnitude. Not surprisingly, there is a rule of thumb that governs how fast these increases take place. It is called Moore's Law, and it deals with the rate at which certain technologies improve (see Figure 1.2).

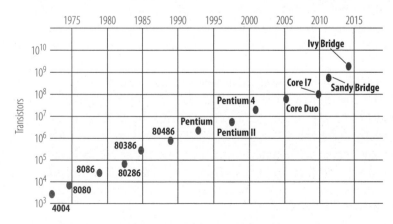

FIGURE 1.2 Moore's Law: transistor count and processor speed

Gordon Moore, one of the founders of Intel, gets credit for recognizing and describing the phenomenon that bears his name. His original thought was publicized back in 1965, and although it has been refined a few times along the way, it is still very true today. Simply stated, Moore's Law says that processing power roughly doubles every 18 months. That means a computer you buy 18 months from now will be twice as powerful as one you buy today. As it turns out, Moore's Law applies not just to *processing power* (the speed and capacity of computer chips) but to many other related technologies as well (such as memory capacity and the megapixel count in digital cameras). You might think that after almost 50 years, we would be hitting some type of technological barrier that would prevent this exponential growth from continuing, but scientists believe that it will hold true for somewhere between 20 years on the low side and centuries on the high. But what does this have to do with straining data centers and ballooning server growth?

Servers are routinely replaced. There are two main models for this process. Companies buy servers and then buy newer models in three to five years when those assets are depreciated. Other corporations lease servers, and when that lease runs its course, they lease newer servers, also in three to five year intervals. The servers that were initially purchased for use were probably sized to do a certain job; in other words, they were bought, for example, to run a database. The model and size of the server was determined with help from an application vendor who provided a recommended server configuration based on the company's specific need. That need was not the company's requirement on the day the server was purchased; it was purchased based on the company's projected need for the future and for emergencies. This extra capacity is also known as *headroom*. To use the server for three to five years, it had to be large enough to handle growth until the end of the server's life, whether it actually ever used that extra capacity or not. When the server was replaced, it was often replaced with a similarly configured model (with the same number of processors and the same amount of memory or more) for the next term, but the newer server was not the same.

Let's take six years as an example span of time and examine the effect of Moore's Law on the change in a server (see Table 1.2). A company that is on a three-year model has replaced the initial server twice—once at the end of year three and again at the end of year six. According to Moore's Law, the processing power of the server has doubled four times, and the server is 16 times more powerful than the original computer! Even if they are on the five-year model, and have only swapped servers once, they now own a machine that is eight times faster than the first server.

TABLE 1.2 Processor Speed Increases Over Six Years

Year	2015	2016	2017	2018	2019	2020
Processor Speed	1x	2x	4x	4x	8x	16x
Three-year plan			purchase			purchase
Five-year plan					purchase	

In addition to faster CPUs and faster processing, newer servers usually have more memory, another benefit of Moore's Law. The bottom line is that the replacement servers are considerably larger and much more powerful than the original server, which was already oversized for the workload it was handling.

The last item you need to understand here is that the server's actual workload does not typically increase at the same rate as the server's capabilities. That means that the headroom in the server also increased substantially. Although that performance safety net began somewhere in the 20 to 50 percent range, that unused capacity after a server refresh or two could be well over 90 percent. Across a data center it was not uncommon to average about 10 to 15 percent utilization, but the distribution was often arranged so that a few servers had very high numbers while the large bulk of servers were actually less than 5 percent utilized. In other words, most CPUs sat around idle for 95 percent of the time, or more!

Understanding the Importance of Virtualization

This is where the two stories come together. There was a wild explosion of data centers overfilled with servers; but as time passed, in a combination of the effect of Moore's Law and the "one server, one application" model, those servers did less and less work. Fortunately, help was on the way in the form of virtualization. The idea and execution of virtualization was not new. It ran on IBM mainframes back in the 1960s but was updated for modern computer systems. We'll come back to the specifics of virtualization in a moment, but in keeping with Popek and Goldberg's definition, virtualization allows many operating system workloads to run on the same server hardware at the same time, while keeping each virtual machine functionally isolated from all the others. The first commercially available solution to provide virtualization for x86 computers came from VMware in 2001.

A parallel open-source offering called Xen arrived two years later. These solutions (VMMs, or hypervisors) took the form of a layer of software that lived either between an operating system and the virtual machines (VMs) or was installed directly onto the hardware, or "bare-metal," just like a traditional operating system such as Windows or Linux. In the next chapter, we'll go into much more depth about hypervisors.

What virtualization brought to those overfull data centers and underutilized servers was the ability to condense multiple physical servers into fewer servers that would run many virtual machines, allowing those physical servers to run at a much higher rate of utilization. This condensing of servers is called *consolidation,* as illustrated in Figure 1.3. A measure of consolidation is called the *consolidation ratio* and is calculated by counting the number of VMs on a server—for example, a server that has eight VMs running on it has a consolidation ratio of 8:1. Consolidation was a boon to beleaguered data centers and operations managers because it solved a number of crucial problems just when a critical threshold had been reached. Even a modest consolidation ratio of 4:1 could remove three-quarters of the servers in a data center.

> The moniker x86 refers to the processor architecture originally based on Intel's 8086 CPU and subsequent chip generations that ended in "86." Other vendors now also produce processors with this architecture.

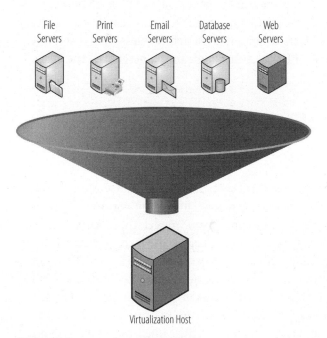

FIGURE 1.3 Server consolidation

In larger data centers, where hundreds or even thousands of servers were housed, virtualization provided a way to decommission a large portion of servers. This reduced the overall footprint of a data center, reduced the power and cooling requirements, and removed the necessity to add to or construct additional data centers. By extension, with fewer servers, it reduced a company's hardware maintenance costs and reduced the time system administrators took to perform many other routine tasks.

CONSOLIDATION DRIVES DOWN COSTS

Many studies show that the total cost of ownership for an individual server is somewhere between 3 and 10 times the cost of the server itself over three years. In other words, if a server costs $5,000, the cost of maintaining that server is at least another $5,000 per year. Over three years, that is $20,000 per server (the initial hardware spend plus three years of maintenance costs). Those ownership costs include software, annual software and hardware maintenance, power, cooling, cables, people costs, and more. So in this example, for every hundred servers the company can consolidate, it can save two million dollars the first year and every year afterward.

Aside from consolidation, a second development took place. As companies began to see the benefits of virtualization, they no longer purchased new hardware when their leases were over, or if they owned the equipment, when their hardware maintenance licenses expired. Instead, they virtualized those server workloads. In other words, they staged these application workloads on their existing virtual infrastructures. This is called *containment*. Containment benefited corporations in multiple ways. They no longer had to refresh large amounts of hardware year after year; and all the costs of managing and maintaining those servers—power, cooling, etc.—were removed from their bottom line from that time on. Until the time when virtualization became commercially viable, Moore's Law worked against the existing application/server/data center model; after it became feasible, it actually helped. The consolidation ratios of the first generation of x86 hypervisors were in the range of 5:1. As time continued to pass, more powerful chips and larger memory enabled much higher consolidation ratios, where a single physical server could host dozens or hundreds of VMs. Instead of removing three out of four servers, virtualization today can comfortably remove nine out of ten; or with sufficiently configured servers, ninety-nine out of a hundred. As a result, most corporate data centers have reclaimed much of the space that they had lost before virtualization.

VIRTUAL SERVERS NOW OUTNUMBER PHYSICAL SERVERS

IDC reported that in 2009, more virtual servers were deployed than physical servers. They predicted that while physical server deployment would remain relatively static over the following five years, virtual machine deployment would double the physical deployments at the end of that span.

Examining Today's Trends

Consolidation and containment are just two of the many examples of how virtualization enhances traditional server usage that we will cover. They are also the two that most analyses deal with because they are the easiest to quantify from a financial standpoint—remove or significantly diminish the associated hardware cost from your budget, and your bottom line will be directly impacted. We'll introduce some of those other examples now and examine them more closely later in the book.

As virtualization takes hold in an organization, its progress takes a very predictable course. The initial beachhead is in infrastructure services and in older servers, two areas where server management and cost issues are typically most acute. Infrastructure servers deliver an organization's technology plumbing in the form of print services, file servers, and domain services. These servers are critical to the day-to-day business but often run on less reliable, less expensive hardware than the tier-one applications that drive the business. Older servers are also a concern. Data centers frequently host applications that do not run on newer operating systems—for example, a 10-year-old Windows NT system running a custom-built analytics system continues to run on its original hardware, which may be obsolete and no longer reliable or even serviceable. A company can also have applications that it no longer knows how to manage (don't laugh, it happens)—the vendor is no longer in business or their internal expert is no longer with the company, but the application runs, so they just hope it will continue to do so. Virtualization, as you will see, makes these applications much more available, scalable, and manageable than they ever were on physical servers, and for less cost as well.

Once the infrastructure services are virtualized and an organization starts to reap some of the fiscal benefits of their new strategy, an active program is put in place to move to the next level. As servers come off their leases, those workloads are migrated to the growing infrastructure. Companies usually adopt virtualization-first policies, which state that as new projects come in house, any server requirements will be satisfied by the virtual resources, rather than by paying for new physical resources. Actual hardware will be purchased only if it can be proven that the need cannot be satisfied with the virtual environment. Right behind the infrastructure services are the test and development servers. For every production application that a corporation runs, there are somewhere between 2 and 10 times as many servers in the data center that support that application. Tier-one applications require many environments for new update testing, quality and assurance tests, user acceptance testing, problem resolution environments, performance tuning, and more. Moving these systems to the virtual infrastructure, aside from again saving costs through consolidation, gives developers and application owners greater flexibility in how they can manage their processes. Preconfigured templates allow them to rapidly deploy new servers in minutes rather than in the weeks it would have taken prior to the change.

At this point, an organization's infrastructure is somewhere between 50 and 75 percent virtualized, at least on the x86 platforms that run their Windows and Linux servers. They have built up expertise and confidence in the virtualization technologies and are still looking to take even further advantage of virtualization. From here companies go in a number of different directions, often simultaneously.

Larger applications often require larger hardware and specialized operating systems to run that hardware. Databases, for example, run on a variety of UNIX systems, each with a vendor-specific version. Sun servers run Solaris, HP servers run HP/UX, and IBM servers run AIX. Companies invest large sums of money for this proprietary hardware, and just as much time and effort in training their people to work with these open but also proprietary operating systems. But again, Moore's Law is working in their favor. In the past, an x86 platform would not be powerful or reliable enough to run this mission-critical type of workload; today that is no longer true. There are almost no workloads today that cannot be run in a virtual environment due to performance limitations. Linux, which is an open source flavor of UNIX, can run the same application software as the vendor-specific hardware and software combinations. Although we'll focus mostly on Microsoft Windows, Linux can also be easily virtualized, and that is leading many companies to migrate these critical workloads to a more flexible, less expensive, and often more available environment.

As we touched on earlier, virtual servers are encapsulated systems, essentially just a set of files that can be copied and moved like any other files. As Internet computing has evolved, availability has become crucial, whether it is maintaining 24/7 operations through enhanced software and features, *disaster recovery* capabilities (restoring operations after an interruption), or even pro-actively shifting workloads out of the areas when time permits, like during the forecasted approach of a hurricane. Virtualization enables availability in a number of ways. Virtual machines can be moved from one physical host to another without interruption. Instead of scheduling application downtime for a physical host to do maintenance, the workload can be moved to another host, the physical work done on the server, and the workload returned, all without interrupting the users. With Linux and newer versions of Microsoft Windows, you can add additional resources, processors, and memory to a virtual machine without having to reboot the operating system. This ability allows an adminis-trator to resolve resource shortages without impacting application uptime. By replicating the files that comprise a server to a secondary site, in the event of an environmental disaster, such as a hurricane or flood, the entire data center can be restored in a matter of hours or even minutes, instead of the days or weeks it would have taken previously. These are just a few examples of the increased availability virtualization provides.

Finally, the remaining physical servers are addressed. These are the ones that run the *tier-one applications,* strategic business applications that give each company its competitive advantage. They take the form of email services such as Microsoft Exchange or Lotus Notes, database servers such as Microsoft SQL Server, Oracle, or MySQL, enterprise business applications such as SAP, business intelligence and analytics systems such as SAS, hospital healthcare applications, financial services applications, custom-built JAVA applications, and on and on. Because the health and well-being of these applications directly affect a com-pany's profitability, administrator and application owners are hesitant to make changes to a time-proven environment or methodology, even if it has flaws. But after working with virtualized servers in test, development, and QA environ-ments, they are comfortable enough to virtualize these remaining workloads.

Moving to an entirely virtualized platform provides enterprises a much greater degree of availability, agility, flexibility, and manageability than they could have in a solely physical environment. You will find out more about many of the capabilities of virtual machines and what a virtual environment can provide throughout this text, but one large benefit of virtualization is that it provides the foundation for the next phase of data center evolution: cloud computing.

Virtualization and Cloud Computing

Five years ago, if you said the words "cloud computing," very few people would have had any idea what you were talking about. Today it would be difficult to find someone who is engaged in the worldwide business or consumer markets who has not heard the term *cloud computing*. Much like the rush to the Internet during the mid-to-late 1990s and early 2000s, many of today's companies are working on cloud enablement for their offerings. Mirroring their actions during the dot-com boom, consumer services are also making the move to the cloud. Apple, for example, offers their iCloud where you can store your music, pictures, books, and other digital possessions and then access them from anywhere. Other companies such as Microsoft, Amazon, and Google offer similar cloud-based services. Rather than define the cloud, which would be outside the scope of this text, let's look at what the cloud is providing: a simplified method for accessing and utilizing resources.

Virtualization is the engine that drives cloud computing by transforming the data center—what used to be a hands-on, people-intensive process—into a self-managing, highly scalable, highly available pool of easily consumable resources. Before virtualization, system administrators spent 70 percent or more of their time on routine functions and reacting to problems, which left little time for innovation or growth. Virtualization and, by extension, cloud computing provide greater automation opportunities that reduce administrative costs and increase a company's ability to dynamically deploy solutions. By being able to abstract the physical layer away from the actual hardware, cloud computing creates the concept of a virtual data center, a construct that contains everything a physical data center would. This virtual data center, deployed in the cloud, offers resources on an as-needed basis, much as a power company provides electricity. In short, these models of computing dramatically simplify the delivery of new applications and allow companies to accelerate their deployments without sacrificing scalability, resiliency, or availability.

Understanding Virtualization Software Operation

Although we've spent the bulk of our time discussing server virtualization and it will be our focus throughout the remainder of the text, there are other methods and areas of virtualization. Personal computers are changing into tablets and thin clients, but the applications that run on PCs still need to be offered to users. One way to achieve this is desktop virtualization. Those applications can also be virtualized, packaged up, and delivered to users. Virtualization is even being pushed down to the other mobile devices such as smart phones.

Virtualizing Servers

The model for server virtualization, as you saw earlier, is composed of physical hardware augmented by two key software solutions. The hypervisor abstracts the physical layer and presents this abstraction for virtualized servers or virtual machines to use. A hypervisor is installed directly onto a server, without any operating system between it and the physical devices. Virtual machines are then *instantiated,* or booted. From the virtual machine's view, it can see and work with a number of hardware resources. The hypervisor becomes the interface between the hardware devices on the physical server and the virtual devices of the virtual machines. The hypervisor presents only some subset of the physical resources to each individual virtual machine and handles the actual I/O from VM to physical device and back again. Hypervisors do more than just provide a platform for running VMs; they enable enhanced availability features and create new and better ways for provisioning and management as well.

While hypervisors are the foundations of virtual environments, virtual machines are the engines that power the applications. Virtual machines contain everything that their physical counterparts do (operating systems, applications, network connections, access to storage, and other necessary resources) but packaged in a set of data files. This packaging makes virtual machines much more flexible and manageable through the use of the traditional file properties in a new way. Virtual machines can be cloned, upgraded, and even moved from place to place, without ever having to disrupt the user applications. We will focus exclusively on hypervisors in Chapter 2, "Understanding Hypervisors," and look closer at virtual machines in Chapter 3, "Understanding Virtual Machines."

Our focus in this book will be on hypervisors and their ability to virtualize servers and the compute function of the data center. They interact with network and storage I/O inside and outside of the physical servers that they reside on. Inside those physical servers, the hypervisors abstract both the network and the storage resources to some degree, but that only reaches to the limits of that physical server. In the past few years, other solutions have appeared that virtualize both the network and storage resources by abstracting them across a data center or further. The lessons that were learned in the compute space are now being applied to other areas of the infrastructure, making these resources more agile as well. We'll examine more about virtualizing storage and network resources in Chapter 9, "Managing Storage for a Virtual Machine," and Chapter 10, "Managing Networking for a Virtual Machine."

Virtualization has not only been disruptive in the number of servers being acquired, but in how servers themselves are being architected. As virtualization became more prevalent, hardware vendors took a closer look at how to create servers that would be an optimal environment for hypervisors to work on. They started to design and offer devices that contained the compute, networking, and storage resources already connected and preconfigured and that could be managed as a single unit. This architecture is described as *converged infrastructure*. These prebuilt blocks allow rapid scalability in a data center. Contrasted with purchasing servers, networking switches, cables, and storage from multiple vendors and then connecting and configuring them all in a time-consuming process, converged infrastructure devices significantly reduce the effort to start or expand a virtual environment. They have been commercially available in a number of forms since 2009 when Cisco offered their first UCS (Universal Computing System) blade. Then VCE was a partnership between Cisco, EMC, and VMware to provide prebuilt reference architecture solutions. Established vendors like HP, EMC, and Dell offer solutions based on their hardware. Lately, offerings have appeared for specialized areas. Oracle offers their Exadata platform, which is a combination of hardware and software focused on solving Oracle database challenges. Similarly, IBM's PureSystems platform addresses the same data analysis space. Newer entrants like Nutanix entered the marketplace also looking to disrupt traditional hardware models, especially in the areas of hosting virtual desktops. Some combination of all these models will be attractive to companies as they continue to drive down costs, increase efficiency, and shorten the time to production.

Virtualizing Desktops

Just as virtualization has changed the model of how traditional server computing is being managed today, virtualization has moved into the desktop computing model as well. Desktop computing for companies is expensive and inefficient on many fronts. It requires staffs of people to handle software update rollouts and patching processes, not to mention hardware support and help desk staffing. Virtual desktops run on servers in the data center; these hardware servers are much more powerful and reliable than traditional PCs. The applications that users connect to are also in the data center running on servers right next door, if you will, so all of the network traffic that previously had to go back and forth to the data center no longer needs to, which greatly reduces network traffic and extends network resources.

Virtual desktops are accessed through thin clients, or other devices, many of which are more reliable and less expensive than PCs. Thin clients have life spans of 7 to 10 years so can be refreshed less frequently. They also only use between

5 and 10 percent of the electricity of a PC. In large companies, those costs add up quickly. If a thin client does break, a user can replace it himself, instead of relying on a specialized hardware engineer to replace it. The virtual desktop where all of the data is kept has not been affected by the hardware failure. In fact, the data no longer leaves the data center, so the risk that a lost or stolen device will cause security issues is also reduced.

That data is now managed and backed up by a professional, instead of an unsophisticated or indifferent user. Creating desktop images as virtual machines brings some of the cost savings of server virtualization but really shines on the desktop management side. A desktop administrator can create and manage fewer images that are shared among hundreds of people. Patches can be applied to these images and are guaranteed to reach a user, whereas that is not always the case with a physical desktop. In the event that a rolled-out patch or other software change breaks an application, an administrator can direct users back to the original image, and a simple logout and login will return them to a functional desktop.

One of the biggest differences comes in the area of security. Today PCs routinely utilize antivirus software applications that help protect their data from malware and more. Virtualization allows new methods of protection. Rather than just loading the anti malware software on individual virtual desktops, there are now *virtual appliances,* specifically designed virtual machines that reside in each host and protect all of the virtual desktops that run there. This new model reduces the overall I/O and processor usage by downloading new definitions once instead of individually by guest. This is an area of rapid change and growth at the moment, and it looks to continue that way as new user devices become more common.

Virtualizing Applications

Computer programs, or applications, can also be virtualized. Like both server and desktop virtualization, there are a number of different solutions for this problem. There are two main reasons for application virtualization; the first is ease of deployment. Think about the number of programs you have on your PC. Some companies must manage hundreds or even thousands of different applications. Every time a new version of each of those applications is available, the company, if it decides to upgrade to that newer version, has to push out a copy to all of its PCs. For one or a small number of computers, this may be a relatively trivial task. But how would you do this to a hundred PCs? Or a thousand? Or ten thousand? Corporate IT staffs have tools that help manage and automate this task to happen repeatedly and reliably.

Two popular solutions for desktop virtualization are Citrix's XenDesktop and VMware's Horizon View. There are other vendors that provide desktops using various combinations of hardware and software.

Some popular application virtualization solutions are Microsoft's App-V, Citrix's Application Streaming, and VMware's ThinApp. Each solution approaches the problem differently but is effective.

The second reason has to do with how different applications interact with each other. Have you ever loaded or updated an application that broke some functionality that had been working just fine? It is difficult to know how an upgrade to one solution may affect other applications. Even simple upgrades such as Adobe Acrobat Reader or Mozilla Firefox can become problematic. Some types of application virtualization can mitigate or even prevent this issue by encapsulating the entire program and process. Many application virtualization strategies and solutions are currently available. This is a rapidly evolving area with new use cases appearing regularly, especially in conjunction with mobile devices such as smart phones and tablets.

On the other end of the spectrum is a new and evolving technology called *containers*. Rather than have discrete virtual machines with individual operating systems in each one, containers allow for one larger software package that includes a shared copy of a single operating system for many workloads to leverage. Depending on the type of workloads needed to be deployed, these new models might be a better fit for a company's strategy. As you can see, this is still a dynamically changing area of technology. We'll see more about containers in Chapter 14, "Understanding Applications in a Virtual Machine."

One final topic to address is how virtualization has not only been disruptive on the architectural side of things, but how it has also shaken up the personnel side of business. In the same way that virtualization has brought about consolidation in the data centers and converged infrastructures have consolidated the various hardware disciplines (compute, network, and storage) into single physical frameworks, virtualization now requires virtualization administrators to manage those virtual infrastructures.

Traditional data centers and infrastructure had organizations that were centered around the specialized technologies deployed. Storage teams focused on deploying and managing data storage in all its many forms. Network teams focused on communications—cabling, switches, and routers, as well as the software side of the operations that manage IP addresses. Network teams often also manage security. Server administrators provisioned and managed the physical servers. They loaded operating systems, patched firmware, and scheduled downtime for maintenance. In larger organizations, these separate teams, like medieval guilds, struggled to find a balance between them and their roles, rarely sharing their duties or access to their particular resources. In addition to these groups, often there were departments that dealt solely with desktop operations, while other groups managed the applications that ran the business. These traditional personnel roles are being replaced by virtualization administrators and virtualization teams.

While working with virtualization does require certain knowledge and experience, as any new technology would, virtualization administrators also need to understand and be adept at working with all of the legacy disciplines. As the hypervisor becomes the hub of the new data center, in order to be timely and effective, the virtualization administrator now needs access into the legacy IT silos of networking, storage, and server administration. In fact, many companies are forming virtualization teams that draw from all of these groups to ensure the viability of their transformation to a virtual environment. We'll cover this topic more in Chapter 14.

THE ESSENTIALS AND BEYOND

Server virtualization is a disruptive technology that allows many logical computers to run on a single physical server. Extreme server population growth driven by application deployment practices, the spread of Microsoft Windows, and Moore's Law have placed physical resource and financial constraints on most of the world's corporations. Virtualization is not a new concept, but was redeveloped and helped relieve those stresses on data centers through server consolidation and containment. Many of the characteristics that server virtualization provides, such as increased availability and scalability, are providing the foundation for corporations as they move to cloud computing.

ADDITIONAL EXERCISES

▶ Using Moore's Law, calculate how much faster processors are today than they were in the year 2000. Calculate how much faster processors will be 10 years from now.

▶ Using the Internet, discover how many different types of server virtualization are publicly available. How many separate architectures are represented in what you found?

▶ At what minimum number of servers does it make sense to virtualize a data center? Will the cost savings and soft cost savings (such as increased manageability and availability) outweigh the initial cost of virtualization, cost of education, and effort to effect the change?

CHAPTER 2

Understanding Hypervisors

In this chapter, you will learn what a hypervisor is, take a closer look at its beginnings more than 40 years ago on mainframe computers, and trace its history. You will examine the different hypervisor types, get a better understanding of what they do, and then compare some of the modern hypervisors that are available today.

▶ **Describing a hypervisor**

▶ **Understanding the role of a hypervisor**

▶ **Comparing today's hypervisors**

Describing a Hypervisor

At the highest level, a hypervisor is an arbiter of resources. It is software that sits between the physical resources on a physical server and the virtual machines that run on that server. In addition to resource allocation, hypervisors provide a virtual environment for those workloads, enable virtual networks for communication between workloads and to the outside world, and offer various forms of clustering for high availability. This is just a small piece of what a hypervisor is; but before looking closer, we need to look at how this all started.

The original virtual machine monitor (VMM) was created to solve a specific problem. However, VMMs have evolved into something quite different, so much so that the term *virtual machine manager* has fallen out of favor and has been replaced with the term *hypervisor*. Today's hypervisors allow us to make better use of the ever-faster processors that regularly appear in the commercial market and to more efficiently use the larger and denser memory offerings that come along with those newer processors. Again, the hypervisor is a layer of software that resides below the virtual machines and above the hardware. Figure 2.1 illustrates where the hypervisor resides.

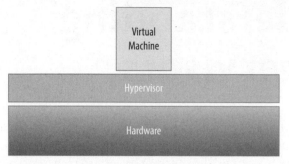

FIGURE 2.1 **Where the hypervisor resides**

Without a hypervisor, an operating system communicates directly with the hardware beneath it. Disk operations go directly to the disk subsystem, and memory calls are fetched directly from the physical memory. Without a hypervisor, more than one operating system from multiple virtual machines would want simultaneous control of the hardware, which would result in chaos. The hypervisor manages the interactions between each virtual machine and the hardware that the guests all share.

Exploring the History of Hypervisors

The first virtualization was performed on IBM mainframes. The code that was developed solved a particular issue by managing available memory resources more effectively, and that code is an ancestor to the much more sophisticated descendants we rely on today. In fact, though our focus will not be around the mainframe at all, virtualization technology has been available on those platforms since the 1960s, has been continuously improved, and is still being widely used today.

The first virtual machine monitors were used for the development and debugging of operating systems because they provided a sandbox for programmers to test rapidly and repeatedly, without using all of the resources of the hardware. Soon they added the ability to run multiple environments concurrently, carving the hardware resources into virtual servers that could each run its own operating system. This model is what evolved into today's hypervisors.

WHY CALL IT A "HYPERVISOR"?

Initially, the problem that the engineers were trying to solve was one of resource allocation, trying to utilize areas of memory that were not normally accessible to programmers. The code they produced was successful and was dubbed a hypervisor because, at the time, operating systems were called supervisors and this code could supersede them.

Thirty years passed before virtualization made any significant move from the mainframe environment. In the 1990s, researchers began investigating the possibility of building a commercially affordable version of a VMM. One large limitation of the mainframes was that they were very expensive when compared to a minicomputer. Providing virtualization atop affordable industry standard hardware would be considerably more cost effective for most businesses. The other half of the challenge was creating a solution that would run a guest operating without any modifications. This was crucial because modifications would open the possibility that a virtual machine was not essentially identical to its physical counterpart, which meant that solutions designed in the virtual environment would not necessarily translate to the physical environment 100 percent of the time, leading to additional complexity in an application's life cycle.

The structure of a VMM is fairly simple. It consists of a layer of software that lives between the hardware, or *host,* and the virtual machines that it supports. These virtual machines, or VMs, which you will learn more about in the next chapter, are also called *guests*. Figure 2.2 is a simple illustration of the virtual machine monitor architecture.

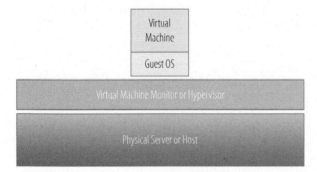

FIGURE 2.2 A virtual machine monitor

There are two classes of hypervisors, and their names, Type 1 and Type 2, give no clue at all to their differences. The only item of note between them is how they are deployed, but it is enough of a variance to point out.

Understanding Type 1 Hypervisors

A Type 1 hypervisor runs directly on the server hardware without an operating system beneath it. Because there is no other intervening layer of software between the hypervisor and the physical hardware, this is also referred to as a *bare-metal* implementation. Without an intermediary, the Type 1 hypervisor can directly communicate with the hardware resources in the stack below it, making it much more efficient than the Type 2 hypervisor. Figure 2.3 illustrates a simple architecture of a Type 1 hypervisor.

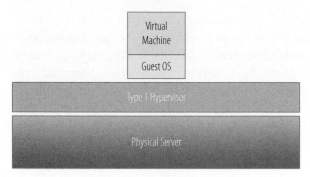

FIGURE 2.3 A Type 1 hypervisor

Examples of Type 1 hypervisors include VMware ESX, Microsoft Hyper-V, and the many Xen variants.

Aside from having better performance characteristics, Type 1 hypervisors are also considered to be more secure than Type 2 hypervisors. Guest operations are handed off and, as such, a guest cannot affect the hypervisor on which it is supported. A virtual machine can damage only itself, causing a single guest crash, but that event does not escape the VM boundaries. Other guests continue processing, and the hypervisor is unaffected as well. A malicious guest, where code is deliberately trying to interfere with the hypervisor or the other guests, would be unable to do so. Figure 2.4 illustrates a guest failure in a Type 1 hypervisor.

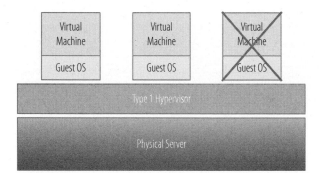

FIGURE 2.4 A guest failure

Less processing overhead is required for a Type 1 hypervisor, which means that more virtual machines can be run on each host. From a pure financial standpoint, a Type 1 hypervisor would not require the cost of a host operating system, although from a practical standpoint, the discussion would be much more complex and involve all of the components and facets that comprise a total cost of ownership calculation.

Understanding Type 2 Hypervisors

A Type 2 hypervisor itself is an application that runs atop a traditional operating system. The first x86 offerings were Type 2 because that was the quickest path to market—the actual operating system already handled all of the hardware resources and the hypervisor would leverage that capability. Figure 2.5 illustrates a Type 2 hypervisor.

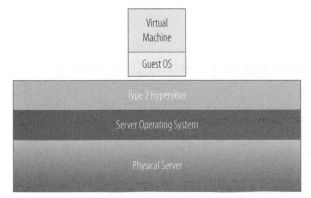

F I G U R E 2 . 5 A Type 2 hypervisor

One benefit of this model is that it can support a large range of hardware because that is inherited from the operating system it uses. Often Type 2 hypervisors are easy to install and deploy because much of the hardware configuration work, such as networking and storage, has already been covered by the operating system.

Type 2 hypervisors are not as efficient as Type 1 hypervisors because of this extra layer between the hypervisor itself and the hardware. Every time a virtual machine performs a disk read, a network operation, or any other hardware interaction, it hands that request off to the hypervisor, just as in a Type 1 hypervisor environment. Unlike that environment, the Type 2 hypervisor must then itself hand off the request to the operating system, which handles the I/O requests. The operating system passes the information back to the hypervisor and then back to the guest, adding two additional steps, extra time and more processing overhead, to every transaction.

Type 2 hypervisors are also less reliable because there are more points of failure: anything that affects the availability of the underlying operating system also can impact the hypervisor and the guests it supports. For example, standard operating system patches that require a system reboot would also force reboots of all the virtual machines on that host.

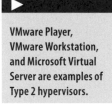

VMware Player, VMware Workstation, and Microsoft Virtual Server are examples of Type 2 hypervisors.

A Type 2 hypervisor deployment uses more physical resources than a Type 1 hypervisor from the standpoint that the underlying operating system consumes system resources in addition to those consumed by the hypervisor's activities.

Type 2 hypervisors are typically used in desktop development environments when a single developer is working on one or more virtual machines in building an application. In this case, the hypervisor is actually just an additional desktop application for that developer. Contrast this with a Type 1 hypervisor deployment where the sole function of the physical server is the hosting of virtual machines and no other applications need to run on that hardware.

Understanding the Role of a Hypervisor

The explanation of a hypervisor up to this point has been fairly simple: it is a layer of software that sits between the hardware and the one or more virtual machines that it supports. Its job is also fairly simple. The three characteristics defined by Popek and Goldberg illustrate these tasks:

▶ Provide an environment identical to the physical environment.

▶ Provide that environment with minimal performance cost.

▶ Retain complete control of the system resources.

Holodecks and Traffic Cops

In order for many guests to share the physical resources of a host, two things must happen. The first thing is that from the guest's perspective, it has to see and have access to the various hardware resources it needs to function effectively. The operating system in the guest should be able to use disk drives, access memory, and make network calls—or at least believe that it can. This is where the hypervisor steps in.

Let's use a quick analogy and go back to the virtual reality technology you've seen in films and television. If the technology is sophisticated enough, and can provide the user with a realistic and accurate enough presentation of reality, that user will not be able to distinguish between reality and the virtual reality. In other words, if you were knocked out and you woke up inside of one of the holodecks on the *Starship Enterprise,* you might not realize that you were actually in a holodeck. From the perspective of a guest operating system, this is what a hypervisor does: it fools the guest into believing that it can actually see and directly interact with the physical devices of the host. This hardware abstraction is illustrated in Figure 2.6.

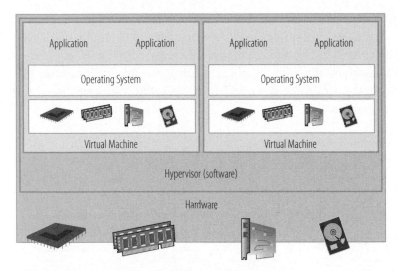

F I G U R E 2 . 6　Abstracting hardware from the guests

In actuality, each guest is presented with only a fraction of the resources of the physical host. A host may have 256 GB of physical memory installed in its frame, but a guest may believe that it has 4 GB. A guest may be writing files to a 250 GB D: drive, but actually be working with a portion of a file system on a much larger storage area network. Processing and network resources work similarly: a guest may have two virtual CPUs and access to a single Network Interface Card (NIC), but the physical host will have many more of both.

The second thing that needs to occur is that the hypervisor not only has to abstract the hardware from each of the virtual guests, but it also needs to balance that workload. Each guest makes constant demands on the various resource subsystems. The hypervisor must service all of those demands by acting as an intermediary between each guest and the physical devices, but also do so in a way that provides timely and adequate resources to all. In that way, the hypervisor acts like a traffic cop, controlling the flow of vehicles so that no one has to wait too long in any one direction and all the roads are used fairly.

Resource Allocation

In a way, a hypervisor has become an operating system of sorts for the hardware, but instead of dealing with application/program requests, the hypervisor services entire (virtual) servers. Figure 2.7 shows how an I/O operation is processed. A guest application calls for a disk read and passes that request to the guest operating system. The guest operating system makes a read to the disk that it sees, shown in the illustration as the C: or D: drive. Here, the hypervisor steps in and traps that call and translates it into a real-world physical equivalent and passes it to the storage subsystem. In the illustration the data actually resides on shared storage array, and the hypervisor makes that request to the proper storage device and file system. When the response returns, the hypervisor passes the data back to the guest operating system, which receives it as if it came directly from the physical device.

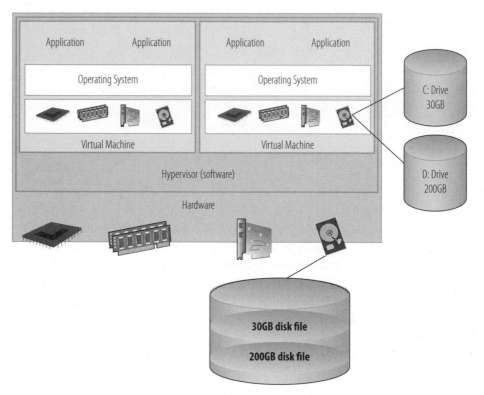

FIGURE 2.7 Processing a guest I/O

Not only does the hypervisor handle all of the storage I/O requests from the guest, but the network I/O, memory processing, and CPU work as well. It does this for all of the guests that are hosted on the physical server on which the hypervisor is running. The hypervisor has a resource scheduling process that ensures all of the requested resources are serviced in a reasonable manner. Some hypervisors have options to prioritize guests so important applications can receive preferential treatment and not suffer performance degradation due to contention.

As part of moving to a virtual infrastructure, this idea of managing and allocating system resources is critical when you determine what the configuration of physical hardware should be. The sum of the resources that all of the guests on the host consume needs to be available on that host. There should even be extra resources available, some to handle periodic performance spikes and growth, and a little for the use of the hypervisor itself.

Comparing Today's Hypervisors

In the early days of the personal computer, there were many choices of operating system; today, there are many solutions available to choose from for a virtualization strategy. Similar to the original mainframe solution, there are vendor- and operating system specific solutions that allow users to carve up a single operating system specific environment into multiple secure environments. Some examples of these are Oracle Solaris Zones, BSD Jails in FreeBSD, HP-UX Containers, and PowerVM on IBM AIX. There are other solutions, such as Virtuozzo and Docker, that virtualize an operating system that all the guests can share.

Because this text focuses on x86 server virtualization rather than some of the other technologies, that is where we will focus as well. Much of the initial shakeout of competitors has already occurred, narrowing the range of choices to a select few. As of this writing, the solutions discussed in this section represent close to 100 percent of the server virtualization market share. The goal of this comparison is to highlight some of the strengths and differences between the solutions, rather than to come to conclusions about which is superior. As you will see, different opportunities often have different solutions.

VMware ESX

Founded in 1998, VMware was the first company to develop a commercially available x86 virtualization solution. The following year, the company released their first product, Workstation 1.0, which allowed developers to create and work with virtual machines on their Windows or Linux desktops. Two years after that, in 2001, both ESX 1.0 and GSX 1.0 were released. ESX was a Type 1 hypervisor and GSX was a Type 2 hypervisor. Both solutions are still around today and are still being enhanced and updated. GSX, though, has been renamed to VMware Server and is available to download at no cost.

> **There have been stories that ESX originally stood for Elastic Sky X and GSX stood for Ground Storm X, although they have been officially known only as ESX and GSX.**
>
>

WHICH IS IT, ESX OR ESXI?

The original architecture of ESX was made up of two parts, the actual hypervisor, which did the virtualization work, and a Linux-based console module that sat alongside the hypervisor and acted as a management interface to the hypervisor. VMware decided that this model was not sustainable for two reasons. The first was that the service console was roughly 30 times the size of the hypervisor—in ESX 3.5, for example, the hypervisor was about 32 MB, while the service console required closer to 900 MB. The second reason was security. Linux is a well-understood environment, and there was concern that the hypervisor could be compromised through the service console. ESXi was developed with the same hypervisor core, but without the service console. The hypervisor is managed through a command-line interface (CLI) and has been re-architected to allow third-party integrations that had been done through agents in the service console. VMware released two versions, classic ESX and ESXi, from version 3.5 in 2007 through version 4.1 in 2010. As of the 2011 release 5, only the ESXi architecture is available.

Market share is not always the best indicator of a solution's viability and capability; however, 15 years after ESX's first appearance, according to Gartner, VMware still holds close to 70 percent of the market. VMware has done a good job of using their first-to-market advantage to develop features and capabilities that many of the other virtualization vendors are still trying to replicate. We'll cover some of those features in a moment, but first let's take a closer look at ESX. Figure 2.8 shows a simplified architecture of VMware ESXi.

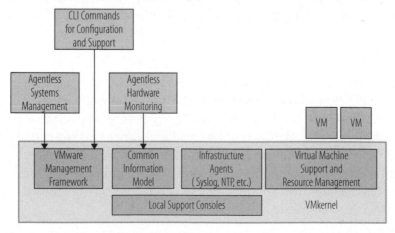

FIGURE 2.8 The ESXi architecture

The VMkernel contains all of the necessary processes to support virtual machines and manage the hardware and availability resources. In addition, infrastructure services, such as timekeeping and logging, integrations with VMware's management tools, and other authorized third-party modules, such as hardware drivers and hardware monitoring tools, can also run in the VMkernel. This model is one of the largest differences between VMware and many of the other solutions.

Being first to the game has also allowed VMware to develop and mature features and capabilities that are either rudimentary in competitive solutions or not available at all. VMotion, introduced in 2003, allows the migration of a running virtual machine from one physical host to another physical host without interrupting the operating system or the applications running on that guest. Transparent page sharing and memory ballooning are just two of the features that facilitate efficient memory usage. High availability and fault tolerance provide enhanced uptime for virtual machines without additional software solutions. These are just a few of the broad range of features that VMware ESX offers.

As you'll see, even though competitors are developing and now offering some of the core capabilities that ESX has, VMware continues to add to and enhance the core functionality of the ESX hypervisor in addition to offering a broad and powerful set of solutions around manageability, security, and availability.

Citrix Xen

The Xen hypervisor began as a research project in the late 1990s at the University of Cambridge, the goal of which was to create an efficient platform for distributed computing. In 2002, the code was made an open-source project, allowing anyone to contribute to improving the features and capabilities. XenSource was founded in 2004 to bring the Xen hypervisor to market, but the open-source project still remained open, as it does to this day. In 2005, Red Hat, Novell, and Sun all added the Xen hypervisor to their product offerings, bringing it to the mainstream. Other solutions like Oracle VM and Amazon Web Services also use Xen as their virtualization framework. Two years later, Citrix Systems acquired XenSource to complement their application delivery solutions. In 2013, it was announced that the development for Xen would become a Linux Foundation Collaborative Project, returning development to the open-source community.

Figure 2.9 provides a closer look at the Xen architecture. The hypervisor is a bare-metal solution and sits directly on the hardware, but the implementation shows some differences from the VMware architecture. The Xen model has a special guest called Domain 0, also referred to as Dom0. This guest gets booted when the hypervisor is booted, and it has management privileges different from the other guests. Because it has direct access to the hardware, it handles all of the I/O for the individual guests. It also handles the hardware device driver support. When additional guests make requests of the underlying hardware resources, those requests go through the hypervisor, up to the Dom0 guest, and then to the resource. Results from those resources reverse that trip to return to the guests.

Having an operating system in the Dom0 guest can affect availability. When OS patching needs to occur, a reboot of Dom0 will interrupt all of the other guests, even if the patches were not related to the virtualization functions. Because Dom0 is also a guest, it consumes resources and contends for resources with the other guests in the system that could lead to performance issues if Dom0 is either short of resources or using guest resources.

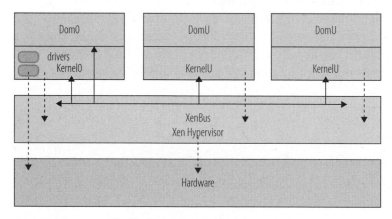

FIGURE 2.9   The Xen hypervisor architecture

Again, the point of this comparison is not to choose which solution is superior (for some people that discussion is akin to picking the Boston Red Sox or the New York Yankees) but rather to explain that there are numerous paths to solve a problem. If the solution you choose resolves whatever problems you had, then it is the correct option for you. As an open-source solution, Xen, and by extension Citrix XenServer, has many proponents; however, as of this writing it has captured less than a 5 percent share of the commercial market, with many of those deployments coupled to their virtual desktop solutions.

Microsoft Hyper-V

Microsoft began in the virtualization space with Virtual Server in 2005, after they had acquired the solution from Connectix a few years earlier. Like GSX, Virtual Server was a Type-2 hypervisor, but has been discontinued in favor of Hyper-V. Microsoft Hyper-V was released in 2008 as an installable part of the Windows Server 2008 operating system. Figure 2.10 shows the architecture of Hyper-V.

Hyper-V is a Type 1 hypervisor because the hypervisor code lives directly on the hardware. The nomenclature is slightly different, though—rather than guests, the virtualized workloads are called *partitions*. Similar to the Xen model, it requires a special parent partition that has direct access to the hardware resources. Like Dom0, the parent partition runs an operating system—in this case, Windows Server. This partition creates and manages the child partitions and handles the system management functions and device drivers. Because it utilizes a model similar to XenServer, it is subject to the same availability vulnerabilities regarding patching and contention.

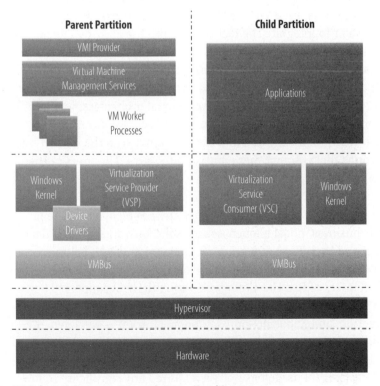

FIGURE 2.10 Microsoft Hyper-V architecture

Despite their relatively late entry into the virtualization space, Microsoft has about 20 percent of the market. Though still not at feature parity with some of the other solutions, Microsoft has used aggressive licensing and packaging policies in their user base to encourage Hyper-V adoption. It is a strategy that they have previously used well, in both the operating system and web browser solution areas.

Other Solutions

In addition to the solutions discussed in the previous sections, there are a large number of other virtualization vendors and solutions that as a group comprise, depending on whose numbers you follow, between 1 percent and 5 percent of the market. Most of the remaining solutions are based on the original open-source Xen code and have been enhanced and updated by the various solution providers.

Oracle offers a number of solutions, both built and acquired. Introduced in 2007, Oracle VM is a bare-metal hypervisor that is based on the open-source Xen code. In 2009, Oracle acquired Virtual Iron, another Xen-based hypervisor solution, with the intent to integrate the technology into the existing Oracle VM. Oracle's acquisition of Sun Microsystems in 2010 brought with it a number of additional virtualization solutions that Sun had developed or acquired as well, including the Solaris-specific Zones and the x86-oriented VirtualBox, a popular workbench tool for developers that we will examine in later chapters. VirtualBox has since been rebranded Oracle VM VirtualBox. The Oracle solutions have not gained mainstream traction, mostly due to their later entry into the market and the variety of solutions that is sometimes confusing to users. The users of these solutions are from strong Oracle shops.

Red Hat is another solution that has gone through a few different permutations over time. Initially, they also used the open-source Xen code because it fit nicely with their business model of open-source solutions. In 2008, Red Hat acquired Qumranet and their Kernel-based Virtual Machine (KVM) solution. KVM, like Linux itself, is also based on the open-source project of the same name. For a time, releases of Red Hat Enterprise Linux (RHEL) supported both the KVM and Xen virtualization technologies. In 2012, Red Hat stated that KVM is their future direction, and Xen is no longer supported. KVM is delivered as a Linux kernel module allowing you to leverage many features of Linux, like the scheduler and memory management, without needing to include them as part of the code. Like Oracle, KVM usage has not yet acquired any significant following and is mostly limited to existing users of Red Hat itself. However, the rise of

OpenStack, an open-source cloud-computing project, has helped as KVM can be used as one of the hypervisor choices.

In addition to these, there are about another dozen or so commercial x86-server virtualization solutions available today. The history of this particular software solution area, and other more mature areas in the past, indicates that many of these solution vendors will either be acquired by one of the market leaders for their technical innovations or fail outright because of the lack of sustainable market share or sufficient financial backing. We are in the midst of this consolidation now, while other areas of the data center—networking and storage, for example—are beginning to accelerate their virtualization journeys. Whatever happens, it is an exciting time to be watching the birth, growth, and maturation of a significant technology that has changed and continues to change the IT industry.

THE ESSENTIALS AND BEYOND

Hypervisors are the glue of virtualization. They connect their virtual guests to the physical world, as well as load balance the resources they administer. Their main function is to abstract the physical devices and act as the intermediary on the guests' behalf by managing all I/O between guests and device. There are two main hypervisor implementations: with and without an additional operating system between it and the hardware. Both have their uses. The commercial virtualization market is currently a growth industry, so new and old solution providers have been vying for a significant share of the business. The winners will be well positioned to support the next iteration of data center computing, support content providers for consumer solutions, and become the foundation for cloud computing.

ADDITIONAL EXERCISES

▶ Using the Internet, find four different Type-2 hypervisor solutions. What differences do they have? Why might you choose one over another?

▶ Hypervisors for server virtualization are just one use for this technology. With microprocessors in many of today's smart devices, where else might a hypervisor and multiple guests be used?

▶ Corporations often have to balance wants and needs based on real-world constraints such as financial budgets and the experience of their personnel. How would you convince your manager who wanted a less-expensive, "good enough" virtualization solution to acquire a fuller featured solution that would cost more? How might you convince your manager who wanted to acquire a more expensive, fuller featured virtualization solution to save some money and acquire a "good enough" solution?

CHAPTER 3

Understanding Virtual Machines

Virtual machines are the fundamental components of virtualization. They are the containers for traditional operating systems and applications that run on top of a hypervisor on a physical server. Inside a virtual machine, things seem very much like the inside of a physical server—but outside, things are very different. In this chapter, we will examine these differences, focus on how virtual machines work in relation to the physical machines they reside on, and take the initial steps in understanding how virtual machines are managed.

▶ **Describing a virtual machine**

▶ **Understanding how a virtual machine works**

▶ **Working with virtual machines**

Describing a Virtual Machine

A virtual machine, also referred to as a VM, has many of the same characteristics as a physical server. Like an actual server, a VM supports an operating system and is configured with a set of resources to which the applications running on the VM can request access. Unlike a physical server (where only one operating system runs at any one time and few, usually related, applications run), many VMs can run simultaneously inside a single physical server, and these VMs can also run many different operating systems supporting many different applications. Also, unlike a physical server, a VM is in actuality nothing more than a set of files that describe and comprise the virtual server.

The main files that make up a VM are the configuration file and the virtual disk files. The configuration file describes the resources that the VM can utilize: it enumerates the virtual hardware that makes up that particular VM. Figure 3.1 is a simplified illustration of a virtual machine. If you think of a virtual machine as an empty server chassis, the configuration file lists which hardware devices would be in that chassis: CPU, memory, storage, networking, CD drive, etc. In fact, as you will see when we build a new virtual machine, it is exactly like a new physical server just off the factory line—some (virtual) iron waiting for software to give it direction and purpose. In Chapter 4, "Creating a Virtual Machine," we will do exactly that.

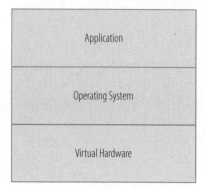

FIGURE 3.1 A virtual machine

Virtual machines have access to various hardware resources, but from their point of view, they don't know that these devices don't actually exist. They access virtual devices, software constructs that represent physical resources abstracted by the hypervisor. The virtual devices they deal with are standard devices—in other words, they are the same within each virtual machine, which makes them portable across various hardware platforms, virtualization solutions, or across vendor solutions, as you will see later in the chapter. In a virtual machine, as in a physical machine, you can configure various types and amounts of peripheral devices. The bulk of this text will cover how to configure and manage these devices. But the real key to understanding virtual machines is to understand that there are two different views of a VM: one from the inside and one from outside.

From outside the virtual machine, what you can see is the composition and configuration of the host server. Whether it is a laptop PC running VMware Fusion, Parallels Desktop, or VMware Workstation or it's a full-fledged enterprise-class server from Dell, HP, IBM, or Cisco running VMware vSphere or Citrix XenServer; the resources to which you have access are all of the systems devices.

From inside a virtual machine, the view is identical to being inside a physical machine. From the operating system's point of view, or an application's point of view, storage, memory, network, and processing are all available for the asking. If you are running Windows and open up the various Control Panel utilities to examine your system, you will find very little that would make you think twice. Storage devices, C: drives, D: drives, etc. are where they should be; network connections are visible and functional; and system services are running. There is some amount of memory in the server along with one or more CPUs, possibly a CD drive, monitor, keyboard, and maybe even a floppy drive. Everything looks just as it ought to, until you dig down and look at Windows Device Manager, as shown in Figure 3.2.

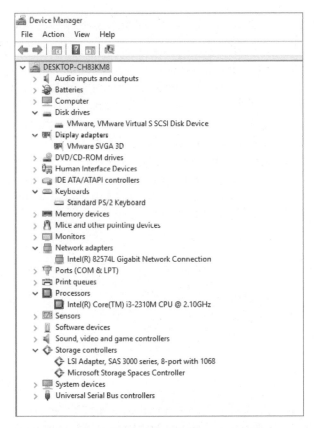

FIGURE 3.2 Windows Device Manager in a VM

Here you can see where real and virtual begin to diverge. Examining the network adapter and the storage adapter reveals industry standard devices. The display adapter is not the same as your actual monitor. It is created as a standard device driver to be used on any monitor. The disk drives and the

DVD/CD drives are also specialized virtual drivers. What happens is that the hypervisor underneath presents the virtual machines with generic resources to which they connect. The specialized device drivers, which we'll examine closely in Chapter 5, "Installing Windows on a Virtual Machine," are added later to help optimize that connection.

When you're buying a new computer, whether it is a laptop or a server, one of your key decisions will be how it should be configured. VMs give you the capability and the flexibility to easily change that configuration without most of the constraints that the same changes would cause in a physical server.

Examining CPUs in a Virtual Machine

Virtual machines are configured to run with one or more processors, depending on the anticipated demand on the system. In the simplest case, a VM will have one CPU and, as you saw earlier, if you examine the hardware from the VM's standpoint, you will see that only one CPU is available. From the host's standpoint, what has been assigned is the virtual machine's ability to schedule CPU cycles on the host's available CPUs. In this case, illustrated in Figure 3.3, the single CPU VM can schedule a single CPU's worth of capacity. The host does not reserve a CPU solely for the use of a particular VM; instead, when the VM needs processing resources, the hypervisor takes the request, schedules the operations, and passes the results back to the VM through the appropriate device driver.

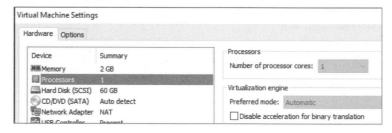

FIGURE 3.3 CPU settings in a VM

It is important to remember that usually the host has many more CPUs available than any one VM, and that the hypervisor is scheduling time on those processors on behalf of the VMs, rather than a VM actually having a dedicated CPU. One of the main reasons for virtualization in the first place was to gain more efficient use of the resources through consolidation, and a dedicated CPU would defeat that purpose. On another quick note, most servers today have multiple socket CPUs, and each one of those sockets contains one or more cores. For our purposes, a VM looks at a core as a single virtual CPU. As you learn more about virtualization, you will see that it is possible to create multi-CPU, multicore VMs, but that is outside the scope of this text. You will learn more about managing and configuring processor resources in Chapter 7, "Managing CPUs for a Virtual Machine."

Examining Memory in a Virtual Machine

RAM (random-access memory), or memory resources, is probably the simplest to understand in the virtual environment. Just as in a physical machine, having enough memory resources in a virtual machine is often the difference between success and failure when evaluating an application's performance. As digital consumers, we are all aware of the value of adequate memory resources, whether it be for our smart phones, tablets, laptops, or other personal electronic devices. More memory is usually better, but there is a fine balance between enough memory and too much memory in a shared virtual environment. As with CPU utilization, hypervisor vendors have added sophisticated memory management techniques to obtain the best use from the available physical memory. As shown in Figure 3.4, a virtual machine is allocated a specific amount of memory, and that is all that it can utilize, even though there might be orders of magnitude more memory available on the physical machine. Unlike physical machines, when a virtual machine requires more memory, you can merely reconfigure the amount and the VM will have access to the added capacity, sometimes without even needing a reboot. You will learn more about managing and configuring memory resources in Chapter 8, "Managing Memory for a Virtual Machine."

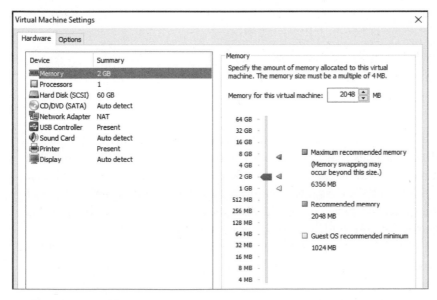

FIGURE 3.4 Memory settings in a VM

Examining Network Resources in a Virtual Machine

Like its physical counterpart, virtual networking provides a VM with a way to communicate with the outside world. Each virtual machine can be configured with one or more network interface cards, or NICs, that represent a connection to a network. These virtual NIC cards, however, don't connect with the physical NIC cards in the host system. The hypervisor supports the creation of a virtual network that connects the virtual NICs to a network that is composed of virtual switches. It is this virtual network that the physical NICs connect to, as shown in Figure 3.5.

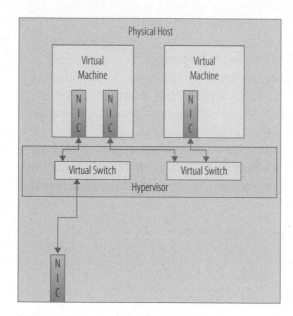

FIGURE 3.5 A simple virtual network

This virtual network is also a vital tool in creating secure environments for the virtual machines that share a host. From a security standpoint, VM-to-VM communications can occur across a virtual switch and never leave the physical host. If a second VM's virtual NIC connects to a virtual switch, and that switch is not connected to a physical NIC, the only way to communicate with that VM is through the first VM, building a protective buffer between the outside world and that VM. If there were a third VM in the picture, unless it was connected to the same virtual switch, it too would have no way to access the protected VM.

Figure 3.6 illustrates the virtual networking options for a virtual machine. You will learn more about managing and configuring network resources in Chapter 9, "Managing Networking for a Virtual Machine."

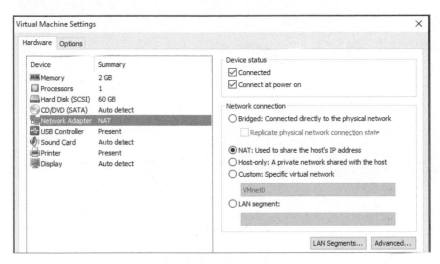

FIGURE 3.6   Network resources in a VM

Examining Storage in a Virtual Machine

Virtual servers need storage to work with, and like the resources you've seen so far, what gets presented to the virtual machine and what the virtual machine believes it is seeing are very different. As shown in Figure 3.7, a virtual machine running Windows will see a C: drive, a D: drive, and maybe many more. In actuality, those "drives" are merely carved out regions of disk space on a shared storage device, and the hypervisor manages the presentation to the VM.

Figure 3.8 illustrates the virtual machine's view of storage resources. As a virtual machine talks to a virtual SCSI disk adapter, the hypervisor passes data blocks to and from the physical storage. That actual connection, from the host to the storage, whether it is local storage on the host or on a storage area network (SAN), is abstracted from the virtual machines. Virtual machines usually don't have to worry about whether they are connected to their storage resources via fibre channel, iSCSI, or Network File System (NFS) because that is configured and managed at the host. You will learn more about managing and configuring storage resources in Chapter 10, "Managing Storage for a Virtual Machine."

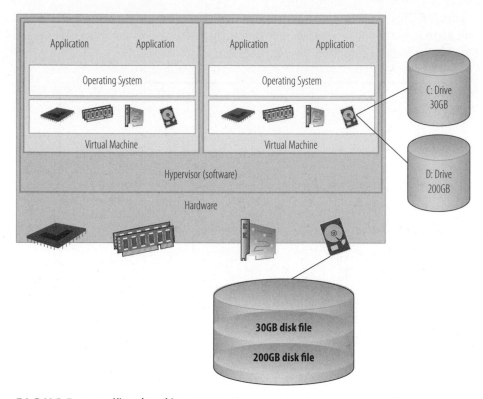

FIGURE 3.7 Virtual machine storage

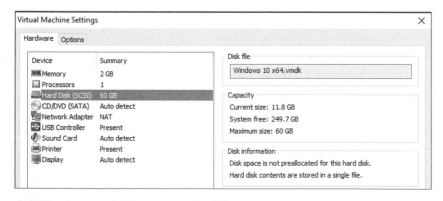

FIGURE 3.8 Storage resources in a VM

Understanding How a Virtual Machine Works

One way to look at how virtualization works is to say that a hypervisor allows the decoupling of traditional operating systems from the hardware. The hypervisor becomes the transporter and regulator of resources to and from the virtual guests it supports. It achieves this capability by fooling the guest operating system into believing that the hypervisor is actually the hardware. In order to understand how the virtual machine works, you need to look more closely at how virtualization works.

Without going too far under the covers, let's examine how a native operating system manages hardware. Figure 3.9 will help illustrate this process. When a program needs some data from a file on a disk, it makes a request through a program language command, such as an fgets() in C, which gets passed through to the operating system. The operating system has file system information available to it and passes the request on to the correct device manager, which then works with the physical disk I/O controller and storage device to retrieve the proper data. The data comes back through the I/O controller and device driver where the operating system returns the data to the requesting program. Not only are data blocks being requested, but memory block transfers, CPU scheduling, and network resources are requested too. At the same time, other programs are making additional requests and it is up to the operating system to keep all of these connections straight.

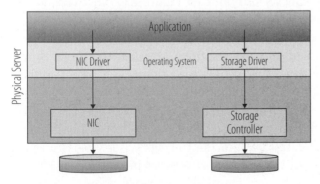

FIGURE 3.9 A simplified data request

Security and safety measures are built into the x86 architecture itself. This is to prevent both accidental and deliberate malicious system calls from co-opting or corrupting the applications or the operating system. The x86 processor's architecture provides protection in the form of four different levels on which processor commands can be executed. These levels are often referred to as *rings*. At the center, Ring 0 is the most privileged ring, where the operating system kernel works. Traditionally, Rings 1 and 2 are where device drivers execute, and Ring 3, the least-trusted level, is where applications run. In practice, Ring 1 and Ring 2 are rarely used. Applications themselves cannot execute processor instructions directly. Those requests are passed through the levels via system calls, where they are executed on behalf of the application, as in the simplified example, or they throw an error because the request would violate a constraint.

If a system program wants to affect some hardware state, it does so by executing privileged instructions in Ring 0. A shutdown request would be one example of this. A hypervisor runs in Ring 0, and the operating systems in the guests believe that they run in Ring 0. If a guest wants to issue a shutdown, the hypervisor intercepts that request and responds to the guest, indicating that the shutdown is proceeding so the operating system can continue through its steps to complete the software shutdown. If the hypervisor did not trap this command, any guest would be able to directly affect the resources and environment of all of the guests on a host, which would violate the isolation rule of Popek and Goldberg's definition, not to mention the difficulties that could ensue.

Like the native operating system that is managing concurrent program requests for resources, hypervisors abstract one layer further and manage multiple operating systems requests for resources. Figure 3.10 illustrates how application requests move in a virtual environment. In one sense, hypervisors decouple an operating system from the hardware, but they still ensure that resource demands are met in an equitable and timely manner. You might think that adding an extra layer of processing would have a significant impact on the performance of applications running in VMs, but you would be wrong. Today's solutions provide very sophisticated algorithms for dealing with this constantly changing and complex I/O flow from guest to hypervisor to host and back again without having to supply noticeable overhead for the hypervisor's needs. Just as in a physical environment, most time performance issues in a virtual environment still come down to correctly provisioning the necessary resources for the application workload.

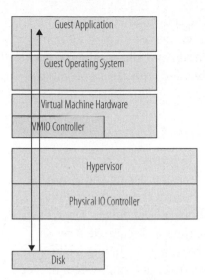

FIGURE 3.10 A simplified data request in a virtual environment

Working with Virtual Machines

Virtual machines exist as two physical entities: the files that make up the configuration of the virtual machines and the instantiation in memory that makes up a running VM once it has been started. In many ways, working with a running virtual machine is very similar to working with an actual physical server. Like a physical server, you can interact with it through some type of network connection to load, manage, and monitor the environment or the various applications that the server supports. Also like a physical server, you can modify the hardware configuration, adding or subtracting capability and capacity, though the methods for doing that and the flexibility for doing that are very different between a physical server and a virtual machine.

We'll defer the "working with a running VM" discussion until the next chapter and focus for now on understanding why the fact that VMs exist as data files is a key enabler in managing and maintaining them. Since the inception of the computer, files have been the method of storing information. Because of that history and knowledge, managing files is routine. If someone needs to move a spreadsheet from one place to another, she moves the file. If she needs to back up a document, she copies that file and moves the copy to another device for archiving. If someone builds a presentation that will serve as a base for many other presentations, he write-locks that presentation and allows other people to duplicate it for their use. By leveraging these same file properties, you can do some remarkable things with virtual machines.

Understanding Virtual Machine Clones

Server provisioning takes considerable resources in terms of time, manpower, and money. Before server virtualization, the process of ordering and acquiring a physical server could take weeks, or even months in certain organizations, not to mention the cost, which often would be thousands of dollars. Once the server physically arrived, additional provisioning time was required. A server administrator would need to perform a long list of chores, including loading an operating system, loading whatever other patches that operating system needed to be up-to-date, configuring additional storage, installing whatever corporate tools and applications the organization decided were crucial to managing their infrastructure, acquiring network information, and connecting the server to the network infrastructure. Finally, the server could be handed off to an application team to install and configure the actual application that would be run on the server. The additional provisioning time could be days, or longer, depending on the complexity of what needed to be installed and what organizational mechanisms were in place to complete the process.

Contrast this with a virtual machine. If you need a new server, you can clone an existing one, as shown in Figure 3.11. The process involves little more than copying the files that make up the existing server. Once that copy exists, the guest operating system only needs some customization in the form of unique system information, such as a system name and IP address, before it can be instantiated. Without those changes, two VMs with the same identity would be running in the network and application space, and that would wreak havoc on many levels. Tools that manage virtual machines have provisions built in to help with the customizations during cloning, which can make the actual effort itself nothing more than a few mouse clicks.

Although it may only take a few moments to request the clone, it will take some time to enact the copy of the files and the guest customization. Depending on a number of factors, it might take minutes or even hours. But, if we contrast this process with the provisioning of a physical server, which takes weeks or longer to acquire and set up, a virtual machine can be built, configured, and provided in mere minutes, at a considerable savings in both man hours and cost. We'll work more with VM clones in Chapter 11, "Copying a Virtual Machine."

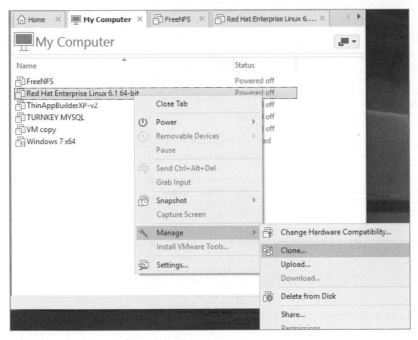

FIGURE 3.11 Cloning a VM

Understanding Templates

Similar to clones, virtual machine templates are another mechanism to rapidly deliver fully configured virtual servers. A template is a mold, a preconfigured, preloaded virtual machine that is used to stamp out copies of a commonly used server. Figure 3.12 shows the Enable Template Mode checkbox to enable this capability. The difference between a template and a clone is that the clone is running and a template is not. In most environments, a template cannot run, and in order to make changes to it (applying patches, for example), a template must first be converted back to a virtual machine. You would then start the virtual machine, apply the necessary patches, shut down the virtual machine, and then convert the VM back to a template. Like cloning, creating a VM from a template also requires a unique identity to be applied to the newly created virtual machine. As in cloning, the time to create a virtual machine from a template is orders of magnitude quicker than building and provisioning a new physical server. Unlike a clone, when a VM is converted to a template, the VM it is created from is gone.

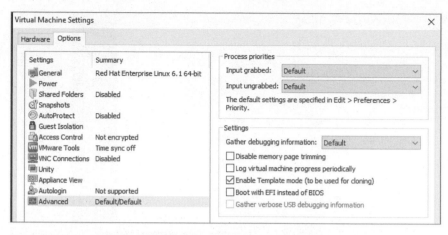

FIGURE 3.12   Creating a VM from a template

Templates are used to do more than just deliver "empty" virtual machines, servers that are composed of the configured virtual machine with an operating system installed; they can deliver VMs that have applications installed and configured as well. When users need their programs to be loaded, a VM created from a prebuilt template can deliver that application or suite of applications to users, ready for immediate use. In fact, many application vendors are beginning to deliver those applications in the form of virtual machine templates that can be downloaded and then deployed in a minimum amount of time. We will look more closely at templates in Chapter 11.

Understanding Snapshots

Snapshots are pretty much just what they sound like, a capturing of a VM's state at a particular point in time. They provide a stake in the ground that you can easily return to in the event that some change made to the VM caused a problem you'd like to undo. If you have ever played any adventure games, the concept of a save point is analogous to a snapshot. Figure 3.13 is a basic illustration of how snapshots work. A snapshot preserves the state of a VM, its data, and its hardware configuration. Once you snapshot a VM, changes that are made no longer go to the virtual machine disk. They go instead to a *delta disk,* sometimes called a *child disk*. This delta disk accumulates all changes until one of two things happens, another snapshot or a consolidation, ending the snapshot process. If another snapshot is taken, a second delta disk is created and all subsequent changes are written there. If a consolidation is done, the delta disk changes are merged with the base virtual machine files and they become the updated VM.

Cisco delivers their Unified Communications solution as a prebuilt download. Oracle currently offers many downloadable templates, including Peoplesoft, Siebel, Oracle E-Business, WebLogic, and Oracle database solutions.

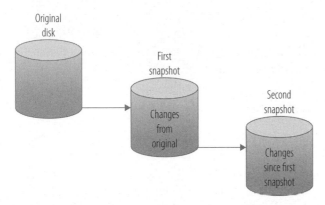

F I G U R E 3 . 1 3 A snapshot disk chain

Finally, you can revert back to the state of a VM at the time when a snapshot was taken, unrolling all of the changes that have been made since that time. Snapshots are very useful in test and development areas, allowing developers to try risky or unknown processes with the ability to restore their environment to a known healthy state. Snapshots can be used to test a patch or an update where the outcome is unsure, and they provide an easy way to undo what was applied. Snapshots are not a substitute for proper backups. Applying multiple snapshots to a VM is fine for a test environment but can cause large headaches and performance issues in a production system. We'll work closer with snapshots in Chapter 11.

Understanding OVF

Another way to package and distribute virtual machines is using the Open Virtualization Format (OVF). OVF is a standard, created by an industry-wide group of people representing key vendors in the various areas of virtualization. The purpose of the standard is to create a platform and vendor-neutral format to bundle up virtual machines into one or more files that can be easily transported from one virtualization platform to another. Put another way, this offers a way to create a VM on a Xen-based system, export it to the neutral OVF standard, and then import in into a VMware or Hyper-V environment. Most virtualization vendors have options to export virtual machines out to OVF format, as well as have the ability to import OVF formatted VMs into their own formats.

The OVF standard supports two different methods for packaging virtual machines. The OVF template creates a number of files that represent the virtual machine, much as the virtual machine itself is composed of a number of files.

The OVF standard body is the Distributed Management Task Force (DMTF). The standard is fairly new and still evolving. See www.dmtf.org for more details.

The OVF standard also supports a second format, OVA, which will encapsulate all of the information in a single file. In fact, the standard states, "An OVF package may be stored as a single file using the TAR format. The extension of that file shall be .ova (open virtual appliance or application)."

Understanding Containers

While containers are not virtual machines, they are close enough in functionality and prevalent enough in application development and business computing that they are worth including here. Like virtual machines, containers offer a platform-independent package to bundle, deliver, and deploy applications. Unlike virtual machines, containers do their abstraction at the operating system level, rather than the hardware level. This means containers can wrap up multiple workloads in a single receptacle, usually supporting a single application.

Although containers do provide great portability and lower resource overhead than virtual machine infrastructure, they do have some limitations. The container model, because it abstracts at the operating system level, has a limitation that all of the workloads in a container must run the same operating system or kernel where a hypervisor can support virtual machines or various operating systems side-by-side. The isolation between workloads in a container is also not nearly as robust as what hypervisors and virtual machines provide.

In certain use cases, containers can offer more rapid deployment and lower overhead than virtual machines. Many of Google's services run in their Let Me Contain That For You (lmctfy) technology. Another popular open-source container technology is Docker (www.docker.com). Working with other like-minded companies, Docker has done a lot to develop standardization within containers in addition to providing numerous other tools and related management technologies to legitimize containers as a mainstream solution.

Much the way virtual machines and virtualization disrupted traditional computing, container technologies are disrupting virtualization and cloud computing. We'll investigate containers again in Chapter 14, "Understanding Applications in a Virtual Machine."

VIRTUAL APPLIANCES

Like many other concepts in technology, *virtual appliance* can represent a range of virtual machine deployments depending on who is doing the defining. Initially, the term referred to a specialized virtual machine that contained an operating system and a preloaded and preconfigured application that was designed for a particular function. The user had little access to the tuning and configuration

(Continues)

VIRTUAL APPLIANCES   *(Continued)*

of the appliance, and upgrades or patches involved a download and replacement of the entire appliance, instead of working inside the VM. BEA's Liquid VM was one such implementation that provided an optimized WebLogic Application Server environment. The definition has since expanded to include ordinary virtual machines that have been preloaded with an operating system and a loaded application, but the user has access to all of the configuration and tuning parameters of both the operating system and application. This model has grown, along with vendor support for their applications running in a virtualized environment.

THE ESSENTIALS AND BEYOND

Virtual machines are the containers that run workloads on top of hypervisors. They are much more manageable and cost effective than their physical counterparts, allowing rapid initial deployment as well as unique configuration alteration capabilities. Traditional server resources are all available in VMs, with the expected interfaces and behaviors, although virtualization provides additional options not possible in physical servers. Application vendors are creating virtual appliances for their customers to download and deploy. The industry standard OVF format allows cross-vendor and cross-platform packaging and distribution of prebuilt, preconfigured servers and applications.

ADDITIONAL EXERCISES

▶ Are there any advantages to physical servers that would preclude someone from using virtual machines? At what point do you think the inherent cost savings and manageability advantages that virtual machines provide would outweigh the physical server advantages you listed?

▶ Using the Internet, investigate the amount and type of virtual appliances that are available for download. What different formats are available? Are they all available in OVF format? Why do or why don't you think this is true?

▶ Examine the OVF standard document. What are the requirements for the VM files to meet the OVF standard? Are they simple or complex?

CHAPTER 4

Creating a Virtual Machine

Virtual machines are the building blocks for today's data centers. Once an infrastructure is in place, the process of populating the environment with workloads begins. There are two main methods of creating those virtual machines, the first being a physical-to-virtual operation (or P2V) and the second being a from-the-ground-up execution. We'll cover both of those and perform the latter to create an initial VM.

▶ **Performing P2V conversions**

▶ **Loading your environment**

▶ **Building a new virtual machine**

Performing P2V Conversions

Virtualization technology and its use by corporations did not spring up instantly out of nowhere. Even though increasing numbers of virtual machines are being deployed today, there are still many millions of physical servers running application workloads in data centers. A significant percentage of new workloads are still being deployed as physical servers as well. As data center administrators initially embraced virtualization, there were two main strategies for using virtualization in their environments.

The first of these was consolidation. *Consolidation* is the practice of taking existing physical servers and converting them into virtual servers that can run atop the hypervisor. As you saw in Chapter 1, "Understanding Virtualization," there were and still are millions of physical servers running business applications. In order to achieve the substantial savings that virtualization provided, corporate IT departments needed to migrate a significant portion of their physical server workloads to the virtual infrastructure. To effect this change, they needed tools and a methodology to convert their existing physical servers into virtual machines. Today, many companies who have begun virtualizing their data centers have more than half of their servers converted into virtual machines.

The second strategy was containment. *Containment* is the practice of initially deploying new application workloads as virtual machines so additional physical servers will not be required, except to expand the virtual infrastructure capacity. You'll learn more about this later when you create new virtual machines.

In the last few years, a third reason for virtualizing existing workloads has appeared in the form of cloud computing. The first step for many companies to take advantage of cloud computing is to either migrate a set of virtual machines to an outside hosting provider or to convert to a subscription application service that is managed by the application company and is usually run outside of the company's physical premises. Some examples of these would be Salesforce .com, Workday, and Microsoft's Office 365 offering. These Software-as-a-Service (SaaS) applications take all of the maintenance and management of the infrastructure from the company, which is part of the vendor's value. We will focus on those infrastructures that require your attention.

Investigating the Physical-to-Virtual Process

The process of converting a physical server to virtual, often shortened to the term P2V, can take a number of paths. The creation of a brand new virtual machine is usually the preferred method. A new virtual machine provides the opportunity to load the latest operating system version and the latest patches as well as rid the existing workload of all the accumulated detritus that an older server acquires over the course of its working lifetime through application installations and upgrades, tool installations and upgrades, and operating system upgrades, not to mention additional work that may have been done and forgotten over time. Also, as part of creating a virtual machine, you will see that certain physical drivers and server processes are no longer needed in the virtual environment. When you create a new VM, part of the process needs to make these adjustments as well.

If you were to perform this process manually for multiple servers, it would be tremendously repetitive, time-consuming, and error prone. To streamline the effort, many vendors have created P2V tools that automate the conversion of existing physical servers into virtual machines. Instead of creating a clean virtual server and installing a new operating system, the tools copy everything into the VM. Older servers that run applications or environments that are no longer well understood by their administrators are at risk when the hardware becomes no longer viable. The operating system version may no longer be supported, or even be capable of running on a newer hardware platform. Here is a perfect situation for a P2V—the ability to transfer that workload in its native state to a new

Aside from P2V, most tools can also perform V2P (for certain debugging cases) and V2V (to change vendor hypervisors). Some editions also cover P2C (Physical to Cloud).

platform-independent environment where it can be operated and managed for the length of its usable application life without concern about aging hardware failing. The other advantage of this process is that a system administrator would not have to migrate the application to a new operating system where it might not function properly, again extending the life and usability of the application with minimal disruption.

One of the disadvantages of a P2V conversion can be an advantage as well. The P2V process is at its very core a cloning of an existing physical server into a virtual machine. There are some changes that occur during the process, translating physical drivers into their virtual counterparts and certain network reconfigurations, but ultimately a P2V copies what is in a source server into the target VM.

In addition to the various hypervisor solution providers, a number of third-party providers also have P2V tools. Here is a partial list of some of the available tools:

▶ VMware Converter

▶ Novell Platespin Migrate

▶ Microsoft Virtual Machine Converter

▶ Citrix XenConvert

▶ Dell vConverter

> Unlike many of the other P2V tools, VMware Converter has no V2P capability. There is no official statement as to why, but V2P is directly opposite of VMware's corporate mission.

Hot and Cold Cloning

There are two ways of performing the P2V process, hot and cold, and there are advantages and disadvantages to both methods. Cold conversions are done with the source machine nonoperational and the application shut down, which ensures that it is pretty much a straight copy operation from old to new. Both types involve a similar process:

▶ Determine the resources being used by the existing server to correctly size the necessary resources for the virtual machine.

▶ Create the virtual machine with the correct configuration.

▶ Copy the data from the source (physical) server to the target (virtual) server.

▶ Run post-conversion cleanup and configuration. This could include network configuration, removal of applications and services that are not required for virtual operations, and inclusion of new drivers and tools.

▶ Make manual adjustments to the configuration, if needed. If an application has outgrown its physical server, the administrator could add more RAM or additional processors. If the workload was overprovisioned in the physical server, here is an opportunity to *right-size* the virtual machine by removing unneeded RAM or processors that can be used more efficiently elsewhere.

Hot cloning, as the name implies, performs the clone operation while the source server is booted and the application is running. One disadvantage to this is that data is constantly changing on the source machine, and it is difficult to ensure that those changes are migrated to the new VM. The advantage here is that not all applications can be suspended for the period of time that is necessary to complete a P2V. A hot clone allows the P2V to complete without disrupting the application. Depending on where the application data is being accessed from, it may be even simpler. If the data is already kept and accessed on a SAN rather than local storage in the server, the physical server could be P2Ved, and when the post-conversion work and validation is completed, the physical server would be shut down, and the disks remounted on the virtual machine. This process would be less time-consuming than migrating the data from the local storage to a SAN along with the P2V.

The length of time to complete a P2V is dependent on the amount of data to be converted, which correlates directly to the size of the disks that need to be migrated to a virtual machine. More disks and larger disks require more time. Times can vary widely from just an hour to maybe a day. Most systems, however, can comfortably be done in just a few hours, and very often P2Vs are run in parallel for efficiency. Vendors and service organizations have years of experience behind them with these conversions and have created P2V factories that allow companies to complete dozens or hundreds of migrations with minimal impact on a company's operation and with a high degree of success. At the end of the process, a data center has a lot fewer physical servers than at the start.

Loading Your Environment

In order to build and configure virtual machines, you'll need a workbench. Although you could download and install a Type-1 hypervisor on your PC, it would be outside the scope of this text as well as unnecessary for the work that you will be doing. In fact, many tools are available that will allow you to create VMs using a Type-2 hypervisor as your environment. The benefit is that you will be able to start up virtual machines when they are required, shut them down

or suspend them when the work is complete, and then return to your usual
PC applications. Many application developers use these tools to create virtual
machines that then get migrated to the larger dedicated virtual environment.
Here is a short list of some of the more popular applications:

- ▶ VMware Workstation Player
- ▶ VMware Workstation Pro
- ▶ VMware Fusion (for Macintosh)
- ▶ Parallels Desktop
- ▶ VirtualBox (open source)
- ▶ Microsoft Windows Virtual PC

> **This chapter uses VMware Workstation Player and VMware Workstation Pro version 12.1.0 and VirtualBox version 5.0.14 for the examples on a Windows 10 system.**

The virtualization workbench tools you choose will depend on several factors,
including what you are running as a desktop operating system and what, if anything, you are willing to pay for the tools. The examples in this text use VMware
Workstation Player for most of the work and VMware Workstation Pro for some
illustrative elements that Player does not have. Just as Adobe Acrobat Reader
allows you to read PDF documents created by other people, VMware Workstation
Player allows you to play virtual machines. It also allows you to create new
VMs. Player is used in these examples for a number of reasons; the first and
foremost is that it is available as a free download. The second is that VMware has
the lion's share of the virtualization market, so it makes sense to use a solution
that would be more prevalent than a lesser-used application. Also, if you are
using this text as part of a university class, many schools have agreements with
various software companies such as Microsoft, Red Hat, Cisco, and VMware to
provide their solutions at little or no cost to students. That means that VMware
Workstation Pro might be available to students at a reduced cost or free. We'll
also use VirtualBox, a free, Oracle-backed, open-source offering that is very
popular in development environments.

> **The latest versions of VMware Workstation Player require a 64-bit computer. If your machine is a 32-bit system, you can use version 10, but your screens will not match the figures. The VMware Workstation Player download page at www.vmware.com/downloads/ has both the latest version available and past editions.**

Loading VMware Workstation Player

As shown in Figure 4.1, you can download VMware Workstation Player from
the VMware website from a number of different links, including www.vmware
.com/downloads. Read the release notes, which are available via the link on the
page, to make sure that your computer meets the requirements for the software. Usually, the resource that your computer needs most is memory. If you
recall that a Type-2 hypervisor sits on top of a native operating system, you will

see that you need to provide memory for the host operating system, VMware Workstation Player, as well as any VMs that you will be running. Because you will typically be running only one VM at a time, processor resources don't usually become a bottleneck. This could change if you do run multiple VMs, which is not unusual in a test or development environment.

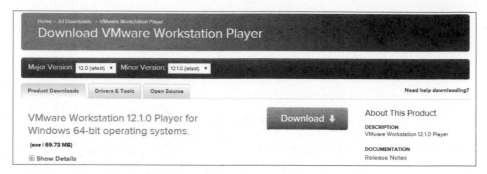

FIGURE 4.1   Downloading VMware Workstation Player

After downloading the Player executable, install it by double-clicking the icon shown in Figure 4.2.

FIGURE 4.2   The VMware Workstation Player package

The Windows User Account Control window appears. Select Yes. The Player Setup screen appears, as shown in Figure 4.3. Select Next to continue.

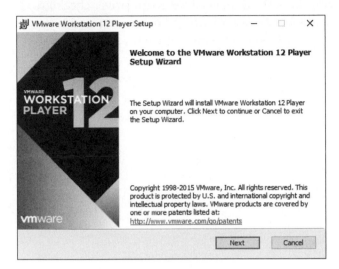

FIGURE 4.3 The Player Setup window

As Figure 4.4 illustrates, you will need to accept the End User License agreement before continuing. Click the I Accept The Terms In The License Agreement checkbox and select Next to continue.

FIGURE 4.4 The License Agreement window

The Custom Setup screen appears, as illustrated in Figure 4.5. Here you can select the destination folder of your choice by clicking the Change button. If you have a Windows host system, check the Enhanced Keyboard Driver checkbox. This provides some additional security, faster keyboard processing, and better handling of international keyboards and keyboards with extra function keys. Select Next to continue.

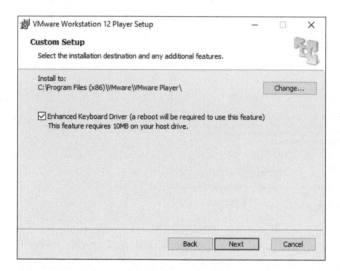

FIGURE 4.5 The Custom Setup window

The User Experience Settings Window appears, as shown in Figure 4.6. Uncheck the first selection box if you do not want to check for product updates on startup. Uncheck the second selection box if you do not want to provide usage statistics to VMware. Select the Learn More link to find out about the feedback process. Choose Next to continue.

The Shortcuts Window appears, as shown in Figure 4.7. Uncheck the selection boxes if you do not want the offered shortcuts created. Choose Next to continue.

As illustrated in Figure 4.8, the Ready to Install window appears. You can review your selections screen by screen using the Back button. Choose Install to install VMware Workstation Player.

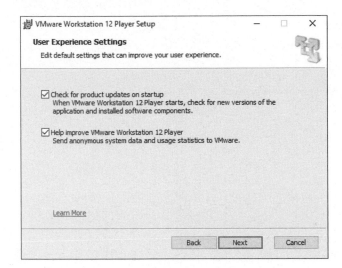

FIGURE 4.6 The User Experience Settings window

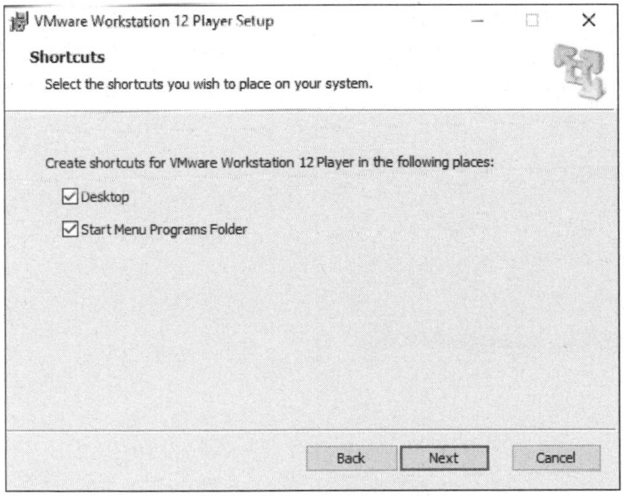

FIGURE 4.7 The Shortcuts window

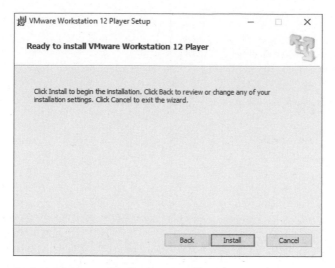

F I G U R E 4 . 8   The Ready to Install window

VMware Workstation Player will be installed, and a series of update screens will display the progress of the installation, as shown in Figure 4.9. This process will take a few minutes.

F I G U R E 4 . 9   The installation progress screen

As illustrated in Figure 4.10, at the completion of the installation, a last screen appears saying the installation is completed. If you chose to retain the shortcut option, a shortcut appears on the desktop. Select Finish to exit the installation process.

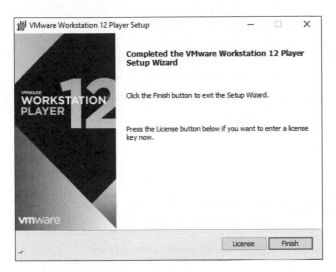

FIGURE 4.10 Installation complete

Exploring VMware Workstation Player

Now that Player is installed, fire it up and take it for a short spin before you start building VMs. Double-click the icon to start VMware Workstation Player. The initial entry prompts you for an email address to use the free version. Enter a valid email address and select Continue. Acknowledge the Thank You window and click Finish.

Figure 4.11 shows the main Workstation Player window. The items along the right side of the screen are a subset of what is available from the Player menu at the top of the screen. You can select either the icons or the text along the right side to choose the action. Selecting the house icon on the left side will return to main window.

Let's look closer at each of the selections under the Player pull-down menu under File. They are

- ▶ Create A New Virtual Machine
- ▶ Open A Virtual Machine
- ▶ Download A Virtual Appliance
- ▶ Player Preferences

As with many Windows applications, there are still keystroke commands that will execute the selected function. Create and Open are both fairly self-explanatory, and you will use both of them extensively. Download A Virtual Appliance will open your default browser to the VMware Virtual Appliance Marketplace where you can search for specific prebuilt VMs, or just browse through the thousands that are available. We'll return to virtual appliances later in Chapter 14, "Understanding Applications in a Virtual Machine." Finally, select Preferences. As shown in Figure 4.12, there are a number of options that can affect how Player behaves as you work with the application.

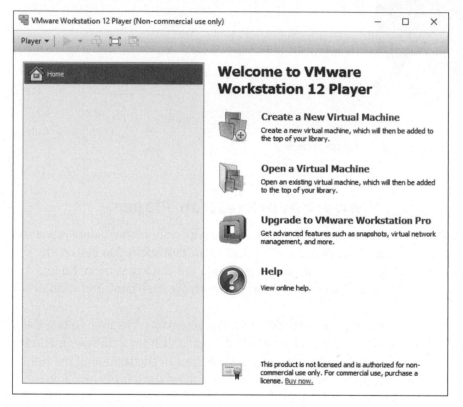

FIGURE 4.11   The VMware Workstation Player main window

Under the Help menu are

- ▶ Help Topics
- ▶ Online Documentation
- ▶ Support
  - ▶ Online Community
  - ▶ Request A Product Feature

- ▶ Upgrade To VMware Workstation Pro

- ▶ Enter License Key

- ▶ Software Updates

- ▶ Hints

- ▶ About VMware Workstation Player

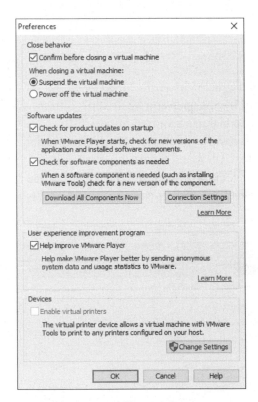

FIGURE 4.12 Player preferences

The Help Topics selection opens an Internet browser and brings you to the appropriate user guides for VMware Workstation Player. Similarly, the Online Documentation selection also opens an Internet browser and brings you to the latest documentation available online for VMware Workstation Player. Under the Support submenu, the Online Community selection provides a link to the VMware Workstation Player online discussion areas. Also under the Support submenu, the Request A Product Feature choice allows you to make feature enhancement suggestions to the VMware Workstation Player product management team. Upgrade To VMware Workstation Pro links you to the VMware Workstation Pro product page for information. Choosing Enter License Key allows you to enter a purchased license key if you are using Workstation Player for a business. Selecting Software Updates will check to see if a newer release of VMware Workstation Player is available for download. The Hints option allows you to toggle the hints capability. Finally, the About VMware Workstation Player window provides information about this particular installation of VMware Workstation Player, including the version number and various bits of host information.

Loading VirtualBox

Another very popular Type-2 hypervisor is Oracle VirtualBox. Developed by Innotek GmbH in Germany, it was offered free as open source in 2007. Sun Microsystems acquired Innotek in 2008, and Oracle acquired Sun in 2010. VirtualBox continues to be open-source software and free of charge. It runs not just on Windows or Linux hosts, but on Mac OS X and Solaris hosts as well. As shown in Figure 4.13, you can download VirtualBox from `http://www.virtualbox.org/`. Choose the Downloads link and select the correct choice for your host machine.

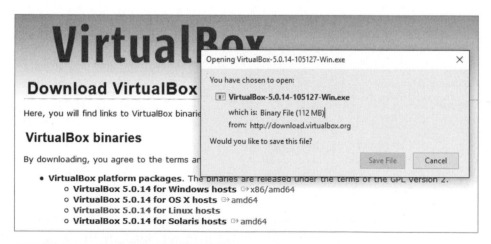

FIGURE 4.13 Downloading VirtualBox

After downloading the VirtualBox executable, begin the installation by double-clicking the icon shown in Figure 4.14. If you are presented with a Windows SmartScreen popup, select More and then Run to continue to the installation.

As shown in Figure 4.15, the VirtualBox Setup window appears. Select Next to continue.

FIGURE 4.14 The VirtualBox installation package

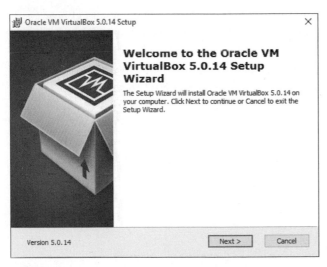

FIGURE 4.15 The VirtualBox Setup window

The Custom Setup screen appears, as illustrated in Figure 4.16. In the feature window, you can select or deselect which features to install. For our purposes, install the default options by making no changes.

You also have the option to change the installation location by choosing the Browse button. The Disk Usage button at the bottom of the screen gives you insight into how much storage will be required for the installation and what is available on your system. Choose Next to continue.

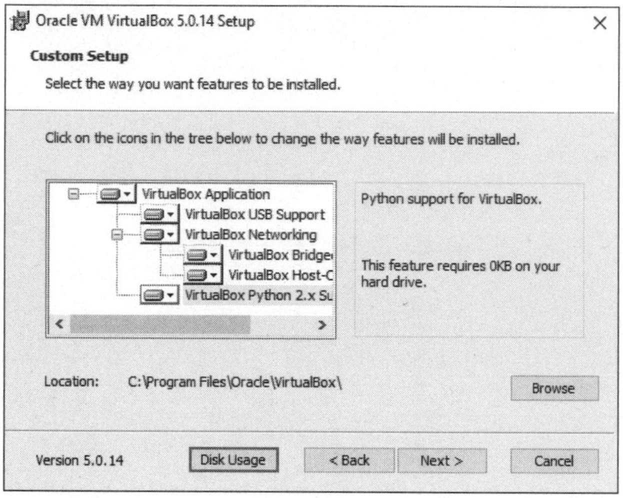

FIGURE 4.16 The Custom Setup screen

Figure 4.17 shows the second Custom Setup window. Here you can choose to keep or unselect the offered shortcuts on the Desktop and the Quick Launch bar. Leave the Register File Associations checkbox selected. This will connect specific file types that VirtualBox uses to the application, much like how Microsoft Excel is associated with .xls and .xlsx file extensions. Select Next to continue.

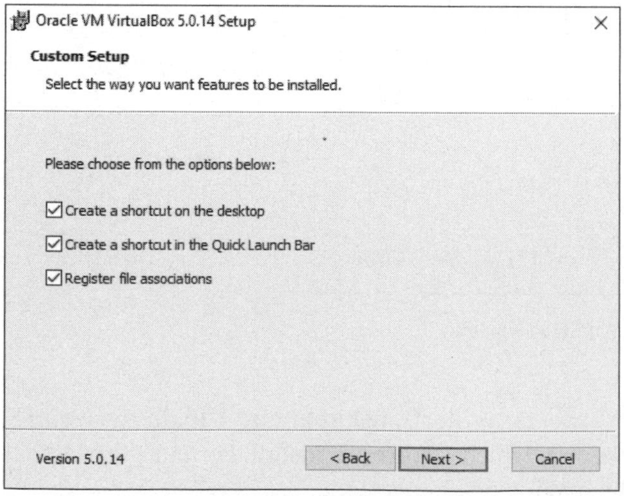

FIGURE 4.17 Another Custom Setup window

The Warning screen, shown in Figure 4.18, appears and explains that VirtualBox will reset the network connection and momentarily disconnect your machine from the network. To proceed with the installation, select Yes.

FIGURE 4.18 The Network Interfaces warning

The Ready to Install window appears as illustrated in Figure 4.19. Click Install to begin the installation process.

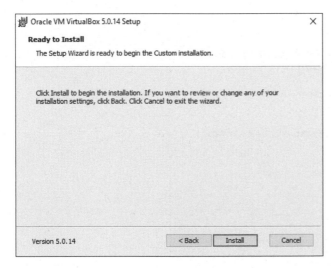

FIGURE 4.19 The Ready to Install window

VirtualBox will be installed, and a series of update screens will display the progress of the installation, as shown in Figure 4.20. During this stage you will be presented with a number of screens to install USB device drivers. Choose Install to allow the drivers to be loaded. This entire process will take a few minutes.

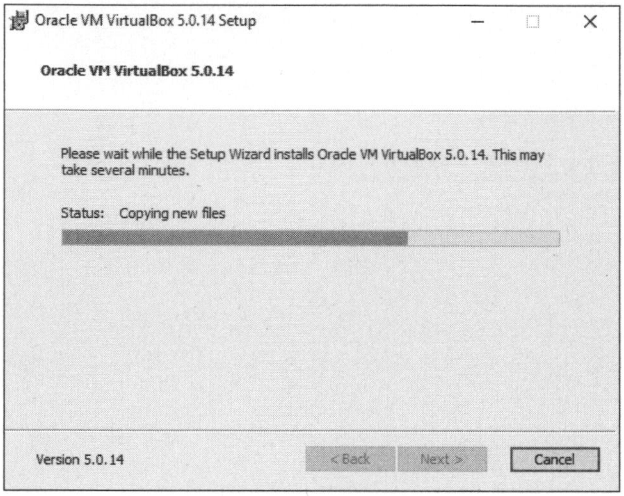

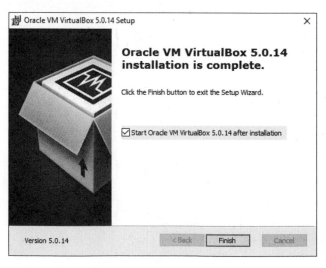

FIGURE 4.20 Installation progress

When the installation is finished, the final screen will display as shown in Figure 4.21. Select Finish to complete the process.

FIGURE 4.21 The VirtualBox installation is completed.

The Installation Wizard closes and VirtualBox is opened for the first time, as shown in Figure 4.22. We'll explore the VirtualBox in Chapter 6, "Installing Linux on a Virtual Machine."

FIGURE 4.22 The Oracle VM VirtualBox Manager

Building a New Virtual Machine

Once they experience the benefits of consolidation in a data center, administrators quickly look to expand the use of virtualization to increase those advantages. *Containment* is the practice of initially deploying new application workloads as virtual machines. One large benefit of a containment strategy is a significant decrease in new hardware acquisition costs because most incoming workloads are now deployed as virtual machines. Some necessary workload-configuration education occurs during this process.

When physical servers are purchased for new applications, their configuration is based on a number of assumptions. The first assumption is how long the server will be in use. A typical server's lifespan is between three and five years, at which point they are replaced by equipment that is newer, faster, and usually less expensive to maintain. In order to configure the system to run for its useful lifespan, you have to take into account two parameters: peak performance and growth.

A server is typically sized to handle what the application owner believes the application will need to handle at the end of its life. For example, if in its initial deployment it will process a thousand transactions a second, and you expect about 10 percent growth every year, at the end of five years, the server will need to process about 1,450 transactions a second. However, from a different perspective, there might be times during that initial year when the expectation is that during peak times, the system would need to process 1,500 transactions per second. That number would grow to about 2,200 transactions per second in the final year. The bottom line is that your server should be sized from day one to handle more than double the need at that time. This is the model that has been in place for many years: the application vendor works with a customer to decide what the long-term need will be, and they configure the hardware for that projection. The company pays for that capacity and hardware, even if that projection is never reached. If that projection is reached earlier, then the existing server needs to have resources added, if that is possible, or a whole new server is needed to replace it.

Thinking about VM Configuration

Virtual machines and virtual infrastructure work differently. The platform is an aggregation of resources that are allocated to the various workloads, but the adjustment of that allocation is often very fluid and dynamic, in sharp contrast to the essentially locked-in configuration of a physical server. Two areas that application owners need to understand as they move their applications into a virtual environment are configuration and resource allocation. Though every application is different and its resource requirements are different, most workloads, when they are migrated to a virtual machine, are configured with less memory and fewer processors than they would have been configured with in the physical world.

There are a number of reasons why this is true, the first being that with the many different aspects of dynamic resource allocation in a virtual environment, they can be sized appropriately for the current need rather than an oversized future need. You'll see later that you can configure cushions of resources that are available if needed but are never used if they aren't required. Those cushions, when they aren't being used, remain as part of the larger resource pool that everyone can use. Both memory management and processor utilization are highly optimized, so the practice is to start smaller with an initial VM and add resources if necessary, rather than start with a larger VM and subtract them. It is a best practice, with few exceptions, to create every new VM with one virtual

CPU (vCPU) and only add additional vCPUs if poor performance dictates the change. Most often, one is more than enough.

Creating a First VM

Taking into account best practices about proper configuration, for your first virtual machine, let's create a VM with one vCPU, 2 GB of memory, 30 GB of storage, and one network connection. Don't forget that the VM is equivalent to a hardware server, so when you are done, you will merely have a container into which you can load an operating system. Chapter 5, "Installing Windows on a Virtual Machine," will cover installing Microsoft Windows 10 into a VM, while Chapter 6, "Installing Linux on a Virtual Machine," will cover loading Ubuntu Linux into a VM.

Let's begin by opening VMware Workstation Player. Select the Create A New Virtual Machine option from the main screen or the File menu. Figure 4.23 shows the New Virtual Machine Wizard. There are three choices here. The first two will load an operating system from either a DVD or an ISO image, but we will defer those methods for now. Select the option "I will install the operating system later" and then select Next.

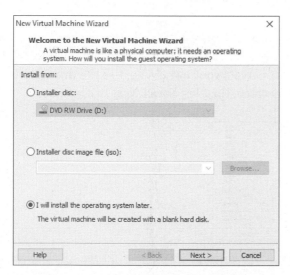

FIGURE 4.23 The New Virtual Machine Wizard

The Select a Guest Operating System screen, shown in Figure 4.24, allows you to choose which operating system you plan to install. You can see there are quite a few operating systems that can be installed in a virtual machine. Choose the Guest Operating System. Choose the Version. This VM will be used as the base for Chapter 5, so Windows 10 x64 is selected. Select Next to continue.

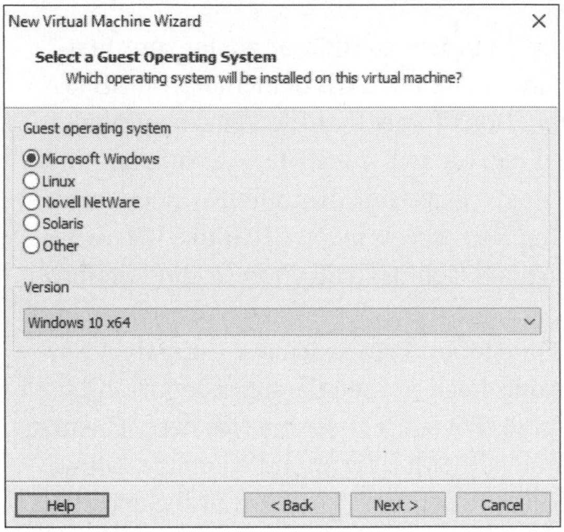

FIGURE 4.24 The Select a Guest Operating System screen

The Name the Virtual Machine screen in Figure 4.25 is where you choose a name for the VM and select where you want the files that comprise the VM to reside. You can choose the defaults or create your own name. Use the Browse button to choose a different place to create the files. Select Next to continue.

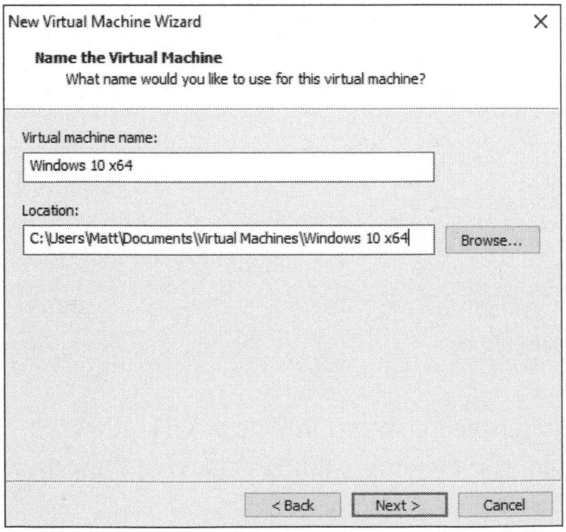

FIGURE 4.25 The Name the Virtual Machine screen

The Specify Disk Capacity screen in Figure 4.26 is where you will size the initial disk for your VM Player. It provides a recommendation, in this case 60 GB, based on the operating system type and version that you plan to install. You should set the maximum disk size to 30 GB. You can choose to create one large file or many smaller files to represent the disk out on the host file system. Because there are no plans to move this VM, store the virtual disk as a single file and choose a smaller amount of storage space for the disk. Choose Next to continue.

The VM is now ready to be created. If you look at the settings, you will see that some virtual devices included in the VM were not selected, such as a floppy drive and a printer. If you want to make additional changes to the default device selections, you can select Customize Hardware. Figure 4.27 shows a summary of the hardware devices that will be configured, as well as the memory settings. You will make adjustments as you go forward, so for the moment just Close the window.

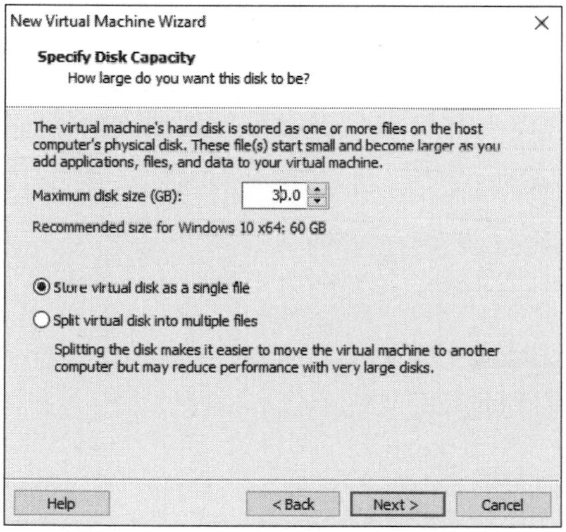

FIGURE 4.26 The Specify Disk Capacity screen

Figure 4.28 shows the final screen. Select Finish to create the VM.

The Virtual Machine is now created. You can see the new VM in the left column. Because the VM is selected, additional information and operational options appear on the right. We will examine these in the next chapter.

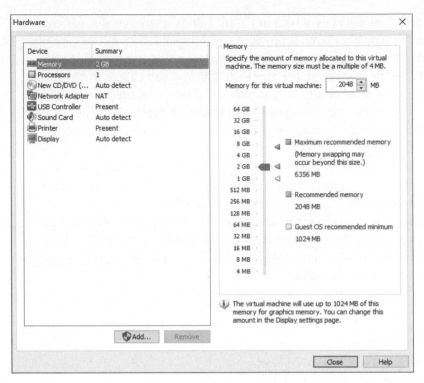

FIGURE 4.27 Customize the hardware.

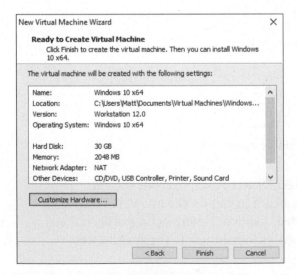

FIGURE 4.28 Create the virtual machine.

THE ESSENTIALS AND BEYOND

The twin drivers of consolidation and containment have accelerated the virtualization efforts of most companies. Because physical servers were being replaced with virtual servers, automated tools were developed to more efficiently effect that translation than manual processes could. Deploying new applications as virtual machines requires the creation of virtual hardware to load the operating system into, as you would do with a physical server. This virtual hardware, though, is much more flexible than a physical server with regard to altering its configuration. Virtual machines are fairly simple to create, whether they are built from scratch or P2Ved from existing physical servers. In fact, they are so easy to generate, some IT departments now struggle with virtual server sprawl. This is forcing many administrators to change their provisioning practices to include life-cycle parameters as they allocate resources to their users. This helps ensure that short-lived projects and their associated VMs are properly terminated rather than left to consume shared resources long past the time they should have.

ADDITIONAL EXERCISES

▶ On the Customize Hardware screen, the memory settings have some minimum and maximum values. How are they determined?

▶ In the initial virtual machine that was created, what hardware devices could be removed without affecting the use of the system? Are any devices missing that should be added?

▶ Use the file system browser to examine the virtual machine files that were created. Examine the .vmx file with a text editor. What can you determine about the VM? Are there other ways to adjust a VM configuration aside from VMware Workstation Player? How could you discover what other options might be available?

CHAPTER 5

Installing Windows on a Virtual Machine

Like a physical server, a virtual machine needs to have an operating system installed to function and run applications. Although there are still dozens of different operating systems that can work on the x86 platform, the bulk of virtualization today is done on the more recent versions of Windows. Understanding how to install Windows and then optimize it for a virtual environment is crucial.

▶ **Loading windows into a virtual machine**

▶ **Understanding configuration options**

▶ **Optimizing a new virtual machine**

Loading Windows into a Virtual Machine

A Windows operating system can be loaded into a virtual machine in a number of ways. In the previous chapter, you saw that during the process of creating a virtual machine, VMware Workstation Player offers the option to install Windows as part of that effort. Most virtual machines are created through a template. *Templates* are virtual machines that already contain an operating system and often are already loaded with application software as well. These prebuilt VMs are stored in a nonexecutable state that allows an administrator to rapidly stamp out copies of the selected configuration. Once a copy is created, a few more personalization and system configuration steps, such as providing a unique system name and network address, will need to be completed before the new VM can be deployed. We will cover more about templates in Chapter 11, "Copying a Virtual Machine."

Periodically, a virtual machine requires a pristine copy of Windows. Some administrators create a new template with every new major release, while others merely power on the existing template and apply the service packs. Some administrators prefer the new install because it forces them to look at the other pieces of software in the VM that might also need updates or refreshes. Others believe that loading a version of Windows with the service packs (SPs) already as part of the distribution is somehow intrinsically superior to applying the service packs separately. There is no incorrect choice here. Most people choose a path that works for them. Instructions for installing VMware Tools follow those for installing Windows 10. These steps are optional but highly recommended.

Installing Windows 10

In order to install Windows, or any operating system, you need the source disks so that you can execute from them. These disks can take the form of actual CDs, DVDs, or image files of the software on other media. In the case of Microsoft Windows, you can purchase a copy at a retail store and come home with the disks, or buy it online and download the images to your computer. That image can be burned to a CD or DVD for backup or execution purposes. If you are using this text as part of a class, you may have access to a student version of Windows. Many universities have agreements with Microsoft to allow students to download Windows for educational use at little or no cost.

The steps that follow are not the only method you can use to create a Windows 10 virtual machine, but rather one of many possible options. For these examples, a 64-bit version of Windows 10 was used (see Figure 5.1). The ISO image is staged on the desktop for the VM to access.

1. Open VMware Workstation Player.

2. Select the Windows 10 x64 virtual machine you created earlier by left-clicking on the Windows 10 x64 VM icon shown in Figure 5.2. You can also select the VM by choosing the Open A Virtual Machine option on the right, navigating to the Windows 10 x64 directory under the Virtual Machines directory, selecting the .vmx file, and clicking Open. Either method will work.

3. Note that the machine state is powered off. You need to tell the VM to boot from the ISO image, much as a physical server needs the CD or DVD drive in the boot sequence so it can find the Windows disks you would stage there. Select Edit Virtual Machine Settings, which results in the screen shown in Figure 5.3.

FIGURE 5.1 The Windows image

4. As shown in Figure 5.4, select CD/DVD.

5. You can see a number of choices regarding the CD/DVD devices. Under Connection, choose Use ISO Image File. This will allow you to have the VM use the ISO image you have staged. Use the Browse button to locate and select the ISO image. Select OK to continue.

6. Now select Play Virtual Machine. You might get a message similar to that shown in Figure 5.5. It means that you have additional hardware devices on your physical computer that could be added to the virtual machine for use. Select OK to continue.

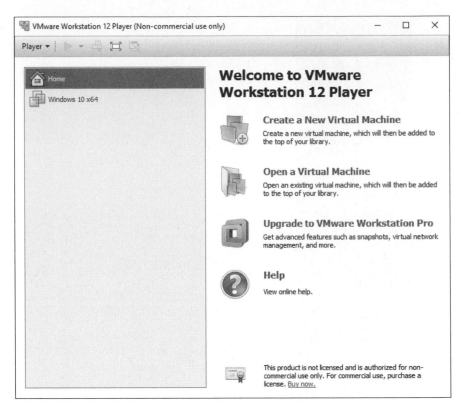

FIGURE 5.2 Select the VM.

7. The virtual machine boots up and connects to the Windows 10 ISO image as if it were a DVD in a disk drive. If you are prompted to download VMware Tools for Windows 2000 and later, you can accept the download by choosing Download And Install and pausing a few moments until it completes the update.

The Windows Setup screen appears, as shown in Figure 5.6. Notice at the bottom of the screen, outside of the virtual machine is an alert bar with some choices regarding the installation of VMware Tools.

We will cover this separately after the installation. Select Remind Me Later and the alert bar disappears.

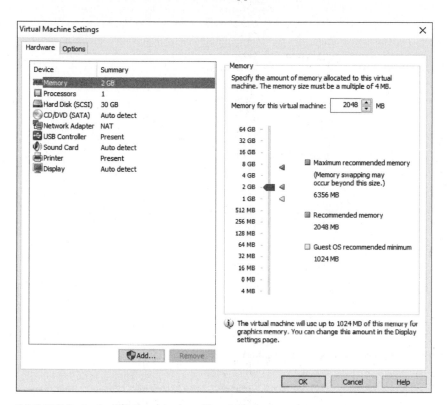

FIGURE 5.3 Edit the virtual machine settings.

8. In the VM Window, click inside the Window Setup window and select your menu choices. Select Next to continue.

9. The next screen, illustrated in Figure 5.7, allows you to Repair Your Computer if needed before continuing. Select Install Now to continue.

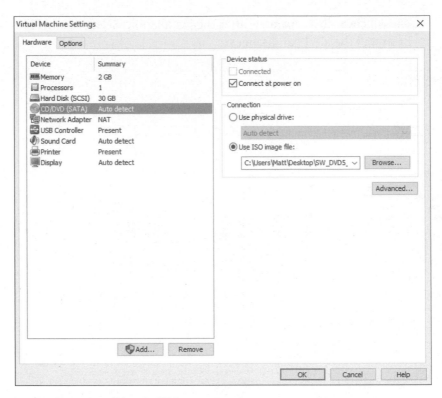

FIGURE 5.4 Using the ISO image to connect

FIGURE 5.5 Removable devices

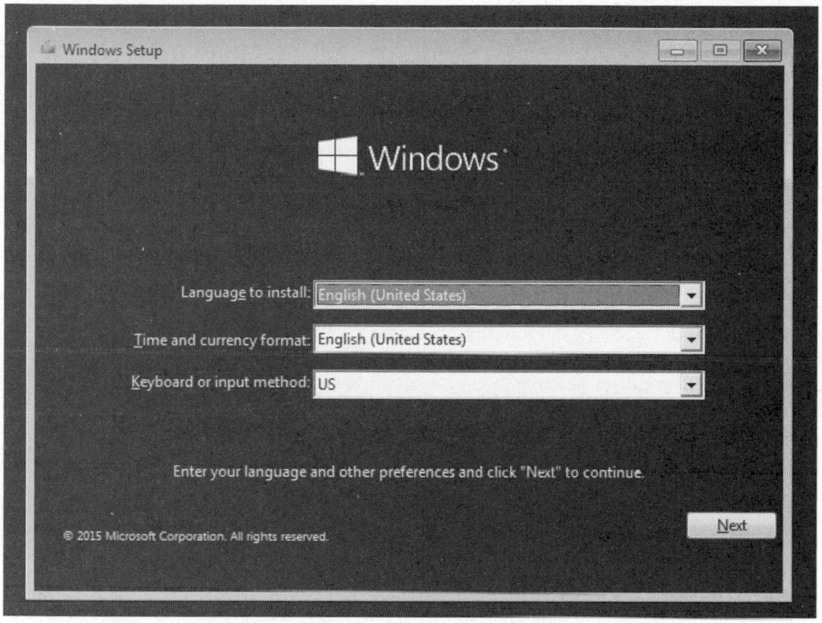

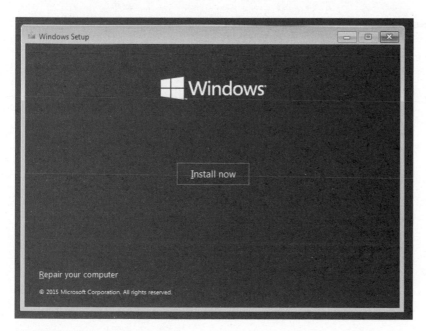

FIGURE 5.6 Windows installation

FIGURE 5.7 Select Install Now.

10. As with most software, you will need to accept the license terms. Select the checkbox as shown in Figure 5.8, and then select Next to continue.

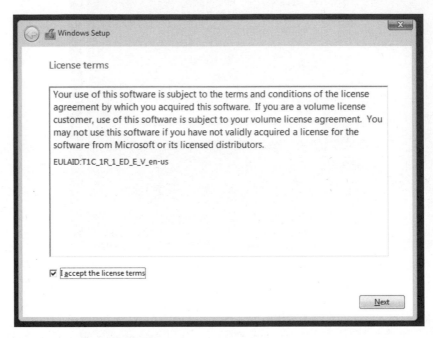

FIGURE 5.8 The license terms

11. Because this is a new installation, you will be doing a Custom installation rather than an upgrade of an existing system. As shown in Figure 5.9, choose Custom to continue.

12. The example VM was created with one 30 GB disk drive. Select Next to continue. (See Figure 5.10.)

13. The Windows installation process will proceed with a number of steps, including formatting the disk storage, creating a file system, and copying the files to the disk. This is usually the most time-consuming step. You can see the steps and the progress in Figure 5.11.

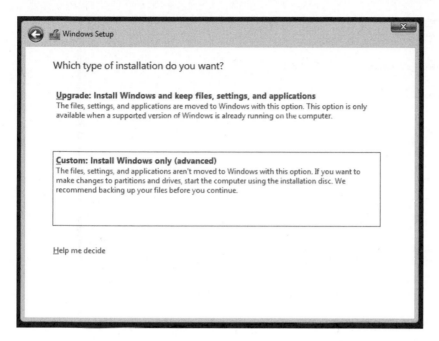

FIGURE 5.9 The installation type

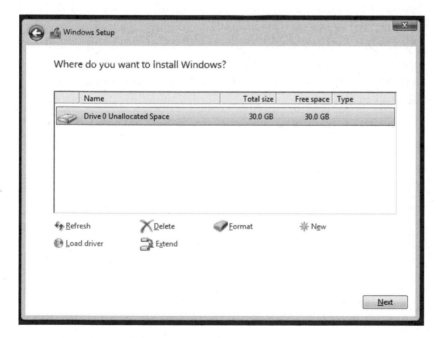

FIGURE 5.10 Disk choice and options

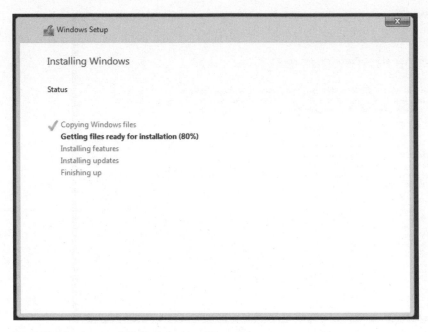

FIGURE 5.11 Installation progress

14. Windows will reboot a number of times during the process. It will then run through a number of first-time use initialization steps. The Express Settings screen, illustrated in Figure 5.12, allows you to streamline the configuration process or to customize all of the settings. For our purposes, streamlining is fine. Select Use Express Settings to continue.

15. After a reboot, you will be prompted to select a connection method. Choose Join A Domain, as shown in Figure 5.13, and then select Next to continue.

16. You will need to choose a username, a password, and a hint for that password for the user you just created. Figure 5.14 shows this screen. Enter a username, a password, and a hint, and then select Next to continue.

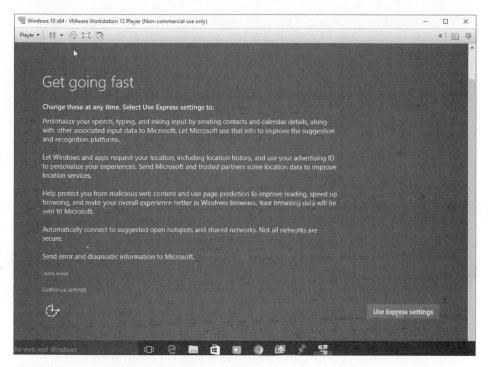

FIGURE 5.12 The Express Settings screen

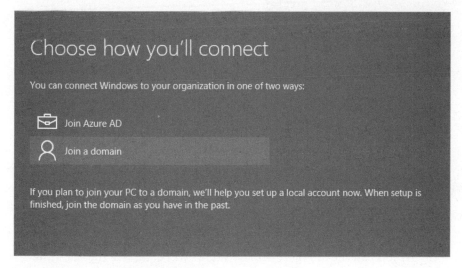

FIGURE 5.13 Connection choices

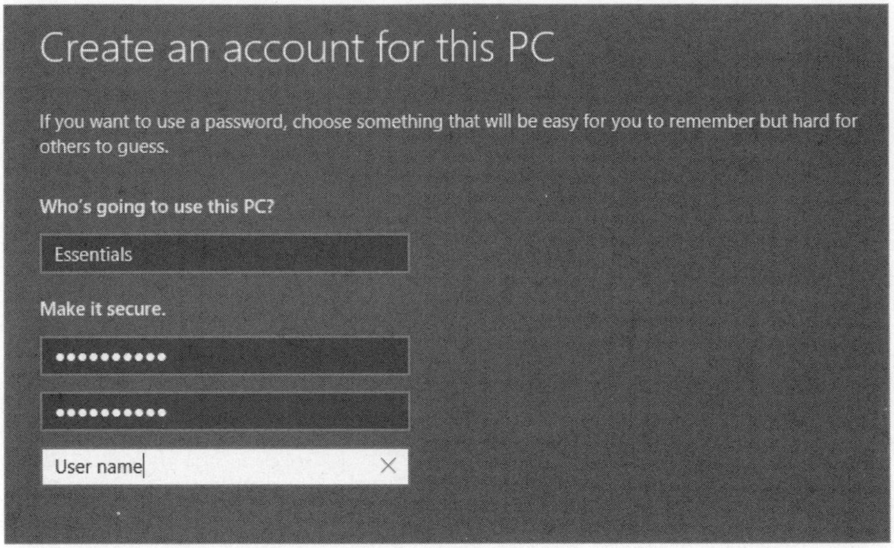

Create an account for this PC

If you want to use a password, choose something that will be easy for you to remember but hard for others to guess.

Who's going to use this PC?

Essentials

Make it secure.

••••••••••

••••••••••

User name

FIGURE 5.14 Create the username, password, and hint.

17. The Windows installation process logs into Windows and does some initial setup. When that is complete, you will be presented with a Network screen, as shown in Figure 5.15. Select Yes to continue.

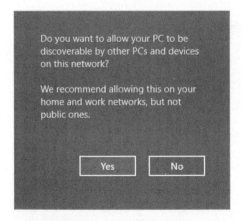

Do you want to allow your PC to be discoverable by other PCs and devices on this network?

We recommend allowing this on your home and work networks, but not public ones.

Yes   No

FIGURE 5.15 Network sharing

18. As you can see in Figure 5.16, Windows will complete the one-time setup and be ready for use.

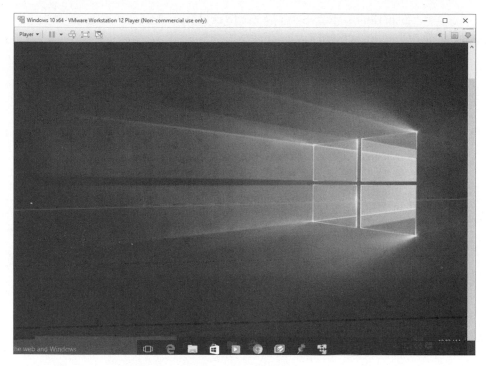

FIGURE 5.16 The completed Windows 10 installation

Installing VMware Tools

You have one more step left to complete before you can work in this virtual machine, and that is adding the VMware Tools. VMware Tools are a combination of device drivers and processes that enhance the user experience with the VM, improve VM performance, and help manage the virtual machine. Although installation of the VMware Tools suite is not mandatory, it is very highly recommended for VMs in any of the VMware environments.

1. Select Player from the menu at the top of the VMware Workstation Player window. Choose the Manage menu option. Select Install VMware Tools as shown in Figure 5.17.

2. The VMware Tools DVD is mounted in the virtual machine. (If you did not download the VMware Tools earlier, you may get a prompt to do so now. Download the Tools and then continue.) Click on the Disc Mounted message. Illustrated in Figure 5.18 are the choices for the

disc. Choose Run Setup64.exe to continue. Answer Yes to the Allow Changes screen.

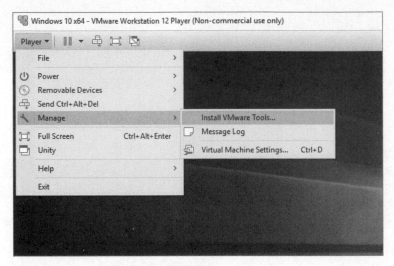

FIGURE 5.17 Install VMware Tools.

FIGURE 5.18 VMware Tools DVD drive options

3. The initial VMware Tools installation screen appears, as illustrated in Figure 5.19. Choose Next to continue.

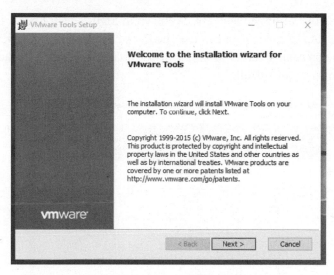

FIGURE 5.19 The VMware Tools Welcome screen

4. Figure 5.20 shows the Setup Type selection window, which offers short descriptions of the three options. The default is Typical, which is sufficient for your needs. Choose Next to continue.

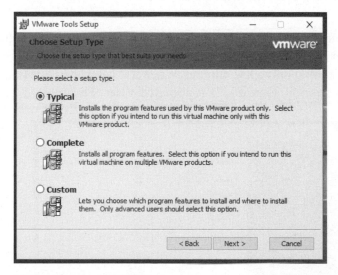

FIGURE 5.20 Setup type

5. The Install screen appears, as shown in Figure 5.21. If any changes need to be made, you can use the Back button to scroll back through the preceding screens to make those changes. If you are ready to continue, select Install.

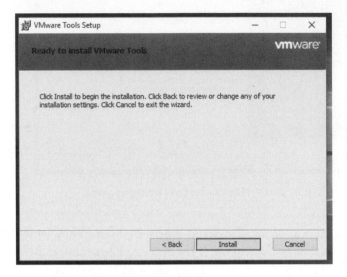

FIGURE 5.21   Ready to install

6. The VMware Tools are installed, and you can mark the progress on the displayed Status screen. It is typically a very short process, requiring only a few minutes. When it is completed, the final screen, as shown in Figure 5.22, is displayed. Select Finish.

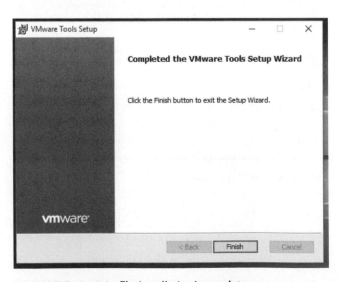

FIGURE 5.22   The installation is complete.

7. Finally, you need to reboot the VM one more time. The system prompts you, as shown in Figure 5.23. Select Yes to restart the VM.

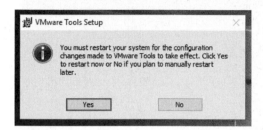

FIGURE 5.23 Restart the system.

Understanding Configuration Options

Now that you have a working VM, let's take a closer look at what you've built. The first thing to observe is that the VM looks identical to the physical desktop, which is exactly what you want. If you select the Start icon, you'll see exactly what you would expect to see in a fresh install of Microsoft Windows 10, as shown in Figure 5.24. It is easy to tell that you are using a virtual machine by looking at the VMware Workstation Player application bar at the top of the VM window. However, most virtual machines are run on servers and are connected to by users who never see the physical or virtual servers with which they work.

If you were to connect to this VM via the network using the Remote Desktop Connection, could you determine if it was a physical or virtual server? The answer is yes. There are a number of key giveaways that you could quickly check to make that determination. First, by highlighting the hidden icons at the bottom right, you will see a VM logo. This indicates that VMware Tools has been installed on this particular VM. You can open the About VMware Tools window to verify that the service is running, as shown in Figure 5.25. Remember, though, that installing the VMware Tools is recommended, but not mandatory. This means that the absence of VMware Tools does not automatically indicate that it is a physical machine. Close the About VMware Tools window.

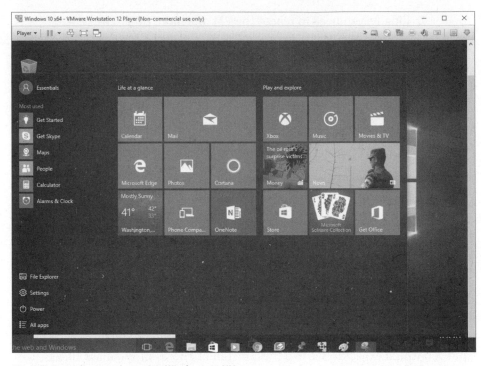

FIGURE 5.24   A running Windows 10 VM

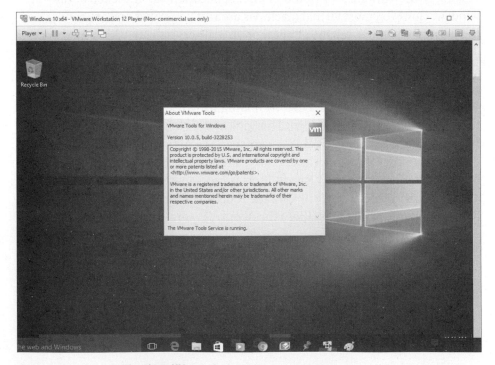

FIGURE 5.25   The About VMware Tools screen

There are ways to more definitively determine what type of system you're using. Choose the Start icon and select Settings and then the Devices icon. Choose Connected Devices and scroll down on the right side of the screen to the bottom. Select Devices And Printers. You can instantly see that some of the devices do not match any physical vendor hardware. Figure 5.26 shows a VMware Virtual USB Mouse, a VMware Virtual S SCSI Disk Drive, and VMware Virtual USB Sensors; but even more telling is that when you select the machine icon on the top left of the devices window.

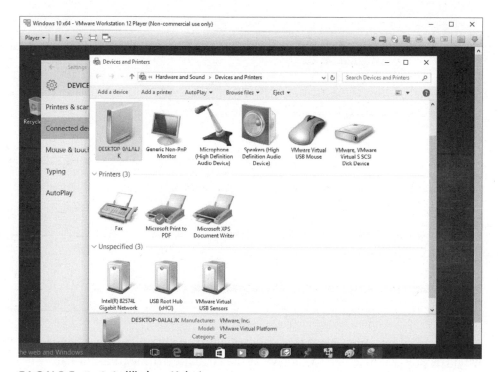

FIGURE 5.26 Windows 10 devices

When you highlight the image, you can see preliminary information at the bottom of the window. It is fairly obvious that this computer is of the virtual variety manufactured by VMware. If you follow the same path on your physical computer, you should see the difference immediately. When you double-click the computer image, a properties window appears, and you can see that the VM is a virtual machine. Select the Hardware tab and scroll through the devices, as shown in Figure 5.27, to confirm that virtual devices compose the system. On your physical computer, obviously only physical devices would be present. Close the windows to continue.

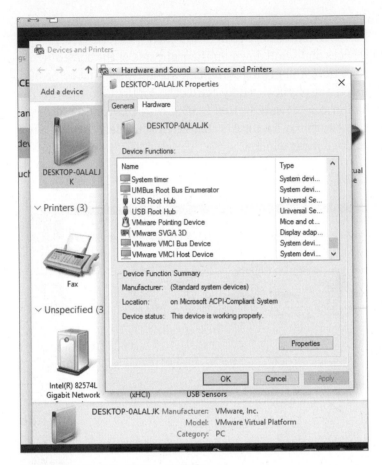

FIGURE 5.27 System properties

Let's look at two more items that will help illustrate the differences between what the physical machine has and what the virtual machine thinks it has. Again, select Start ≻ Settings ≻ System ≻ Storage. Here you can see the single disk drive that you created; the C: drive still has about 20 GB free out of the 30 GB it has. But what is the actual size of the storage on this physical system? By following the same steps for the physical system, as shown in Figure 5.28, you can see that the physical C: drive is considerably larger. We'll look closer at this in Chapter 9, "Managing Storage for a Virtual Machine." Close both the physical and virtual Storage windows.

1. Enter **Control Panel** into the search bar of your virtual machine. When the program appears in the list, select it. Navigate to System

and Security ➤ System. The key information is displayed. The Windows version is, as you'd expect, Windows 10. You have 2 GB of memory (RAM), just as you configured. The processor information is also available.

2. Now, in your physical environment, duplicate the previous steps to show the Control Panel on your computer. As you can see in Figure 5.29, this physical machine actually has 8 GB of memory, again more than what is configured for the virtual machine.

3. You can examine some of the other similarities and differences and then close those windows when you are done.

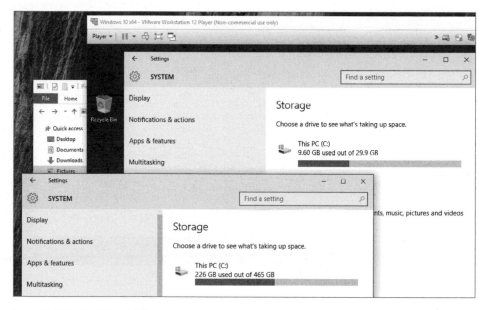

FIGURE 5.28 Disk sizes

Now let's make one small adjustment to the VM just to experience the flexibility of changing the configuration. You've allocated 2 GB of memory to the VM, but if you look at the Microsoft Windows 10 system requirements, a 64-bit implementation, which is what is deployed, should have a minimum of 2 GB. You haven't done anything yet to stress the VM from a performance standpoint, so the 2 GB has been sufficient to operate without any ill effects.

1. Select Player from the VMware Workstation Player menu bar.

The minimum system requirements for Windows 10 are available at https://www.microsoft.com/en-us/windows/windows-10-specifications.

2. Select Manage from the menu and then select Virtual Machine Settings.

3. As shown in Figure 5.30, highlighting the Memory device in the Hardware tab shows the controls for adjusting the memory in the VM. There are values that are selected by VMware Workstation Player as minimum, recommended, and maximum values. You can adjust the memory right to those values by selecting the colored boxes next to those suggestions. You can also manually adjust memory by moving the slider up or down, or by entering a specific value into the field indicated by Memory for this virtual machine.

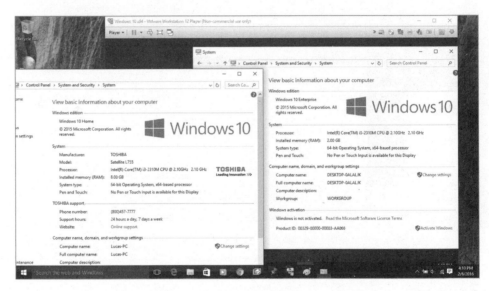

FIGURE 5.29 Memory sizes

4. Adjust the memory value to 1.5 GB by entering **1536** into the Memory For This Virtual Machine field. Notice the warning at the bottom of window that states the change will not occur until the VM is restarted. This is an operating system requirement, not a virtual machine requirement. In certain versions of the hypervisor applications, the VM would automatically accept the additional memory and show the new larger value. Here, we would need to shut down the VM, change the amount of memory, and then reboot the VM for the change to take effect. To perform the equivalent reconfiguration in a physical server would require not only the same system restart but

actual hardware changes, installing additional memory, which would take anywhere from tens of minutes to hours, depending on the environment. Multiply the time of that operation by dozens of servers, or hundreds, and it is easy to see why rapid reconfiguration is one of the many strengths of virtualization.

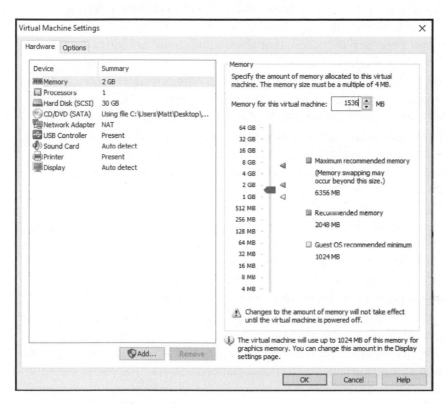

FIGURE 5.30 Adjusting the memory in a VM

Optimizing a New Virtual Machine

The process we just executed is not very different from what system administrators go through as they deploy workloads onto a virtual platform. There are automation options and other methods of improving their operational efficiency available, and we'll cover some of these as we progress, but the basic template is here. This, however, is only the first step in creating an application's virtual machine. You have completed a fairly generic Microsoft Windows installation, but there are two more important steps you need to take to help the VM perform its very best for the application that will run there. The first is specific to virtual machines, while the second is just good practice for physical or virtual servers.

Many services that run as part of the Windows operating system help optimize how the physical environment runs. Some of these services don't optimize a virtual environment, so it makes good sense to just disable them. Many of the wireless networking services, for example, while perfectly reasonable for a Windows 10 implementation running on a local laptop, do nothing for a Windows 10 VM running on a host server because that physical hardware wouldn't normally have access to a wireless network. There are other physical world features that PCs have that don't translate to a virtual world. Administrators routinely disable power management features because they don't apply to a VM. Virtualized servers often have many of the personalization features removed or disabled because fancy fonts and customized sounds are not necessary for an application server. They also take up disk space and use CPU and memory resources.

Wallpapers are removed, as are screen savers. Various visual effects, such as Aero, are often disabled for virtual application servers. The intent of all of these modifications is to provide VMs that do not needlessly consume extra CPU cycles, memory blocks, I/O bandwidth, or disk space. On one virtual machine, all of these savings are small, but when you stack many multiple VMs on a physical server, they provide significant efficiencies—and virtualization is all about improving efficiencies. Administrators apply these optimizations into their templates so they can be replicated again and again to newly provisioned VMs.

The second step could apply to either physical or virtual machines. One of the best practices for moving physical application workloads to virtual machines is to ensure that enough resources are allocated to the virtual machine to provide equal or better performance on a virtual platform. So that you can understand what those resource requirements are, some type of performance metrics need to be collected while the application is still staged in a physical environment. There are professional services engagements as well as automated tools that can help gather this information and translate it into recommendations for virtual machine configuration sizes and even host server configurations.

However those metrics are acquired, the information is vital to properly configuring the virtual machine. Then there are certain applications that seem to have been created for virtualization. Very often web servers, which in the physical world typically each require their own server, can be densely packed onto a single host, because of memory optimization technologies available within certain hypervisors. We'll cover this in more depth in Chapter 8, "Managing Memory for a Virtual Machine."

One guide to honing an operating system is the Optimization Guide for Windows available at http://www.vmware.com/files/pdf/VMware-View-Optimization Guide Windows7-EN.pdf. The document comes with links to a tool to automate the optimizations. The guide undergoes periodic updates and is currently in the process of being revised to address Windows 10 optimization.

THE ESSENTIALS AND BEYOND

The steps to install a Windows operating system into a VM are at times tedious, but necessary. Both tools and processes make this step in the creation of a functional virtual machine less and less mandatory, requiring less time than in the past when a manual install was more the norm than the exception. Although we've spent time examining the ways to identify a VM, with best practices and proper resource allocation, today there is little reason to be concerned whether an application is staged on a physical platform or a virtual one.

ADDITIONAL EXERCISES

▶ Examine the supported versions of Windows for a particular vendor's virtualization platform. Are there advantages to supporting older versions of various operating systems?

▶ Compare your results from the previous exercise with another vendor. Do all vendors support the same operating systems? Do they support the same operating system versions? Are these differences a reason to select one virtualization vendor's platform over another?

CHAPTER 6

Installing Linux on a Virtual Machine

While a large number of virtual machines today are running with Microsoft Windows, an increasing number have Linux installed. Linux has been adopted in many corporate data centers as a way to decrease license costs and decrease dependency on Microsoft as a single source for operating systems. Because many of today's modern applications run on a number of different operating systems, the choice is up to the customer, rather than the vendor. The slow and steady adoption of open-source solutions also has contributed to this shift.

▶ **Loading Linux into a virtual machine**

▶ **Understanding configuration options**

▶ **Optimizing a new Linux virtual machine**

Loading Linux into a Virtual Machine

Why Linux? Although Microsoft Windows is still the predominant operating system in the x86 server arena, and by extension the x86 virtualization space, there is an ongoing decline of that position, in part because of devices like smart phones and tablets that do not run Windows. In the desktop space, there is no discussion when it comes to who owns the market; however, the server space is a bit more dynamic. The original push into the server space for Windows came because companies were tired of being forced into paying premium prices to purchase proprietary hardware along with proprietary operating systems to run their applications. Even though many of the operating systems were UNIX derivatives, vendors had enhanced them to run for their specific server hardware. That hardware was much more expensive than generic Windows servers that a company could acquire from a number

▶ Though still a significant portion of the server market, the various vendor-specific versions of UNIX such as HP/UX, IBM's AIX, and Oracle/Sun's Solaris continue to shrink.

of different vendors. In addition to offering a choice, competition drove the hardware cost of those servers down, making the Windows choice a better financial option as well.

Today, a similar trend is continuing. As before, the cost disparity between legacy UNIX platforms and Windows continues to increase. Applications that have been tied to those systems now have a lower cost, open-source option in Linux—and as before, they can run Linux on a generic hardware server that is available from a number of vendors. In a virtual environment, Linux servers can be converted to virtual machines and run alongside Windows servers on the same hardware hosts. While this trend of migrating UNIX to Linux continues, Windows users, now feeling the same operating system lock-in issues earlier proprietary operating systems felt, are looking to Linux as a less-expensive option to their ongoing Microsoft licensing costs.

The recent explosion of cloud computing has only accelerated this trend. In addition to a lower cost, companies cite better security and a broader feature set as the main drivers for deploying Linux servers. Larger next-generation cloud providers who run massive data centers to provide scalable and available services to mobile applications or Software-as-a-Service solutions also rely on Linux. New open-source models such as OpenStack have Linux as a foundational element. Other open-source solutions—for example, databases such as MySQL, Hadoop, and MongoDB—are all becoming more widely adopted as they mature, and they all run happily on Linux. While the PC desktop space still belongs to Microsoft Windows, the data center and cloud computing arenas are rapidly moving to Linux.

> A 2014 study by the Linux Foundation found that Linux had over 70 percent of the server operating system market share compared to 30 percent for Windows.

Exploring Oracle VM VirtualBox

We installed VirtualBox as part of Chapter 4, "Creating a Virtual Machine," and we'll use this for our exercise of loading Linux into a VM. VirtualBox is available for free as an open-source distribution and is widely used in application testing and development environments. As a Type-2 hypervisor, it can be installed on machines running Windows, Linux, Mac OSX, and Solaris. It also supports a wide variety of guest operating systems, including multiple versions of Microsoft Windows and many Linux distributions.

Open VirtualBox by double-clicking the icon. Figure 6.1 shows the main window. Across the top are the File, Machine, and Help drop-down menus, which we'll examine in a moment. Of the icons displayed, at the moment, only New is not grayed out. New will allow you to create a new VM. Settings provides access to change the VM settings. Discard removes VMs, while Start, as its name implies, powers on a selected virtual machine. On the left side, empty now, is where the list of VMs will be, while the largest part of the screen is reserved for displaying and working with VMs. This section of the screen also indicates that Help is available via the F1 key.

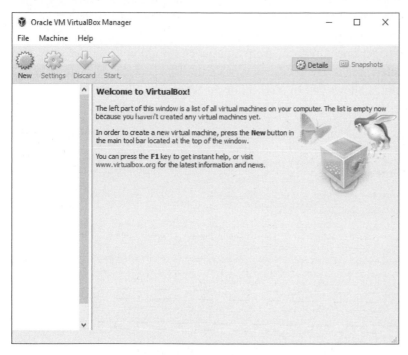

FIGURE 6.1 The VirtualBox main window

Let's look more closely at the selections under the File menu. They are

- ▶ Preferences
- ▶ Import Appliance
- ▶ Export Appliance
- ▶ Virtual Media Manager
- ▶ Network Operations Manager
- ▶ Check For Updates
- ▶ Reset All Warnings
- ▶ Exit

As with many applications, there are keystroke shortcuts that will execute the selected functions.

Preferences, as shown in Figure 6.2, controls how VirtualBox interacts with your environment, allowing you to determine which changes to which devices to use, what language to display in, and where the virtual machines should be kept. Import Appliance and Export Appliance are fairly straightforward, offering the ability to import or export Open Virtualization Format (OVF) packages. The Virtual Media Manager handles storage for the VMs, and the Network Operations Manager does the same from a network standpoint. Check For Updates will determine if a newer version of VirtualBox is available to download. Reset All Warnings allows you to reset all of the warnings. Finally, Exit will close the application.

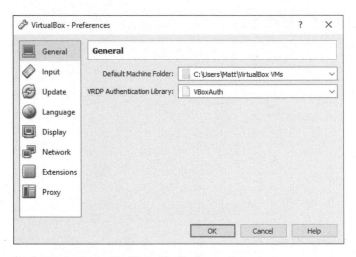

FIGURE 6.2 The VirtualBox Preferences screen

Under the Machine menu are

- ► New
- ► Add
- ► Settings
- ► Clone
- ► Remove
- ► Group
- ► Start
- ► Pause
- ► Reset

- ▶ Close

- ▶ Discard Saved State

- ▶ Show Log

- ▶ Refresh

- ▶ Show In Explorer

- ▶ Create Shortcut On Desktop

- ▶ Sort

Because there are no virtual machines currently in the library, all of the options except New and Add are grayed out. We will look more closely at many of these as we work with virtual machines.

Under the Help Menu are

- ▶ Contents

- ▶ VirtualBox Web Site

- ▶ About VirtualBox

Contents will return the same Help application as the F1 key. It is fairly extensive and detailed enough for both the novice and the more experienced user. VirtualBox Web Site will open a browser and bring you to the VirtualBox home page, `https://www.virtualbox.org`, where you can find all the latest documentation, additional downloads, and more. Finally, About VirtualBox will return the version information about this particular installation.

Installing Linux into a Virtual Machine

There are a few things you need to do before loading Linux into a VM. First, you will need to create a virtual machine to use. The configuration is similar to the virtual machine we created for the Windows installation: 1 CPU, 1 GB of memory, and 20 GB of disk space. The disk setup is slightly different because of Linux's requirements; you will learn about that during the installation. As with the Windows procedure, you will need to have the Linux installation images to use. There are many different providers of open-source Linux. The examples will be using Ubuntu Linux, which you can download from the Ubuntu website. The download is free, but you may be prompted to donate funds for the continued development and improvement of this distribution. Unlike with Windows, you do not have to pay licensing costs, only support costs, if you choose to use this operating system in production.

> Other popular versions of Linux to use include SUSE, Red Hat, Debian, and CentOS, but dozens of other free distributions are available.

For the purposes of this demonstration, you can download a version at `http://www.ubuntu.com`.

The example will use the 64-bit version of Ubuntu Linux version 15.10, the Desktop Edition. The steps that follow should not be considered the only path to create a Linux VM, but rather a possible outline of the steps to follow. The ISO image is staged on the desktop, as you can see in Figure 6.3.

FIGURE 6.3 The Ubuntu Linux ISO image

1. Open Oracle VM VirtualBox.

2. Select the New icon. You could also choose New from the Machine menu at the top of the window or use the Ctrl+N keyboard shortcut.

3. The Create Virtual Machine Wizard appears, as shown in Figure 6.4. Here you will need to choose a VM name, the operating system type, and the version. Choose Next to continue.

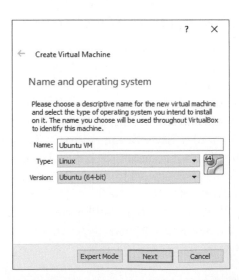

FIGURE 6.4 The Create Virtual Machine Wizard

4. Here you can adjust the memory size, as illustrated in Figure 6.5. The recommendation is 768 MB, but change it to 1024 MB or 1 GB. Select Next to continue.

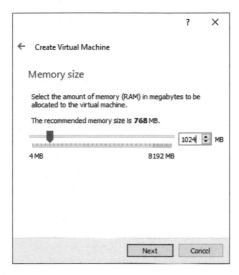

FIGURE 6.5 **The Memory Size screen**

5. Figure 6.6 shows the hard disk selection. Note the recommendation is only 8 GB. Leave the default setting, Create a virtual hard disk now, and choose Create to continue.

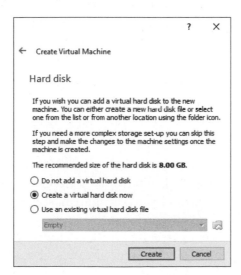

FIGURE 6.6 **Creating a hard disk**

6. The Hard Disk File Type screen gives you multiple options for the type of disk file type to create. As shown in Figure 6.7, keep the default with the VirtualBox Disk Image (VDI) and select Next to continue.

FIGURE 6.7 The Hard Disk File Type screen

7. Figure 6.8 show the two choices for how storage allocation should be handled and what the differences are. Leave the default as Dynamically Allocated and select Next to continue.

8. Figure 6.9 shows the File Location and Size screen. Here you can choose where in the file system to create the virtual machine and change the size of the virtual disk. Leave the default file location but adjust the disk size to 20 GB. Choose Create to complete the virtual machine.

9. The virtual machine is created. Figure 6.10 shows that now there is an Ubuntu VM entry in the VM list in the left panel of VirtualBox. Notice too, that the Settings and Start icons are now active and no longer grayed out. The main panel has the details of the virtual hardware that was just configured. It says that Ubuntu (64-bit) is the operating system, but that is only because we said we planned to

install Ubuntu as part of the configuration. The operating system has not been loaded yet.

FIGURE 6.8 Hard disk storage type

FIGURE 6.9 Hard disk location and size

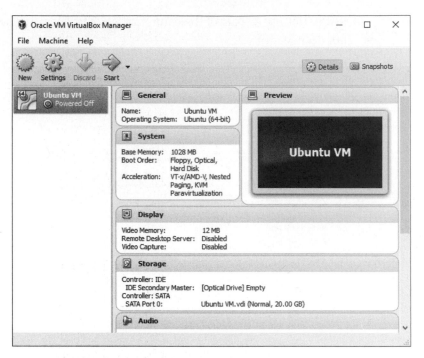

FIGURE 6.10 The Ubuntu virtual machine

10. As with the Windows installation in the previous chapter, we need to virtually insert the installation disk into the VM's CD/DVD drive. We do the same here and point the CD/DVD drive to the ISO image of the Ubuntu installation disk that we have staged on the desktop. As Figure 6.11 illustrates, in the Storage section of the VM's settings, click on the [Optical Drive] Empty hyperlink and select Choose Disk Image.

11. A file browser window appears. Navigate and select the Ubuntu ISO disk image as shown in Figure 6.12. Select Open to continue.

12. In the Storage section of the VM settings, the Ubuntu ISO file is now virtually inserted into the disk drive. Just as with a physical server, all we need to do now is turn it on. Select the Start icon to power on the virtual machine.

FIGURE 6.11   Choose Disk Image

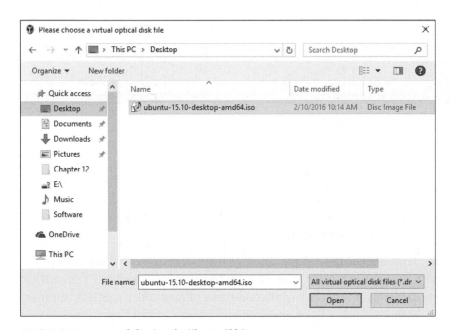

FIGURE 6.12   Selecting the Ubuntu ISO image

13. While the machine powers on, a number of informative messages appear at the top of the screen. You can read them and then remove them by clicking the X at the right side of each alert. The VM screen resizes and the Welcome screen appears, as shown in Figure 6.13. We are going to install the operating system, so choose Install Ubuntu to continue.

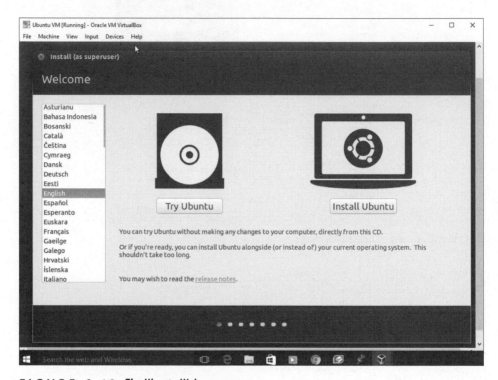

FIGURE 6.13 The Ubuntu Welcome screen

14. The next screen, shown in Figure 6.14, has some minimum requirements in order to continue. Make sure you comply or the installation will fail. Select the Download Updates While Installing checkbox to ensure that the completed installation is up-to-date. Choose Continue to move forward.

15. The installer has determined that no operating system is present, which confirms that this is a brand-new virtual machine. Figure 6.15 displays some of the installation types offered. Keep the default Erase Disk And Install Ubuntu option and choose Install Now to continue.

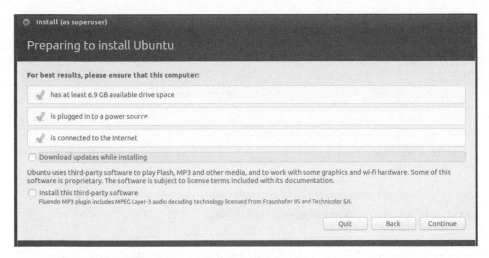

FIGURE 6.14 Preparing to Install Ubuntu screen

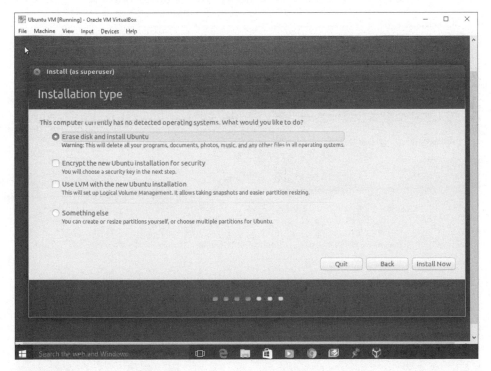

FIGURE 6.15 Installation types

16. A warning screen appears, shown in Figure 6.16, asking if you want to make these changes. Select Continue to proceed.

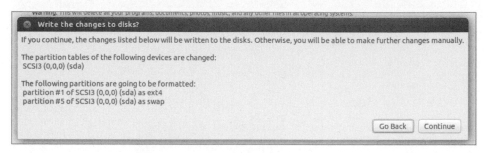

FIGURE 6.16 The Write the Changes to Disks screen

17. The installer asks which time zone your installation is in, as illustrated in Figure 6.17. If you need to alter the presented default, select the map area to make the change. Then choose Continue.

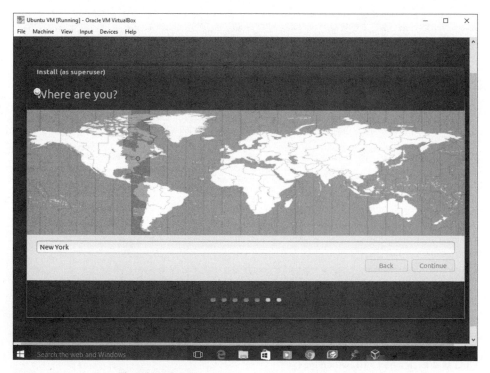

FIGURE 6.17 The Where Are You screen

18. A keyboard layout screen appears, and U.S. English is highlighted. Select Continue to proceed.

19. Next, you must create a machine name for the VM along with a username and a password for that user. As shown in Figure 6.18, there are additional login and encryption options to choose. Enter a username, a machine name, and a password. Select Continue to proceed.

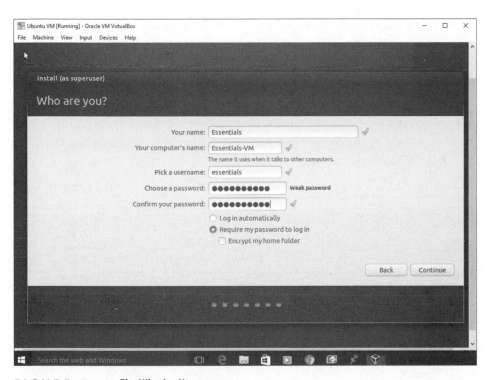

FIGURE 6.18 The Who Are You screen

20. The installation begins and the process gives you the opportunity to examine some of the features while it loads and configures the system. A progress bar at the bottom of the screen shows what is occurring and how far the installation has proceeded.

21. When the installation is complete, the installer prompts you to reboot the virtual machine as shown in Figure 6.19. Select Restart Now to reboot the VM.

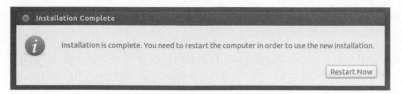

FIGURE 6.19 Rebooting the VM

22. If the reboot returns an error, shut down the virtual machine, make sure that the Ubuntu ISO is no longer connected to the virtual CD/DVD drive, and then restart the virtual machine. When the VM successfully reboots, enter the password into the login screen.

23. The Ubuntu desktop is presented along with some keyboard shortcuts, as shown in Figure 6.20. Close the shortcuts display by clicking the X at the top-left corner. The installation is complete, and the Ubuntu virtual machine is now live.

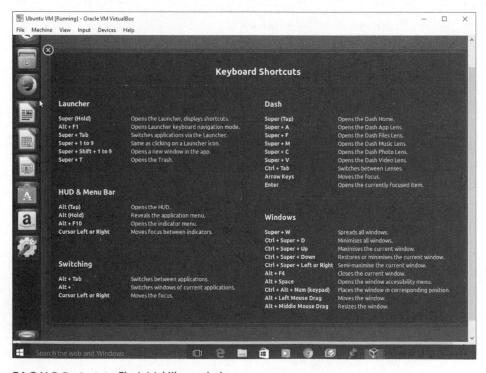

FIGURE 6.20 The initial Ubuntu desktop

Installing VirtualBox Guest Additions

Installing the VirtualBox Guest Additions into a VM will enhance the user experience, improve performance, and help manage the VM. These improvements are offered through a set of device drivers and system applications that include better mouse integration and video support, optimized VM time synchronization, expanded host system and guest interactions via shared folders, Clipboard support, and more. More details are available in the VirtualBox User Manual. Although installing the Guest Additions is not mandatory, it is very highly recommended for VMs running on VirtualBox. There are similar utilities for all virtualization platforms, and we will discuss these further in Chapter 12, "Managing Additional Devices in Virtual Machines."

1. Choose the Insert Guest Additions CD Image option from the Devices menu on the VirtualBox window, as shown in Figure 6.21.

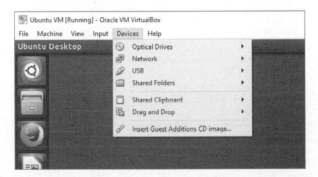

FIGURE 6.21 The Insert Guest Additions CD Image option

2. The disk image is mounted and an alert window appears, allowing you to run the Guest Additions utility software, as shown in Figure 6.22. Choose Run to continue.

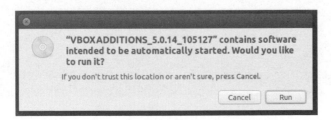

FIGURE 6.22 Automatically run the disk image.

3. Permission is needed to run the utility, and the program prompts you for the user password, as illustrated in Figure 6.23. Enter the password and select Authenticate to continue.

FIGURE 6.23 The Authenticate screen

4. As shown in Figure 6.24, a number of packages are downloaded, uncompressed, recompiled, and installed. When it is complete, the utility prompts you to press Return to continue. Do so.

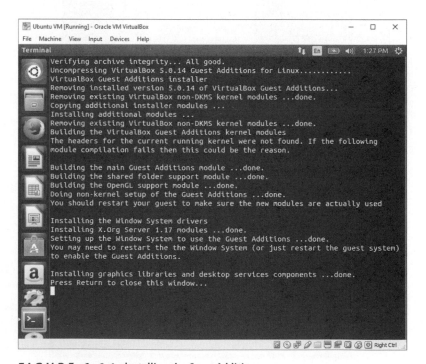

FIGURE 6.24 Installing the Guest Additions

5. The Guest Additions installation is complete. The final step just involves some cleanup. Right-click on the CD image at the bottom of the left panel. As illustrated in in Figure 6.25, the Disk Action menu will appear. Choose Eject to unmount the Guest Additions image from the virtual CD/DVD drive. A message appears, confirming that the disk has been ejected.

FIGURE 6.25 Unmounting the disk image

Understanding Configuration Options

Now that you have a working Linux VM, let's take a closer look at what you have built. The first thing to observe is that the virtual machine looks identical to a physical server, which is exactly what you want. It is easy to tell that you are using a virtual machine in this case. Just look at the VirtualBox application bar at the top of the VM window. Most virtual machines, however, are run on servers and are connected to by users who never see the physical servers on which the VMs are hosted.

1. There are a few quick adjustments you might want to make before you examine the VM configuration. The first is the screen resolution. The installation process did a good job for the example, but your results may have varied. If necessary, the screen can be adjusted in a few steps. First, open the System Settings, which is the icon on the left side of the screen with the gear and wrench.

2. Here, much as with the Microsoft Windows Control Panel, is where adjustments can be made for all aspects of the operating system.

Select the Displays icon in the Hardware area of the screen. The Displays utility is displayed in Figure 6.26.

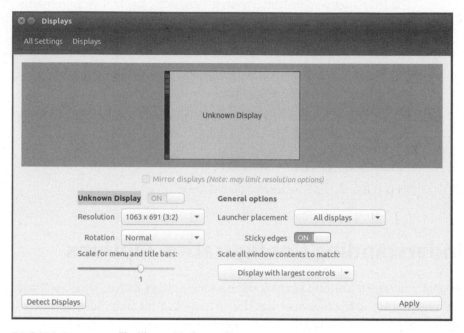

FIGURE 6.26 The Ubuntu Displays utility

3. Most commonly, the resolution will need to be adjusted. When you change the resolution and select Apply, the screen resolution will change and a message box will appear, asking if the display looks okay. If it does, accept the change. If it doesn't, cancel the change and repeat until the display is correct.

4. Close the Displays utility to continue.

GETTING THE STATUS OF THE LINUX DEVICES

You can get a quick overview of most of your devices by looking at the icons at the bottom right of the window. When you hover the cursor over each image, the system provides you with some basic information about the selected device and the state of that device. Adjustments to the devices, however, are usually done through the Systems Setting Utilities.

5. Select the top icon in the left panel, also known as the Dash. If you hover over the icon, it will display "Search your computer and online sources."

6. In the text bar, enter the word **system**. A number of choices, both utilities in your virtual machine and other things the extended search system has found, are displayed.

7. Select System Monitor. The System Monitor appears, as shown in Figure 6.27. If it isn't already selected, choose the Processes tab. The programs that are running on the Linux VM are displayed. They are presented in process name order, but you can change that by selecting any of the column headers. In addition to the name, real-time information is provided about the CPU and memory usage, owner name, process ID, and the priority at which the process is running.

System Monitor

	Processes	Resources	File Systems		

Process Name ▲	User	% CPU	ID	Memory	Priority
at-spi2-registryd	essentials	0	1334	344.0 KiB	Normal
at-spi-bus-launcher	essentials	0	1324	N/A	Normal
bamfdaemon	essentials	0	1378	4.2 MiB	Normal
compiz	essentials	3	1335	194.2 MiB	Normal
dbus-daemon	essentials	0	1332	280.0 KiB	Normal
dbus-daemon	essentials	0	1232	1.2 MiB	Normal
dconf-service	essentials	0	1471	564.0 KiB	Normal
deja-dup-monitor	essentials	0	1791	1.0 MiB	Normal
evolution-addressbook-factory	essentials	0	1623	4.9 MiB	Normal
evolution-addressbook-factory	essentials	0	1637	4.4 MiB	Normal
evolution-calendar-factory	essentials	0	1582	38.6 MiB	Normal
evolution-calendar-factory-sub	essentials	0	1614	2.2 MiB	Normal
evolution-calendar-factory-sub	essentials	0	1605	6.3 MiB	Normal
evolution-source-registry	essentials	0	1452	3.7 MiB	Normal
gconfd-2	essentials	0	1545	1.4 MiB	Normal
gnome-keyring-daemon	essentials	0	1074	460.0 KiB	Normal
gnome-session	essentials	0	1325	1.2 MiB	Normal
gnome-system-monitor	essentials	2	2334	15.9 MiB	Normal
gvfs-afc-volume-monitor	essentials	0	1561	1008.0 KiB	Normal
gvfsd	essentials	0	1273	532.0 KiB	Normal
gvfsd-burn	essentials	0	1593	620.0 KiB	Normal

FIGURE 6.27   Processes in the System Monitor

8. Select the Resources tab. The Resources tab, as illustrated in Figure 6.28, shows real-time resource usage in three areas: CPU, memory, and network activity. The charts are updated continually, and this provides a great visual snapshot into how stressed the virtual machine is and where the stress is (if there is any). Our VM is fairly idle at the moment, and the metrics indicate that.

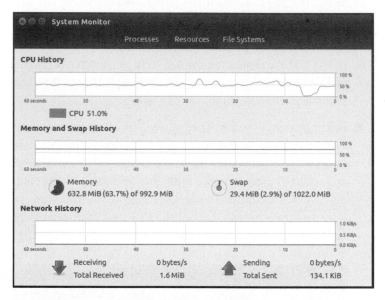

FIGURE 6.28   Resources in the System Monitor

9. Select the File Systems tab. The File Systems tab, as illustrated in Figure 6.29, displays all of the mounted file systems on the virtual machine. Here, we have only the one that is mounted on the root directory represented by the backslash (/).

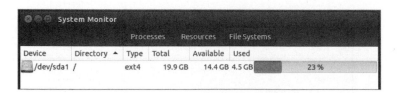

FIGURE 6.29   File Systems in the System Monitor

10. Finally, when you double-click on the disk icon under the Device column, the file browser opens. You can also get to this utility by selecting the file drawer icon in the left panel on the desktop.

11. Close the File Browser.

12. Close the System Monitor.

Now you have a complete, functional, Linux virtual machine. From inside the virtual machine, Linux can see the processor and memory resources that you've assigned to it, and the amount of those resources are only a subset of what are available in the physical machine. The VM has access to storage that is also abstracted from what the actual physical storage has available—and there is access to the network, through the physical machines network port.

Optimizing a New Linux Virtual Machine

While a generic install of Linux as you have just done will be fine for educational, or even for test and development purposes, production systems should be modified to be as efficient as possible. Inefficient VMs waste system resources and, when multiplied over many VMs, waste data center resources. The economies of scale that come with virtualization and consolidation also apply to performance. Ensuring that VMs are as efficient as possible multiplies these performance gains and leads to higher consolidation ratios and greater ongoing cost savings.

Linux comes "out-of-the-box" with a number of processes (or in the Linux/ Unix parlance, *daemons*) that are automatically started as part of the operating system boot. The Processes tab in the System Monitor utility you used earlier shows the list of these processes and also provides a short description of their individual functions. Disabling some of these processes should be a standard practice when creating VMs for production systems. Other published resources are available that can itemize which daemons should be eliminated based on the deployed applications and hardware configuration. One example might choose the NOOP scheduler, which passes all the I/O through the system in a first-in, first-out manner, assuming that optimization will occur somewhere else. Another might be disabling NFS daemons if you are using a different method to access storage.

Linux distributions are made up of packages. Each *package* contains an application suite or a set of functionality to be installed. Installing only the packages necessary to the operation of a particular virtual machine will save space on the storage side and usually will require fewer daemons running, which means less CPU and memory utilization as well. Everything that runs in the VM uses resources; slimming down the operating system is a good practice on many levels.

One parameter that has been of particular interest with Linux virtual machines is that of time synchronization. Computers have always used time to monitor and control many of the operations that occur on a subsecond basis. Closer to home, applications use time voraciously, for everything from time-stamping business transactions, to ensuring that clustered technologies work effectively. If a computer's clock is not reliable, the work it performs will also be unreliable. To ensure that computers stay in time with each other, time servers are available on the Internet that you can synchronize with using the Network Time Protocol (NTP). Even if your computer's CPU is slightly off-tune and tends to drift out of sync, the NTP server provides a steady source of reliable time with which to align. Virtual machines have no physical processors, so the guest operating systems need a way to tie to a time source. They do this through the host machine that can be synchronized to an NTP server. This way, all of the virtual machines on a host will have the same time. Groups of machines tied to the same NTP server also guarantee synchronization. Linux systems, because of the way timekeeping is implemented in the Linux kernel, have always had some challenges in a virtual environment. Numerous best practices concerning NTP configuration are available at the Network Time Protocol project website, www.ntp.org, but the various hypervisor vendor sites and knowledge bases have more current information. As Linux kernels have matured, these issues have mostly been resolved, but it is definitely something about which you should be aware. For our deployment on VirtualBox, the installation of the Guest Additions will manage the synchronization between the host system and the Linux guest.

Finally, as in the physical world, there is no way to effectively judge the performance of a virtual machine without metrics. Before an application is P2Ved, performance measurements should be taken so that a baseline is in place to measure against. Once in place, those measurements should be periodically repeated to determine how an application is faring in the virtual environment. As the application gets updated, workload requirements change, or hardware alterations occur, physical or virtual, the metrics will prove an invaluable tool to ensuring good continued performance and satisfied users.

THE ESSENTIALS AND BEYOND

The Linux operating system continues to increase its share of the data-center server market based on a number of factors including cost, performance, and open-source heritage. Applications that in the past were tied to proprietary UNIX versions are now available or being ported to the various Linux editions. Vendors are also taking the open-source versions and customizing them for use on their platforms. Two examples of these are the Red Hat–based Oracle Linux and IBM's z/Linux, which are run on mainframe systems. As these trends continue, expect to see Linux usage grow significantly in the data center as a platform for key business applications. Virtualization of these workloads will continue to grow as well.

ADDITIONAL EXERCISES

▶ Change the VM memory to 2.5 GB (2,560 KB) in the Virtual Machine Settings. Will the memory be applied?

▶ Open the System Monitor as described in the "Getting the Status of the Linux Devices" section. Select the Processes tab and examine the various processes there. By convention, daemon processes usually end in the letter *d* or sometimes with the word *daemon*. How many daemons do you see? Now, switch users to the root user. You can do this beneath System. Select the drop-down box at the top-right side of the System Monitor and select All Processes. Are there more daemon processes or fewer? Why do you think that is?

CHAPTER 7

Managing CPUs for a Virtual Machine

The CPU is the heart of any computer, whether it is a server, a laptop, tablet, or mobile device. As such, virtualization of the processor is a critical part of achieving good performance of the virtual machine, as well as good overall use of the physical resources. Not only is the actual virtualization operation important, but so is the correct allocation and configuration of the VM's CPU. A poorly implemented deployment will cause performance issues and undermine the virtualization effort.

▶ **Understanding CPU virtualization**

▶ **Configuring VM CPU options**

▶ **Tuning practices for VM CPUs**

Understanding CPU Virtualization

Along with memory, network I/O, and storage I/O, CPUs are some of the main resources used to help size and then determine how well a server is behaving. One of the core properties of virtualization, as defined by Popek and Goldberg, is that there should be little or no difference in the *performance* between the virtual machine and its physical counterpart. If any one of the resources is suffering *contention,* or is constrained, then the entire performance of that virtual server appears degraded, even though only one of these resources may be bottlenecked. The CPU is the first of these that we will examine.

The first electronic computers were very large, covering almost 2,000 square feet of space and weighing almost 30 tons. Most of the machine was directed at supporting the actual processing work—the calculations that provided results. Those initial computers were literally programmed by hand, having wires and patch panels that were reconfigured by an aptly named computer scientist to provide a certain set of calculations. When the

program was changed, the wires were unplugged and reconnected in a different arrangement to accommodate the updated calculation set. Today's microprocessors are both more powerful and faster by orders of magnitude than those room-sized behemoths.

The CPU, or *Central Processing Unit*, is the computer inside the computer, and its function is to execute the programs passed to it from the various programs running on the machine. Programs run on the CPU in the form of a relatively small instruction set. These instructions perform bits of work on the data that accompanies the instructions passed to the CPU. The speed at which these instructions execute directly relates to the apparent performance of the CPU, although it would be more accurate to say that performance is more a measure of the number of instructions executed in a certain amount of time rather than the actual number of instructions being executed. If a particular application's workload requirements cannot execute within a certain amount of time, it appears slow; whether it is because the CPU is older or the application demands more processing time than is available is irrelevant. One solution to this issue is a well-known tradition: throw more hardware at the problem by adding a second CPU. There are other strategies to handle this—for example, hyper-threading, which we'll cover shortly, and resource pooling, which we'll cover in Chapter 14, "Understanding Applications in a Virtual Machine."

In the context of virtualization, the question is, "How do you virtualize a CPU?" The short answer is, most times you don't. There are virtualization solutions that attempt to emulate the CPU itself, but emulation often suffers from performance and scalability issues because large amounts of processing overhead are devoted to the effort. Instead, the hypervisor schedules slices of time on the available processors in the physical host server for the virtual instructions to run. A simple example is illustrated in Figure 7.1. The first virtual machine needs to execute a set of commands on the virtual hardware, and that request is directed to the hypervisor. The hypervisor schedules an execution session for that virtual machine's request. The physical CPU executes the instructions on the associated data and passes the results back to the hypervisor, which returns them to the first virtual machine. As the physical CPU frees up, the hypervisor schedules the next set of instructions from the second virtual machine to be performed. In this way, the virtual machines are serviced in a timely and efficient manner while the physical resource, the CPU, is also utilized most effectively. Also, virtual CPUs are not mapped to physical CPUs. A hypervisor will schedule work on behalf of a virtual machine on any available physical CPU, so the work from a particular virtual machine might actually be run on any and all of the host processors over a period of time.

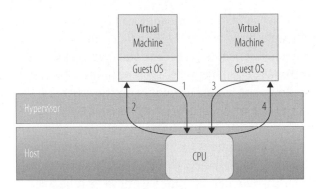

FIGURE 7.1 VMs using a host CPU

If each virtual machine had only one virtual CPU and each physical server had only one physical processor, the model would be that simple. Of course, reality is much more complex. The first wrinkle is that most servers today are configured with more than one processor. That does not greatly affect this model aside from providing additional resources in the form of CPU time that can be allocated by the hypervisor. The next change is that most of today's modern CPUs contain more than one processor in their makeup. Each of these processors in the CPU is called a *core,* and even today's personal computers have multicore CPUs. Table 7.1 illustrates the number of cores available in various processor configurations. Early releases had two (dual-core) or four (quad-core) processors, but servers today have eight, twelve, or more cores. Again, adding more cores to each CPU adds more available processing resources for the virtual machines to utilize.

TABLE 7.1 Cores Available in Various Processor Configurations

# of processors	single core	dual core	quad core
1	1	2	4
2	2	4	8
4	4	8	16
8	8	16	32

To distinguish between physical server CPUs and virtual machine CPUs, we'll refer to the latter as vCPUs. What happens when you add vCPUs to virtual machines? If you have a virtual machine with two vCPUs, the hypervisor will need to schedule work on two physical CPUs. That means two physical CPUs would need to be available at the same time for the work to be performed. Don't forget, virtualizing a CPU is really just scheduling slices of time on the physical CPU. In the case of a VM with more than one vCPU, you need more than one physical CPU to be available to do the work. Depending on the scheduling algorithm, which might be an issue in a busy system or a system with a limited number of CPUs, a multi-vCPU system might wait a long time to be scheduled. As an example, if a virtual machine is configured with four vCPUs and it was running on a host that had four physical CPUs, all of those physical CPUs would need to be idle for that virtual machine's work to be scheduled. On a system with other virtual machines, those single vCPU VMs get to grab resources sooner because they only need to hold one CPU. Even VMs configured with two vCPUs would have an easier time being scheduled than the four vCPU VMs. Relaxed scheduling models have made that challenge less likely, allowing CPUs to be allocated in a staggered manner rather than in strict lockstep, which would penalize virtual machines configured with multiple vCPUs. In addition, there are facilities within the hypervisor for prioritization so that important workloads, even if they are "challenged" with multiple processors, can receive adequate scheduling time on the physical processors.

So far, even with multi-vCPU systems, we have kept things fairly simple when it comes to scheduling time on the physical CPUs, but we have only been discussing unicore processors. When multicore processors are added to the equation, things get more complex. As chip technology has matured, manufacturers have learned to deliver more processing power into compact packages. A "processor" today is usually a package of multiple CPUs, also known as multiple "cores." The mapping of a vCPU to a physical CPU changes by matching a vCPU to one core of the physical CPU. In the previous example, a four-CPU server that had four cores per CPU (quad-core) would have sixteen resources that could be scheduled by the hypervisor. Obviously, the odds of four out of sixteen processors being available at a particular moment in time are much greater than four out of four being free. Since virtualizing CPUs is really just a time scheduling exercise, from a performance standpoint, the more efficiently you can schedule, the better throughput you can receive. Even with multiple cores on both the physical and virtual side of things, which might complicate that scheduling, more resources are better.

Looking at this a little closer, when you plan for how many virtual machines can fit on a host, one of the criteria is the number of vCPUs and physical CPUs. In this simple model, with four unicore physical CPUs on the host, you actually can allocate more than four vCPUs for the guests because individual guests don't monopolize a physical CPU. If they did, you would need to assign them additional vCPUs. Instead, each guest uses a portion of a physical CPU, and you can allocate more than one vCPU for each physical CPU in your server. The question then becomes: how many more vCPUs can you allocate?

Each vendor has different supported recommendations and different limitations. Vendors have a total number of vCPUs that can be allocated on each individual host, although that theoretical limit is rarely reached. More often, that limit is the vendor's recommended value of vCPUs you can allocate per physical CPU. VMware ESXi supports 32 vCPUs per physical core. In a four CPU unicore server, it can support up to 128 single vCPU VMs. If you were to go through the same exercise with a multicore machine, four CPUs with four cores, you would have sixteen physical CPU resources on which to schedule, and the numbers would increase appropriately. Again, these numbers would vary depending on the workloads that the actual deployed virtual machines required.

One last fly in the ointment is hyper-threading, an Intel technology that improves parallel operations in each core by making it appear as two logical cores, almost doubling the throughput available. It does require that the operating system support multiple processors as well as the hyper-thread technology. Most hypervisors support both requirements. Both virtual machines and the hypervisors they are supported on can take advantage of hyper-threading.

The examples illustrated here are considered guidelines, but actual performance is dependent on the host server hardware configuration, as well as workloads of the guest VMs. An underconfigured host will be able to support fewer VMs than a correctly sized host. Likewise, a host will be able to support more virtual machines that require fewer CPU resources than those that require more. Processing is a key resource and if not planned for properly, contention will cause a bottleneck and overall performance will suffer.

Configuring VM CPU Options

In the case of virtual CPUs, there are very few items that you can adjust to affect the virtual machine's performance. In fact, as part of the virtual machine, there is really only one parameter that you can adjust: the actual number of vCPUs. Until recently, you could increase the number of processors in a virtual machine only when the virtual machine was shut down. This was because the operating systems would not recognize additional processors when they were added. Certain operating systems today, like Linux and Windows Server 2012, will allow you to hot-add resources such as additional processors. This is a welcome capability because it means that processor resources can be added to a server without needing to interrupt the application or the users, while providing more horsepower for the work to be done. Currently, you cannot similarly reduce the number of CPU resources in a running virtual machine. In that case, you would need to shut down the VM, change the number of CPUs, and then restart the system. Again, this is because the operating systems do not support a hot-remove capability.

To examine or change the number of processors in your virtual machine, you can perform the following:

1. Select Virtual Machine from the VMware Player menu bar.

2. Select Virtual Machine Settings from the menu.

3. As shown in Figure 7.2, selecting the Processors line on the left side of the screen under the Hardware window will display the Processor options.

4. By selecting the Number of Processor Cores drop-down menu, you can choose up to 16 vCPUs for your virtual machine. If you have an application that requires more than a single vCPU, you can increase its number of vCPUs at this time. VMware Player limits you to 16 vCPUs in a single virtual machine, but other Tier-1 hypervisor solutions, from VMware and others, allow you to configure many more.

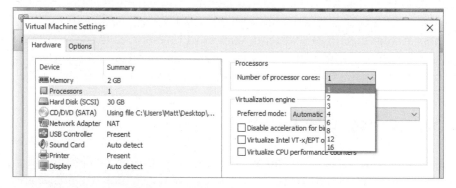

FIGURE 7.2 Processors in a virtual machine

Tuning Practices for VM CPUs

Although a CPU is one of the core resources for correctly sizing and managing virtual machine performance, it is also the one with the fewest number of moving parts when it comes to tuning. Essentially, you can affect the number of vCPUs that you allocate to a virtual machine and you have some ability to control how those vCPUs are seen by the virtual machine. Aside from that, there are few factors on the physical server that are changeable that affect how well the virtual machines perform.

Choosing Multiple vCPUs vs. a Single vCPU

When you're building a virtual machine, one of your initial configuration choices is the number of virtual CPUs that will be allocated to the VM. The choice would seem to be fairly simple, either one or more than one, but this is one of the largest areas of discussion when it comes to virtual machine performance. As with physical servers, having multiple CPUs in virtual machines would provide more CPU resources to utilize; but as you have seen, having additional vCPUs can actually hinder performance because the additional vCPUs need to be scheduled simultaneously, which is not always possible on a busy system. Despite this, administrators often overallocate the number of vCPUs in a virtual machine.

The reason this happens is primarily due to demands from the application owner or the application vendor who may not be knowledgeable about virtualization performance. The history of an application in the physical world is usually one of "more is better." Even though processor speed and efficiency increase regularly, the use of those processor resources does not. Compounding the effect is the fact that hardware vendors have configured more processors and more cores per processor into each server, so very often an application is using a mere fraction of the CPU power available to it. So, when a company undertakes a virtualization project, it is not unusual for application owners to push back on the virtual machine configurations that are allocated to them. Their thinking is that the application is currently running on a physical server that has two dual-core processors, so the virtual machine should also have four vCPUs, even though that physical server may be using less than 5 percent of those processors.

This is not to imply that there are not applications that require multiple vCPUs. There definitely are, and they should be configured accordingly. But the majority of virtual machines can be and should be configured with one vCPU. Before workloads are P2Ved, a number of different performance tools can be run to determine a baseline of expected CPU performance. One advantage of a virtual machine is that its configuration can be modified quickly and easily as capacity requirements change. Instead of sizing the virtual machine for a future workload three years down the line, as you would do with a physical server, the VM can be adjusted on an as-needed basis. vCPUs can potentially be hot-added without interrupting the application at all. Again, it is best to begin with a single

It is outside the scope of this text and beyond VMware Player's capability to create a multicore vCPU. For more information, go to http://kb.vmware.com/kb/1010184.

vCPU and then adjust upward if circumstances demand it, rather than to start with many and work downward.

Finally, some operating systems can run only on a limited number of CPUs. In the case of Windows XP Professional Edition, the maximum physical processor limit that is supported is two. If you load Windows XP Professional Edition on a server with four processors, it will use only two of them. Similarly, if you create a virtual machine with four vCPUs, Windows XP Professional Edition will utilize only two of them. However, it will take advantage of multicore processors, so if you could build a VM with multicore vCPUs, you could use more resources. Fortunately, certain hypervisors have this capability, allowing you to create a dual-core vCPU, for example. Creating a virtual machine with two dual-core vCPUs would allow Windows XP Professional Edition to use four CPUs, much the same as it would if it were installed on a physical server with two dual-core CPUs.

Hyper-Threading

Hyper-threading is an Intel microprocessor technology that improves performance by making more efficient use of the processor scheduling. Prior to hyper-threading technology, only one set of instructions could be executed on a processor at a time. For each physical processor, hyper-threading presents two logical processors. Each logical processor can process an individual *thread* of work, so for each physical core, two threads of work can be scheduled. Hyper-threading doesn't double the capability of a processor, but it might provide an additional 30 percent efficiency under the right circumstances.

A few prerequisites are required for hyper-threading to work. First, the processor must be an Intel microprocessor that is capable of hyper-threading. The operating system must support multiple processors, and it must be capable of supporting hyper-threading. Windows and Linux support hyper-threading, as do most hypervisors. This means that a hypervisor can schedule two threads of work on each physical processor or core on the physical server. Let's check your system to see if hyper-threading is enabled.

1. From the Windows search box, enter **Task Manager**.

2. Select the Task Manager to open the application.

3. Choose the Performance tab at the top of the application.

4. As shown in Figure 7.3, if it isn't already highlighted, select the CPU graph on the left panel.

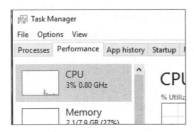

FIGURE 7.3 CPU in the Task Manager

In Figure 7.4, just below the performance graph, you can see that the example system contains two processor cores and four logical processors, which translates back to two threads per core. Hyper-threading is enabled on the physical system.

Maximum speed:	2.10 GHz
Sockets:	1
Cores:	2
Logical processors:	4
Virtualization:	Enabled
L1 cache:	128 KB

FIGURE 7.4 Physical and logical CPU information

Working with Intel and AMD Servers

When it comes to virtualization, questions often arise regarding which x86 chipset is best for performance. At present, the best answer is that no x86 chipset is particularly better than another. As a proof point, companies are not making hardware decisions based on the chipset in the server. Companies refresh their server hardware and improve the platforms on which they run either through a consolidation effort as they move to a virtualized environment or by replacing their virtualized environment. Sometimes these upgrades involve switching to a vendor that uses a different x86 microprocessor—for example, when going from Intel to AMD. From a performance standpoint, typically there is not that much fluctuation in CPU performance, but there is a potential change in operational performance.

Hypervisors will run just as well on either an AMD or Intel platform; in fact, there is no way to discern what chip you are running on from an operational standpoint. However, issues can arise when you are working in a mixed environment, supporting both Intel-based and AMD-based servers. In Chapter 13,

"Understanding Availability," you'll learn about *clustering* hosts for increased performance and availability. For now, you just need to know that one feature of clustering is the ability to migrate a virtual machine from one physical server to another, while the virtual machine is still running, without interrupting the application on that virtual machine. This capability is used for dynamically load balancing virtual machines across a number of physical hosts and for evacuating a physical host so that maintenance can be done. This is true for a cluster made up of physical servers that share the same vendor microprocessor. In a mixed environment, the instruction sets of the different microprocessors are not identical, so you cannot live-migrate the virtual machines from an AMD host to an Intel host, or vice versa. In order to move a virtual machine from an AMD host to an Intel host, or the reverse, you need to shut down that virtual machine, and then you can restart it on the second host with the different chipset.

THE ESSENTIALS AND BEYOND

CPUs are the engines that drive computers in all of their many forms. Virtual machines depend on their CPUs even more than their physical counterparts because of the way they are shared among many VMs. Poor configurations on both the physical and virtual side can magnify performance issues, causing problems for applications and users alike. Modern physical servers are configured with CPUs that contain multiple processors or cores. Each of these cores can be used to schedule work on behalf of a single vCPU, adding additional capacity and flexibility when you're planning for performance. Capabilities that physical CPUs can take advantage of, such as hyper-threading, can also be utilized by virtual machines and their vCPUs.

ADDITIONAL EXERCISES

▶ You have a virtualization host that has four processors and each processor has four cores. According to the vendor guidelines, the virtualization solution you've chosen will support up to 18 vCPUs per physical CPU. If you want to keep about 20 percent of your CPU capacity in reserve for growth and performance spikes, how many single vCPU virtual machines will you be able to deploy on this host?

▶ At the last moment, your procurement group was able to contribute additional monies for the host and, instead of a quad-core server, you are able to acquire a virtualization with four eight-core CPUs. The trade-off is that you will need to support an additional application that consists of 17 virtual machines configured with four vCPUs each. Keeping that same 20 percent reserve, in addition to the 17 larger VMs, how many single-vCPU virtual machines will you be able to deploy on this host?

CHAPTER 8

Managing Memory for a Virtual Machine

Memory, like the central processing unit (CPU), is a crucial part of the virtual machine. Unlike the CPU, memory is usually the resource that is consumed the fastest. Hypervisors abstract memory by handling data blocks between the server's physical memory and what has been allocated to the virtual machines. The management of memory resources by both the hypervisor and the administrator is important for effective use of the physical resources.

▶ **Understanding memory virtualization**

▶ **Configuring VM memory options**

▶ **Tuning practices for VM memory**

Understanding Memory Virtualization

Fifteen years ago, the concept of computer memory was isolated in a few pockets of people who, in some way or another, were involved with computer technology. They didn't even refer to it as memory but rather as RAM, which stands for Random Access Memory. RAM was thought of and treated as another storage device, like a disk, but it was much faster and you could access data in memory with a more flexible model than accessing data from disk storage devices. System memory sizes were much smaller as well, measured in kilobytes and then megabytes. Let's contrast that with today's environment. Personal computers and smart phones routinely are offered with gigabytes of memory. iPads and other tablets are similarly provisioned as well. In addition to those items, many other devices that are part of our daily experience have memory as part of their configurations. Digital cameras, mp3 players, and game systems have all added to our pool of common consumer electronics. Currently, we are on the cusp of a wave of all-new consumer devices enabled for the Internet of Things offering us web-enabled automobiles, refrigerators, and even lightbulbs. Each of these will require memory to store information and have a workspace to operate on that data. With the spread of these commercial devices, the understanding of what memory provides to computing has also spread throughout the population so that today both 12-year-old children and 70-year-old grandparents are aware of, and often knowledgeable about, memory.

MEMORY GROWTH IN CONSUMER DEVICES

The initial commercial personal computers in the 1980s came with 64 KB of memory. One popular model was named the Commodore 64 because that amount of RAM came configured with the system. Like today, initial limitations in memory size were due to cost, the ability of the chip (CPU) to manage large amounts of memory, and the ability of operating systems to address large amounts of memory. The Apple iPad Pro offers 128 GB of memory, which is two million times larger than the memory offered in a Commodore 64.

Memory is a computer's workspace. When an operating system boots up, certain regularly used routines are loaded into memory and stay there. As programs are executed, those routines are copied into memory as well for speed of execution and quick access for reuse. When programs work on information, that data is also moved into memory so all of the calculation's various parts and pieces can be quickly transferred to the CPU for processing and then written back to memory after whatever transformations the CPU has performed. With more memory, computers can access and process larger amounts of data faster. In game systems, DVD players, and digital video recorders (DVRs), memory is used as a buffer to stage data so it can be smoothly presented to a screen. With the growing spread of real-time multimedia streaming in the consumer marketplace, memory is a critical part of the equation.

The same holds true in virtualization. More than any other resource, memory is the one with the largest impact on how well or how poorly the virtual environment will perform. As with CPU virtualization, the hypervisor abstracts memory by using the physical server's memory on behalf of the virtual machines it supports. To understand how memory works in a virtual environment, we need to return to the Windows virtual machine that was created in Chapter 5, "Installing Windows on a Virtual Machine." We began with 1 GB of memory, and, as shown in Figure 8.1, we later adjusted that to 1.5 GB. The physical system on which the virtual machine is hosted has more than that, whether it is the 8 GB that the test system is using, or the hundreds of gigabytes with which current servers are outfitted. The point is that the virtual machine, and by extension, the operating system in the virtual machine, is only aware of the 1.5 GB that is allocated.

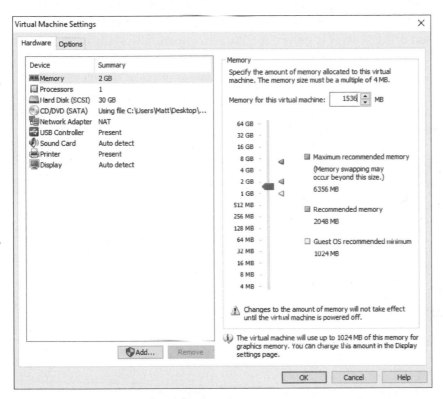

FIGURE 8.1 Memory in a virtual machine

But that 1.5 GB is not nearly enough working area to hold an operating system, some applications (for example, Microsoft Word, Adobe Acrobat Reader, and Mozilla Firefox), and the data that you might be using with those applications. Because of this, operating systems have been developed to constantly shuttle program and data information between physical memory and disk storage. Memory blocks are referred to as *pages,* and they are usually moved around in uniform sizes; in today's architecture, a typical memory page size is 4 KB. This 4 KB page size is based on the processor type and architecture, but it can be adjusted. There are applications that benefit from having larger blocks of data shuttled in and out of memory, but there is usually little need to configure larger pages.

When memory blocks need to be freed up so newer information can be loaded, the older, less-recently used blocks are written to disk. The disk acts as an extension of the physical memory, and the process of copying the pages to the disk is called *paging.* The file that the memory pages are copied to is usually called the *page file.* Processors have physical memory, called *cache,* as part of their makeup, where work is queued up before entering the CPU. A very simplified illustration of the process is shown in Figure 8.2. Because working with disk storage is much slower than working with memory, from a performance standpoint, paging is an expensive process. Even today, as physical storage is transforming from the spinning disks that have been prevalent for the last 50 years to solid state drives without moving parts, having data already in memory is orders of magnitude faster than retrieving it from a disk.

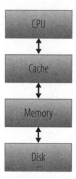

FIGURE 8.2 Moving memory pages

Configuring VM Memory Options

For such an important part of the virtual machine, it is a bit ironic that there is only one adjustment that can be made to a virtual machine's memory and that is to either increase or decrease the size. Additional elements are built into the hypervisor that can be adjusted on a macro level to adjust memory usage throughout the host, but we'll cover them in the next section. Just as with a physical server, a virtual server must be configured with enough resources to do the job it has been assigned. If too much memory is assigned, then memory could be wasted, not being available to other virtual machines. If too little memory has been configured, then memory will constantly be paging to the physical disk and affect the performance of the applications. The trick is to find the sweet spot between too much and too little. Fortunately, best practices and performance tools are available to help guide the way.

1. Although we went through this exercise when you created your virtual machine, let's take another look at setting the memory in a virtual machine. In VMware Player, select the Windows 10 virtual machine.

2. At the bottom right or from the Virtual Machine menu, select Edit Virtual Machine Settings.

3. The first hardware device highlighted is Memory. As shown in Figure 8.3, you can see the memory configuration for the Windows 10 virtual machine. You can adjust the memory up or down by using the slider or by directly changing the value in the Memory For This Virtual Machine text box.

4. VMware Player provides three default values: a minimum recommended memory value, a recommended memory value, and a maximum recommended memory value. The minimum and recommended values are based on the guest operating system, while the maximum amount is based on the amount of memory in the host server.

5. Select Cancel to close the Virtual Machine Settings window.

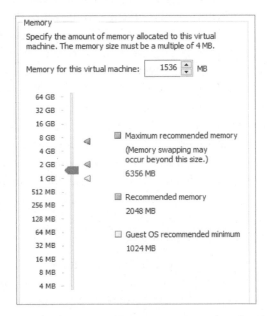

FIGURE 8.3 Memory management in a virtual machine

Memory adjustments are dependent on the operating system installed in the virtual machine. Dynamic additions of memory without a reboot are possible in operating systems that support this capability. Windows Server 2003, 2008, and 2012, and newer distributions of Linux support hot-add memory. Windows versions will recognize the additional memory without intervention. At this time, the Linux versions usually need to have a command executed to set the memory status to online before it will be available to the system, physical or virtual. Although you can also edit a virtual machine to remove memory, current operating system releases require a system reboot to make the adjustment. Depending on the Type-2 hypervisor being used, you might still need to reboot the virtual machine for hot-add changes to be applied, even if the guest operating system supports hot-add capabilities.

 TIP   Many videos are available on YouTube that demonstrate most of the covered capabilities. One that shows how to hot-add memory in a production environment is at http://www.youtube.com/watch?v=NdpWjAIjgoA.

Tuning Practices for VM Memory

Context is important when you're working with memory in a virtual environment. So far we have looked at memory only from the standpoint of the virtual machine looking outward. The amount of memory that has been allocated to the virtual machine is what it can use. The physical host it resides on may have hundreds of gigabytes available, but each individual virtual machine is unaware of the greater resources. Figure 8.4 shows a simple illustration of this model. The two virtual machines have been allocated 4 GB and 2 GB of memory, respectively, and that is all the memory that the guest operating systems in those virtual machines are aware of. The physical host actually has 16 GB of physical memory. With 6 GB of memory already spoken for by the two virtual machines, there are still 10 GB of memory available on the host for use—but that isn't entirely accurate.

Calculating Memory Overhead

The hypervisor itself needs to reserve some portion of the memory for its own processes, much as an operating system reserves memory. In the past, this would be a significant portion of physical memory, upward of 20 percent in some cases, but newer hypervisor technology has drastically reduced that amount. For each virtual machine running on the host, a small portion of memory is also reserved, in addition to the memory allocated for the use of the virtual machine. This additional memory is used for operational functions such as memory mapping tables—connecting the virtual machine memory addresses to the physical memory addresses. The actual overhead numbers vary by hypervisor implementation and the memory configurations of the individual virtual machines. For this discussion, we can use the round number of 1 GB of memory to cover both the hypervisor overhead and the virtual machine overhead and be comfortable that we've allocated enough memory whatever parameters we change. That would reduce the available memory to 9 GB.

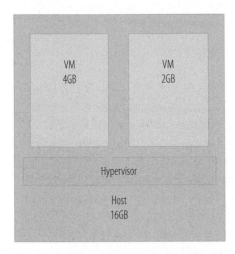

FIGURE 8.4 Memory in virtual machines and their host

Now let's add a few more virtual machines. Two additional 4 GB virtual machines and one 1 GB virtual machine will consume the remainder of the available physical memory. In practice, most systems are never fully utilized in this way for a number of reasons, the primary one being that administrators always keep resources in reserve for a rainy day. As virtual machines grow, or unanticipated performance demands appear, having a reserve pool of memory, or any resource, to supplement from makes good business sense. This model now has five guests that are utilizing 15 GB of physical memory, but that is not very efficient. From a strict virtualization standpoint, we haven't improved the utilization of the shared resource, memory, since we aren't sharing it. Each virtual machine is, from a memory standpoint, still behaving like a physical server with a defined amount of dedicated memory. If you compare CPU virtualization and memory virtualization, they are very similar. Both resources depend on the hypervisor to manage the allocation of the larger physical device, while providing the appearance of servicing the virtual device.

The hypervisor determines which pages are written into physical memory, and it keeps track of how each virtual machine's allocated memory is mapped to the physical server's memory through the previously mentioned tables. This holistic view of memory in both the physical and virtual environments puts the hypervisor in a unique position to provide some interesting capabilities. Instead of having a fixed amount of memory, what if you could vary memory up and down depending on the workload? As part of that process, there would be need for a way to reclaim memory pages that were no longer needed. Storage technologies today routinely use deduplication and compression technologies for improved performance and cost savings. Could you do this with memory as well? The answer to both of those questions is yes.

Memory Optimizations

The five virtual machines are allocated 15 GB of memory among them, but in reality they are probably using much less. Application owners routinely ask for more memory than normally required to handle growth and performance spikes. Physical servers, because of the static nature of their configuration, are sized with additional memory for future capacity and potential need. These ingrained practices often find their way into the virtual world as well. The result is that virtual machines often are unnecessarily allocated more memory. The hypervisor has the ability to circumvent that issue. Because the hypervisor controls all of the physical memory operations and the virtual machine's view of those operations, it is simple to tell the virtual machine that it has a certain amount of memory, but then work behind the scenes to make that amount flexible.

Even though a virtual machine is allocated an amount of memory, say 2 GB, the memory is not hard reserved for the VM. The hypervisor can use any of that memory for other virtual machines. The memory allocation is like a high-water mark, and the hypervisor raises and lowers the actual memory amount that is being used. From the guest operating system standpoint, the virtual machine has 2 GB and behaves accordingly. One technique that is used to reclaim memory from the virtual machine is called *ballooning*. A simple illustration of ballooning memory is shown in Figure 8.5. In order to take the physical memory back from a virtual machine, the pages that are in memory need to be flushed back to a different storage device, in this case, the paging area of the disk. The balloon driver is activated and (virtually) inflates, forcing the operating system to flush pages from memory. The operating system chooses the pages to flush because it knows which pages are the least recently used and are stale, making them good candidates to remove. Once the pages are flushed, the balloon driver deflates, and the hypervisor reclaims the physical memory for use. Usually, this process only happens when there is contention for memory.

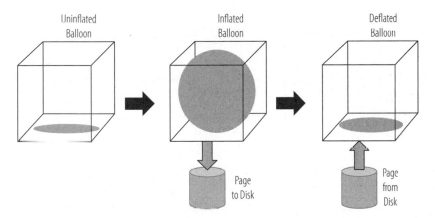

FIGURE 8.5 Ballooning memory

One by-product of this memory agility is that much less physical memory is used than the amount allocated to the virtual machines. If the five virtual machines used half their memory as an average, you would actually have 7.5 GB of additional memory to use. You wouldn't want to allocate 100 percent of the memory—that would leave no headroom for performance spikes. If you conservatively reserve 10 percent of the physical RAM for a buffer, that would still leave about 6 GB of additional memory. Because each virtual machine uses half its allocated amount, you can actually put more virtual machines with an aggregate 12 GB of memory on the host. In this model, we might add another 4 GB VM and four more 2 GB VMs, doubling the five existing VMs to ten. This ability to allocate more virtual memory on a host than physically exists is called *memory overcommitment*. A simpler example is shown in Figure 8.6. Each of the thin blocks represents memory blocks specific to a particular VM. Here, the host has 16 GB of memory, but the three virtual machines have an allocated total of 24 GB.

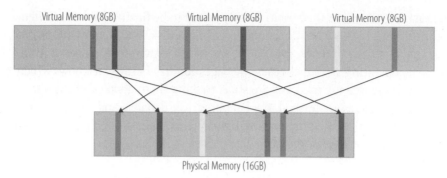

Virtual Memory (8GB)   Virtual Memory (8GB)   Virtual Memory (8GB)

Physical Memory (16GB)

FIGURE 8.6 Memory overcommitment

Memory overcommitment is a powerful virtualization technique, but it is important to understand the memory usage characteristics of your virtual machines in order for it to be effective. Idle virtual machines, or VMs with more memory allocated than they use, allow the hypervisor to manage the memory resource across more virtual machines for a better consolidation ratio, as you saw in the example. The example with the virtual machines using half of their memory is considered to be a 2-to-1 overcommitment ratio. Many mature virtual environments use memory overcommitment, and those that do run somewhere between a 1.5:1 and that 2-to-1 ratio. Application environments that are well understood can run at significantly higher ratios, 10-to-1 or even 20-to-1, although these are definitely the far edge exceptions to the rule.

In addition to overcommitment, there are other methods to help increase effective memory utilization in a virtual environment. One of these is page sharing. *Page sharing* is analogous to data deduplication, which is a technique that storage vendors use to reduce data blocks and save disk space by storing only one copy of a duplicated data block. With ten virtual machines, it would not be unusual for many of them to be running the same version of their guest operating system, or even the same applications. Large Internet providers often run dozens if not hundreds or thousands of application webservers, each of which is identically configured from the hardware, to the operating system, and to the application programs. When the virtual machine loads operating system pages or application program pages into memory, many of these pages are identical from one virtual machine to another. Because the hypervisor manages all of the page transfers between virtual machines and the physical memory, it can determine which pages are already in physical memory and use that page instead of writing yet another copy to physical memory. Figure 8.7 illustrates this sharing process. Some memory pages contain operating system or application program code that will never be altered by a user or system process. Other memory pages contain application- or user-specific data that can be dynamically updated. If a virtual machine needs to write to a memory page that has already been designated as a shared page, the hypervisor will create a new copy of that page for that virtual machine's exclusive use. This process is called *Copy-on-Write*.

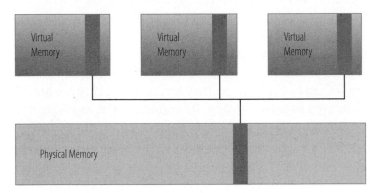

FIGURE 8.7 Page sharing

Not only does page sharing work between different virtual machines, but within the same virtual machine as well. Without having to duplicate these shared pages, even more memory is reclaimed by the hypervisor for use by the virtual machines. In practice, page sharing can save an additional 10 to more than 40 percent of the available physical memory. Virtualization not only allowed the Internet providers mentioned earlier to consolidate those hundreds of application web servers into a much smaller and less costly physical environment, but through the use of memory overcommitment and page sharing, a much more efficient one. Another utilization that benefits from page sharing is VDI, or Virtual Desktop Infrastructures. VDI is the virtualization of a company's desktop computers, as opposed to the server virtualization on which we've focused. VDI creates virtual machines that are composed of a Windows or Linux operating system and an approved set of applications. Creating all of the virtual desktop machines to be essentially identical makes VDI an excellent use case for page sharing.

When a virtual machine is initially booted, the hypervisor reserves an amount of disk storage called a swap space. The *swap space* is for storing memory pages in the event that paging is required. If the hypervisor needs to reclaim memory, it will use the balloon driver to free up memory pages. If activation of the balloon driver hasn't provided enough free memory, the hypervisor can swap all of the virtual machine's memory pages out of physical memory and write them to physical disk. As you might imagine, since disk reads and writes take much longer than memory I/O, the virtual machine's performance during a swapping event is not good. Swapping is the last resort action in a system with memory contention. This is why proper memory configuration and ongoing monitoring is vitally important for good performance in a virtual environment.

Another available memory technique is memory compression. The goal of *compression* is to defer swapping pages out to disk since that is a more expensive time- and resource-consuming operation. The hypervisor reserves a portion of memory to use as a compression cache. When it determines that paging needs to occur, it examines the pages with algorithms to see the viability of compression. If the pages can be compressed, they are, and then they are moved to the cache, instead of being paged out to disk. Restoring them reverses the process. Compression and decompression is a much faster activity than page swapping would be.

Through the use of all of these memory management techniques, virtualization provides a much more efficient use of memory than physical servers. Without these mechanisms, server configurations would need to have more memory configured in order to handle the memory allocated to the virtual machines. The example server had about 12 GB of memory to work with after we put aside a portion for performance spikes and the hypervisor overhead. With page sharing and ballooning, we were able to effectively double utilization of that memory. If we needed to buy that additional memory, it would cost a few thousand dollars, even for the lightly configured host. Enterprise-class systems routinely are outfitted with 128 GB, 256 GB, and even terabytes of memory. Not having these memory optimization capabilities for servers of this size would require not just additional memory, but purchasing additional servers that would add tens of thousands of dollars to the budget for each server. In a large environment, the cost savings these capabilities provide are considerable.

VENDOR MEMORY OPTIMIZATION TECHNIQUES

In describing the various memory optimization techniques that virtualization can provide, we did not cover which particular hypervisor offers what techniques. One reason is that with each new release, vendors add capabilities that they did not have in the previous release. Vendors also provide similar capabilities, but implemented in different ways. Three popular solutions shown in Table 8.1 have some memory overcommit capability, but they are all architected differently. Even though every capability is not available in every vendor's offerings today, they might be added in the future. Likewise, new techniques will continue to be added as vendors continue to innovate.

TABLE 8.1 Memory Optimization Techniques

Techniques	VMware vSphere (vSphere 6.0)	Microsoft Hyper-V (Server 2012 R2)	Xen Variants (XenServer 6.5)
Overcommit	Yes	Yes	Yes
Ballooning	Yes	Yes	Yes
Page sharing	Yes	No	No
Compression	Yes	No	No

THE ESSENTIALS AND BEYOND

Memory is one of the key resources in virtualization. Not enough memory or poor configurations can create and magnify performance issues in a virtual environment. In the last few years, the effect of Moore's Law has provided virtual environments with larger amounts of memory, allowing companies to get more virtual machines on each physical host, and to virtualize much larger servers that were not candidates for virtualization just a few years back. In addition to basic memory virtualization capabilities, vendors have developed a number of memory optimizations to further increase memory usage for better performance and higher consolidation ratios.

ADDITIONAL EXERCISES

You have a 128 GB server to use as a virtualization host. You have thirty-two application servers that you plan to P2V to this host. Each application server is currently on a physical server that has 6 GB of memory. The application servers all run Windows Server 2012.

▶ Without taking advantage of any memory optimization techniques, what is the maximum number of virtual machines you can host on your server?

▶ With page sharing and ballooning, you can take advantage of memory overcommit. If you overcommit memory at a 1.25:1 ratio, how many virtual machines can you now host?

▶ While gathering baseline performance metrics for the move to the virtual environment, you find that on average, each system is actually using only 1 GB of memory. Keeping the same overcommit ratio, how many virtual machines can be hosted?

▶ You decide to leave some additional memory available for growth or emergency. At a 90 percent utilization limit, how many virtual machines can you have?

CHAPTER 9

Managing Storage for a Virtual Machine

Data storage is everywhere in today's world. Whether for the more obvious places like our computers and smart phones, or the less obvious like our DVRs and GPSs, having somewhere to store the information we need to access is part of many routine tasks we perform. In virtualization, abstracting the storage resources requires good planning; but with many choices and strategies, storage virtualization is often an area where many deployments come up short. The good news is that most of the current storage technologies and practices translate well to a virtualization environment so there are many technologies to leverage as you architect your model.

▶ **Understanding storage virtualization**

▶ **Configuring VM storage options**

▶ **Tuning practices for VM storage**

Understanding Storage Virtualization

Data storage is an ever-expanding resource. You only need to examine your personal environment over the past five to ten years to understand how necessary and pervasive data storage has become. Everything from refrigerators to automobiles now contains some amount of data storage. Appliances like GPSs (Geographic Positioning Systems) or DVRs (Digital Video Recorders) have become part of our daily routines, adding to the amount of data storage we consume. Computing devices like PCs, smart phones, music players, and tablets have experienced storage growth as each new generation of the devices appears. The same holds true in the traditional corporate data center where the amount of data being handled and stored today is far greater than just a few years back. One reason for this growth is that the type of data is vastly different than in the past. Originally, only text information, words and numbers, were stored and processed. Today, visit any website and you'll find a vast array of visual information: movie clips and motion pictures; aural information, music and speech; as well a whole host of graphics, animated and static; in addition to the textual information that is presented in all of the many fonts, colors, and sizes available to today's web page designer. All of these elements take up much more space than mere text information. Social media like Facebook and Twitter continue the trend. Wikipedia, eBay, Amazon, Google, and Apple's iCloud are all examples of the current data explosion.

HOW MUCH DIGITAL INFORMATION IS THERE?

A University of California at Berkeley study in 2008 determined the amount of digital information generated for that year to be about 8 exabytes (8 quintillion bytes), or 57,000 times the size of the Library of Congress. In addition, they concluded that the amount would double roughly every six months. The rate of increase has accelerated, and as of 2010 that amount had passed 1 zettabyte (1 sextillion bytes), or roughly a thousand times greater in that short span. The IDC Digital Universe Report stated that in 2011, the amount of digital data generated was close to 2 zettabytes (2 sextillion bytes). They forecast that by 2020 we will be generating 40 zettabytes annually.

From a computer standpoint, whatever the computing device, the process to obtain stored information to work on is very similar. The operating system, as you have seen previously, controls the access to the various I/O devices. An application program is loaded into the memory and, based on the functions it must perform, makes a request to the operating system for information to process. The operating system then passes that request on to the storage subsystem, usually a storage device (or group of devices) with a microprocessor at the front end of the system to help optimize the requests. The subsystem locates the information and then passes it back to the operating system in the form of like-sized data blocks. The operating system transfers those data blocks to the program. The program does its work, and as it needs more information, the process is repeated. If it changes the information in the data blocks, the blocks can then be shipped back through the operating system to the storage subsystem where the altered information will be rewritten to the physical storage device, until it is requested again. This path is similar whether you are using email on a PC or watching a movie that was recorded on the DVR.

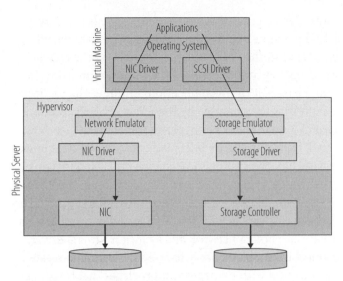

FIGURE 9.1 Virtual storage pathway

How does this work in a virtual environment? Let's take the example of acquiring information from a disk drive. Figure 9.1 illustrates the path that a request for data makes from the application program to the storage controller. The request goes to the operating system, which determines the I/O device to which the request needs to go. Direct attached storage (DAS), disk storage internal to the host system, is managed by a storage *controller,* a physical processor card that is part of a computer's hardware. A SAN (Storage Area Network) or NAS (Network Attached Storage) is a disk storage device that is connected to a computer through a dedicated storage network or through the NIC (Network Interface Controller), a physical card that connects the computer to the network. A SAN usually connects via a specialized controller, sometimes called a Fibre-Channel Controller (FCC), or a Host-Bus Adapter (HBA). Each of these physical I/O cards, the storage controller and the network controllers, utilize device drivers that the operating system uses to communicate with them. In the case of a request for information that resides on a local disk, or internal to the computer, that request goes to the to the SCSI driver. The SCSI driver request, which in a physical server goes to the physical storage controller, is taken by the hypervisor in the virtualized environment. The virtual machine sees a SCSI controller presented by the hardware, but in actuality it is merely an abstraction that the hypervisor uses to send and receive storage I/O requests. The SCSI emulator catalogs the request and places it in a queue with storage I/O from all of the virtual machines on the host. The requests are then passed to the hypervisor's storage device driver, which is connected to the physical host's storage controller. The storage controller executes the request and receives the data blocks that satisfy the virtual machine application's request. The data blocks then follow the reverse path, sent to the correct requesting VM by the hypervisor. The virtual machine's operating system receives the information from the virtual storage controller and passes it to the application, fulfilling the request.

The previously described model is the one used by the VMware hypervisor; but one major difference between VMware and other hypervisor technologies is how I/O throughput is architected. Shown in Figure 9.2 is the data path for a request in the Xen model, but the basic blueprint is the same for the other Xen variants or Microsoft Hyper-V. Here, the request is generated by the application in the virtual machine, designated a user domain. The request is passed through the guest operating system to a front-end device driver. As with the storage and network drivers in the last example, this model has both a network and a block front-end driver. These front-end drivers connect to complementary back-end drivers that reside in the Dom0 guest, the unique guest with management privileges that has direct access to the hardware. The back-end device driver receives the request from all of the user guests (user domains) and passes it to the Dom0 device driver. The device driver connects directly to the appropriate hardware device that then makes the data request to the storage devices. In this model, the hypervisor is bypassed because Dom0 is the entity that is connected to the storage devices. As with the previous example, the return trip of the data blocks back to the requesting guest application is a reversal of the request's path.

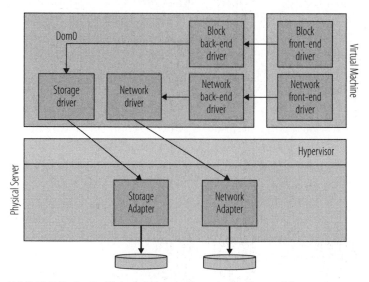

FIGURE 9.2 Virtual storage pathway in the Xen model

Similar to the processor and memory virtualization you saw earlier, storage virtualization is an abstraction of the physical resources presented to the virtual machines as if they actually controlled the physical devices. When you configure virtual storage, you will see that the Windows D: drive with which the virtual machine interacts is a logical representation of a physical Windows drive as it appears to the guest operating system. From a physical perspective, the data blocks on the physical storage device might be on any one of a number of storage options and connected to the hypervisor-controlled host through a variety of connection types. From the virtual perspective, from the viewpoint of the virtual machine's operating system and applications, it looks and acts like a Windows D: drive.

One key portion of virtualization storage architecture is the concept of clustering and shared storage. SAN or NAS solutions allow a server to access disk storage that is not part of its hardware configuration. They also allow multiple computers to access the same physical drives. Both physical and virtual infrastructures can simultaneously leverage a SAN or NAS device, often making the transition to a virtual environment smoother. For example, a physical server with its data located on internal storage can be P2Ved and spun up as a virtual machine. The data disks would also have to be migrated to the new environment, either as part of the virtual machine or moved to the shared storage. A physical server with data already on the SAN would also need to be P2Ved. Rather than needing to copy all of the data disks, they merely need to be remounted by the virtual machine for access. For testing purposes, it gives administrators a simple way to try a virtual environment and fall back to the original server if there are issues. Companies sometimes do periodic P2Vs of physical hosts as a disaster recovery option in case of a hardware failure. We'll cover more about clustering in Chapter 13, "Understanding Availability."

FILE SYSTEM OPTIONS

Each hypervisor offers a file system for use by the virtual machines that abstracts the physical storage so it is simpler to manage than if each VM had direct access to the storage array. VMware uses VMFS (Virtual Machine File System), Hyper-V has CSV (Cluster Shared Volumes), Xen has XFS, and each is used to store their guests' virtual hard drives. There is a way to present storage directly to a virtual machine and bypass a hypervisor that uses a raw device mapping (RDM) or a pass-through disk. RDMs are usually the exception rather than the rule, being useful in certain situations such as the earlier-referenced example of moving storage between a physical and virtual machine via remounting. In earlier releases of these file systems, there was sometimes a bias for raw device mappings where storage I/O performance was a concern due to perceived virtualization overhead. Current releases now offer virtually identical performance for either choice.

In addition to the configurations we covered earlier, there are some newer solutions that can help in virtual environments that are cost constrained. Smaller businesses often cannot afford to purchase shared storage solutions and are limited to virtualizing inside individual hosts. While this may be cost effective, it does decrease overall availability by increasing the number of workloads that will be affected if a single host fails. This possibility sometimes becomes a barrier to entry, causing companies to delay their virtualization efforts until they can acquire traditional shared-storage solutions. These solutions allow a group of separate disks, like the internal server disk drives, to be pooled into a shared resource that can be seen and utilized by multiple systems. A simple illustration of this is shown in Figure 9.3. Two examples of these are HP's StoreVirtual VSA solutions and VMware's Virtual SAN (VSAN). Both use the existing internal storage of individual servers to create a shared pool of storage resources that is available to all of the servers. The acquisition of a costlier storage array is no longer necessary.

Internal Storage   Logical SAN

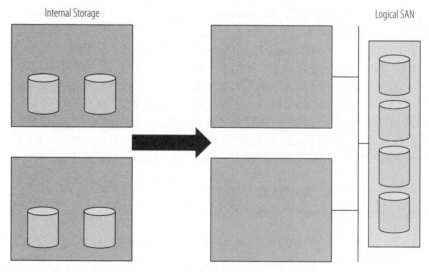

FIGURE 9.3 Pooled storage without a storage array

Configuring VM Storage Options

Just as with memory and CPUs, there are limited options for changing the storage of a virtual machine. That is, there are many, many ways to connect and configure storage to virtual machines, but these are all methods that are possible in a physical environment as well. We will cover a number of these in the next section, but here we will focus on the changes you can make to the virtual storage from the management interface.

1. If your virtual machine is still running, shut it down. Once it is powered down, edit the Virtual Machine Settings and highlight the Hard Disk option. As shown in Figure 9.4, you can see some basic information about the C: drive: some capacity information, the name of the file that comprises the hard disk in the physical system's file system, and a small selection of utilities. The utilities menu shows a number of tools.

2. Defragment is similar to the physical disk tool in that it will rearrange the data files in the virtual disk in a more compact configuration, but it will not reclaim that newly emptied space. Expand will allow you to add space to a virtual disk drive. Compact will reduce the size of a virtual disk by reclaiming empty space, but the virtual machine must be powered down to use this capability.

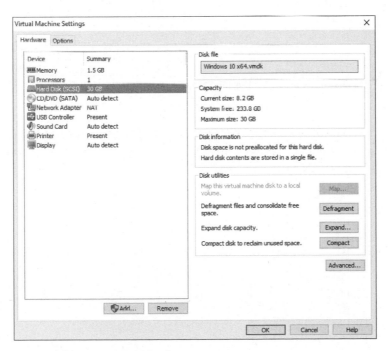

FIGURE 9.4 Virtual hard disk options

3. Let's add a second disk drive to the system. Below the Device Summary on the left side of the screen, select Add. If your host system requests permission for VMware Workstation Player to make changes on the computer because it will be creating a new disk file, allow it to do so by selecting Yes.

4. Figure 9.5 shows the initial screen of the Add Hardware Wizard. Hard Disk is already highlighted, so select Next to continue.

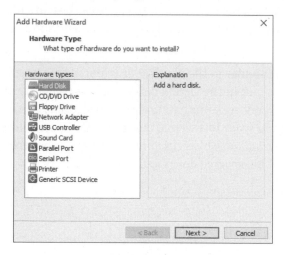

FIGURE 9.5 The Add Hardware Wizard

5. The Select a Disk Type window appears, as shown in Figure 9.6. You can choose between bus types, but stay with the recommended SCSI. Select Next to continue.

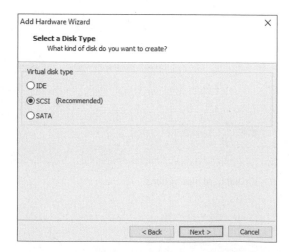

FIGURE 9.6 Select a disk type.

6. Figure 9.7 displays the Select a Disk screen. The first radio button is already selected to Create A New Virtual Disk by creating a file on the host operating system. Notice the other selections as well. Use An Existing Virtual Disk would allow you to connect or reuse a previously created disk. Use A Physical Disk would allow the virtual disk direct access to a physical device. Select Next to continue.

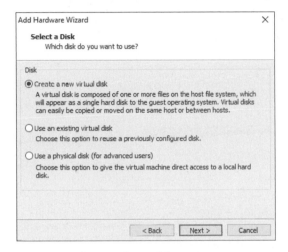

FIGURE 9.7 Select a disk.

7. Next, you get to choose how much storage space you'd like to allocate to the new drive. You can see in Figure 9.8 that both maximum and recommended sizes are presented as guidelines. You have an option to allocate all of the space on the disk at once, or have it grow incrementally as it is required. As with the C: drive during the original virtual machine creation, you also have the option to keep the disk file as one single file or split it into multiple smaller ones. The plusses and minuses are stated in the description. For this exercise, enter 5 GB and then choose to Store Virtual Disk As A Single file. Select Next to continue.

8. The final screen of the Add Hardware Wizard, illustrated in Figure 9.9, allows you to select the name and placement of the virtual disk files. The wizard takes the existing virtual disk name and increments it by default. Also by default, the disk will be placed in the existing virtual machine folder. You can select Browse to examine the folder and existing files there already. When you are done, close the Browse window and then select Finish to complete the process.

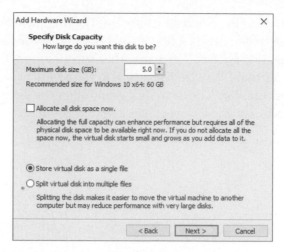

FIGURE 9.8 Specify the disk capacity.

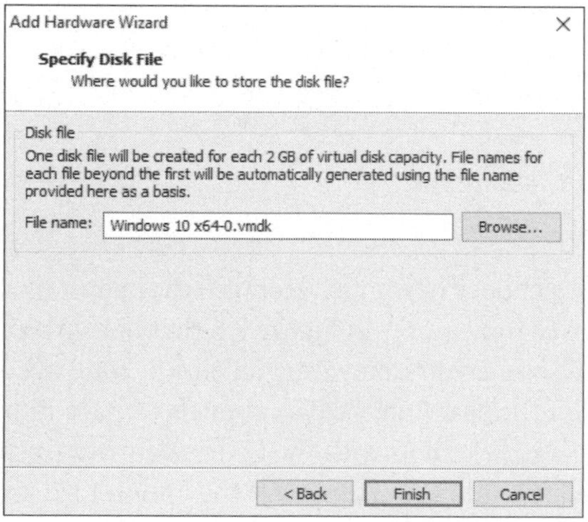

FIGURE 9.9 Specify the disk file.

9. Back on the Virtual Machine Settings window, you can see that the new disk has appeared. As shown in Figure 9.10, examine the capacity of the new disk and note that the maximum size and the actual size are different because you didn't pre-allocate the space. If you highlight the Utilities, you can see that the only option available is to

expand the disk size. One reason why is that the job of creating a new disk is not complete. The disk is now configured and connected to the virtual machine, but you haven't formatted and initialized it for Window's use.

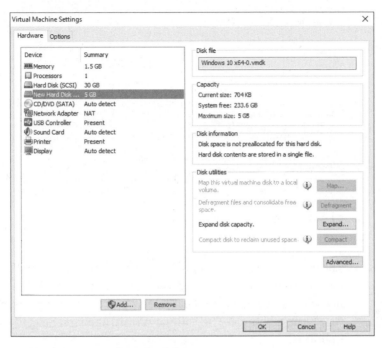

FIGURE 9.10 A new hard disk

10. Select OK to close the Virtual Machine Settings window and power on the virtual machine by selecting Play Virtual Machine. Note that there are now two disk icons at the top of the VMware Workstation Player window. If you hover over them with your cursor, you will see both the original 30 GB C: drive and the new 5 GB drive.

11. Once the virtual machine is powered on, click the Windows Start button and select All Apps. Expand the Windows Administrative Tools folder and double-click Computer Management. In the left-hand windowpane, expand the Storage item if it isn't already done and select Disk Management.

12. The utility recognizes that the new storage device, Disk 1, has not yet been initialized and, as shown in Figure 9.11, offers to do so. You can move the window to uncover the existing devices and verify that the disk to be initialized is the correct one. Select OK to proceed.

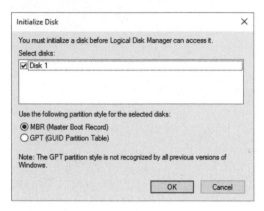

FIGURE 9.11   Initialize the new disk.

13. The new drive is now recognized by the system and is online, but it is still not usable by Windows. As illustrated in Figure 9.12, right-click in the Unallocated portion of the disk and a menu appears. Select New Simple Volume. The Volume Wizard appears. Select Next to Continue.

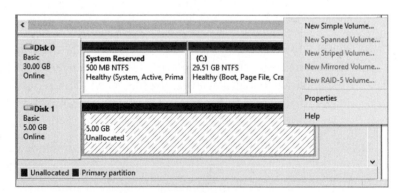

FIGURE 9.12   The New Simple Volume option

14. The maximum and minimum volume sizes are presented, and you can choose a value in MB between those limits. Leave the default, which is the maximum value, and then choose Next to continue.

15. The next screen allows you to assign a drive letter to the new disk. E: has already been selected, but you can change that if you like by choosing another letter from the remaining choices in the drop-down menu. Select Next to continue.

16. The next screen has formatting options. For our purposes, the defaults are fine, but change the Volume label to Second Drive. Select Next to continue.

17. The final screen of the wizard allows you to review the selections you have made. Check your work and then select Finish. After a few moments, as you can see in Figure 9.13, the new disk, Second Drive, has been formatted and mounted to the file system as Drive E.

FIGURE 9.13 The new drive is ready.

18. When the drive was mounted, Windows 10 automatically recognized it and an AutoPlay window appeared when the format was complete. Close the Computer Management utility. You can also see the drive by clicking the Windows File Explorer icon and choosing This PC, as shown in Figure 9.14. The drive is completely empty aside from the overhead Windows maintains for management structures.

FIGURE 9.14 Both hard drives

Tuning Practices for VM Storage

As mentioned earlier, storage is one area where performance issues often arise. The reasons are manifold but usually due to a misunderstanding of how virtualization will affect the overall storage throughput of the environment.

These issues are not isolated to any particular storage choice or connection protocol. The main reason performance issues occur in a virtual environment is consolidation. The same benefit that allows data centers to remove hundreds of physical servers also creates the problem that causes the most headaches. By moving multiple workloads in the form of virtual machines to a single physical host server, we've not only aggregated the memory and processing requirements for those workloads, but the storage I/O requirements as well. Virtualization beginners understand the need for host servers with many processors and cores, and much larger amounts of memory, but often neglect the storage and, as we'll discuss in the next chapter, the network throughput needs a consolidated environment.

Imagine a fire truck answering an alarm. The pumper truck squeals to a halt at the curb; firemen clad in protective gear clamber out and begin to deploy their equipment. Two men attach the hose to the nearby hydrant and station themselves to attack the blaze. But when the water flow is opened, you see that the hose they have chosen is a common garden hose, and the amount of water arriving is not nearly enough to quench the fire. This is very much like a virtualization server without enough storage throughput capacity to handle the requests of the many virtual machines it hosts. Consolidation reduces the number of physical servers, but it does not reduce the amount of I/O. Often, it is compressed across fewer channels, making the problem more acute. To compound things even more, virtualization typically increases the amount of I/O needed because the creation of virtual machines is usually so quick and easy that there are more virtual machines in the virtual environment than were in the original physical environment.

Fortunately, providing enough *pipe* (capacity for throughput) is a fairly well-understood and well-documented process whatever storage choices are in place. Good practices in the physical environment translate directly to good practices in the virtual environment. There are some basic maxims that apply today that have been around for a long time. The first of these is that more spindles are usually better. When faced with a choice between many smaller disks and fewer larger disks, even if those larger disks have better performance characteristics, the choice of the many is usually the best one. The reason is that storage arrays have many strategies to quickly and efficiently read and write data blocks to their disks, and they can do this in parallel, meaning that more disks can allow more simultaneous work to be done.

Other storage techniques and capabilities that are used to good effect in a physical environment also can be utilized for virtual infrastructures. For example, storage vendors have developed availability techniques to prevent data loss in case of a disk failure. Our investigation here is merely an exposure to the many types of storage optimizations and not an in-depth discovery that would be necessary to understand all the details of dealing with data storage. One such optimization is disk mirroring. *Disk mirroring* is the use of a second disk to perfectly mirror the data blocks of a disk. In the event that the physical disk fails, the identical mirror-copy contains all of the information, preventing data loss and interruption of data access. Mirrored drives also provide the benefit of having two copies to read from, halving the contention a single disk copy might have. *Disk striping* is another common technique. Here, a single file system is striped in pieces across multiple disks, and when data is written or read back, the multiple drives can work in tandem, significantly decreasing the through-put time. Marrying the two can both increase the availability of the data and increase the performance, though at a cost of doubling the disk drives.

RAID BASICS FOR AVAILABILITY AND PERFORMANCE

Many of the storage technologies that address increasing availability and through-put fall under the broad title of RAID. RAID originally stood for a Redundant Array of Inexpensive Disks, and it deals with how data is spread over multiple disks. Different RAID levels were defined and evolved over time. Each level describes a different architecture of data distribution, the degree of protection, and the performance it afforded. For example, the striping you saw earlier is considered RAID level 0. Likewise, the mirroring is defined as RAID level 1. Sometimes the combination is referred to as RAID 1+0 or RAID 10. There are other more sophisticated RAID techniques involving writing individual parts (bits, bytes, or blocks) on separate disks and providing data integrity through a separate disk that contains information to re-create the lost data if any single disk fails.

Another strategy used for efficient storage usage is data deduplication. *Deduplication* is similar to the memory page sharing that you saw in the last chapter. Imagine the email server in a corporation. The vice president of human resources sends a 12-page document outlining changes in corporate policies to the five thousand employees. All five thousand employees, knowing that it is an important document, save the 2 MB document. The document is now occupying 10 GB of corporate disk space. Ten gigabytes may not seem like that much, but multiply that one example by the thousands of documents that are sent and stored every day over years of time and you can see how fast it adds up. Deduplication technology locates identical chunks of data in the storage system, flags the original, and replaces the duplicates with pointers back to the original document. Chunks of data can be small byte-sized data strings, larger blocks of data, or even full files. In each case, only one copy of the actual data is now stored. Instead of 10 GB, the storage space has been compressed to 2 MB plus the five thousand pointers, which is fairly negligible. Figure 9.15 displays a simple before and after deduplication scenario. In practice, data deduplication has been shown to reclaim between 30 and 90 percent of used disk space, depending on the composition and the redundancy of the data.

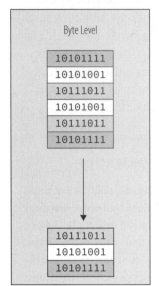 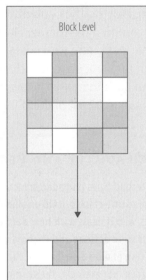 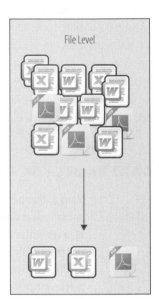

FIGURE 9.15 Deduplication

When file systems are initially configured, the administrator has to choose how much storage to allocate for that space, just as we did earlier when we added the second disk drive. Once that space has been allocated, it is removed from the usable storage pool. As an example, if you have 300 GB of storage and you create three 100 GB file systems, you have consumed all of the disk storage. This is called *thick provisioning*. The downside of thick provisioning is that each file system is pre-allocated the entire amount of disk space upon creation and it is dedicated to that file system. If you eventually use only half of each file system, 150 GB, or half the space, has been wasted.

Figure 9.16 shows one possible solution to this issue: thin-provisioned disks. If you *thin provision* the same three disks at 100 GB and they each use the same 50 GB apiece, only 150 GB of the disk has been allocated. Much like the memory-overcommit technology we discussed earlier, thin provisioning actually allows you to overprovision the storage space you physically possess. With the same ratio as the previous file systems, you could provision two additional 100 GB file systems and still not use all of your physical storage. Thin provisioning usually has minimal impact on performance, but the downside of thin provisioning is much more acute than that of thick provisioning. Each file system believes that it has more space available than it actually does. If they consume all of the allocated space, problems will occur. Obviously, you need to have a thorough understanding of your storage usage before implementing thin provisioning; but done wisely, it can be a powerful tool to prevent wasted space.

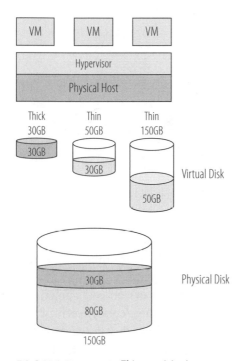

FIGURE 9.16 Thin provisioning

An additional challenge related to piling many workloads into fewer servers is that these workloads now share the access paths to the storage resources. The requests and data blocks flow through the same pipes with little control over priority. Figure 9.17 shows a simple illustration of this problem. If you have an application that is requesting most of the storage bandwidth, it could negatively impact other applications that are actually more important to the business. Similar to how regularly overcrowded highways have added high-occupancy vehicle (HOV) lanes to ease congestion during rush hour, there are analogous solutions to this problem in the virtual infrastructure. Sometimes, depending on the storage solution, either the storage vendors or network vendors can overlay some QoS (quality of service) policies that can give certain traffic types greater bandwidth when contention is detected. From a hypervisor standpoint, VMware's hypervisor has the ability to assign storage I/O priority on a VM-by-VM basis, guaranteeing appropriate resources for applications that have been designated more critical in resource-constrained situations. At the moment, it is the only solution with this capability.

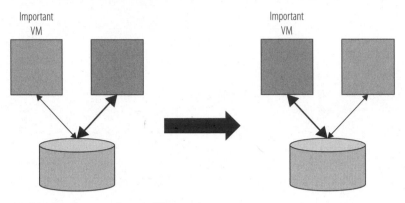

FIGURE 9.17 Storage I/O control

Virtualization can take advantage of other hardware storage devices as well. Solid-state disk drives (SSDs) are storage devices that contain solid-state memory instead of spinning disk platters to store information. In a way, these are products of Moore's Law; as memory technology has driven costs down and provided us with denser, larger memory chips, it is now cost effective to store data in memory. SSDs, though not yet offering as much storage space as traditional disk storage technologies, can offer data access that is much faster. Today's hard disk can read information from a device in about 5 ms. An SSD can read that same information in .1 ms, about fifty times faster than its predecessor. As virtual environments are designed, architects are using SSDs in tactical positions to offer greater speeds to certain functions. Virtual desktop implementations often use a small number of operating system images that are stamped out as needed, over and over again—a fresh template for each user that only needs a small amount of customization before deployment. Staging the desktop template on a SSD can significantly decrease the deployment time of a new desktop. Hypervisors themselves can also be stored on SSDs, so that when a host is booted, or if necessary rebooted, the instantiation time is also much faster than if it were booted from disk.

Finally, storage vendors have developed the concept of *tiered storage*, using different types of storage with varying performance and availability properties, to service an application's requirements. An application that requires top-notch performance and availability would be deployed on faster storage, with some type of RAID capability. An application with less stringent demands might be placed on a slower set of disks, with little or no availability options. Often, all of these storage types are contained within the same data storage array. The data that comprises particular applications can be migrated from one tier of storage to another, as the application requirements change. Depending on the vendor solution, this can be done dynamically if circumstances require better response time, or low utilization over a period of time merits a demotion of service. Virtual machines can take advantage of this quality of service flexibility on the physical layer itself. Newer hypervisor releases communicate with the storage array and pass requests, not just for data blocks to be read and written, but for large data moves from one disk to another, file system initializations, locking operations, and other functions that were once performed by the hypervisor. By allowing the storage array to execute functions it was designed for, work is removed from the hypervisor and many of the functions are executed more rapidly than when the hypervisor performed them.

You might be wondering, "Why not just put all the applications and their data on the fastest and most available storage?" The answer is in the cost. Storage solutions that have the highest availability and/or provide the best performance also come at the highest premiums. Also, not every application actually needs the highest availability or super performance. Sometimes "good enough" actually *is* good enough. The art is in allocating the appropriate resources, with respect to speed and availability, to all of the applications and doing so within the available budget.

While none of the technologies described previously are specific to virtualization, they are all important in architecting and maintaining a highly available, resource-efficient, and well-performing environment. The basic principles that apply to good storage practice in a physical environment are just as important in the virtual environment. The virtual infrastructure adds the complexities of compacting workloads on fewer hosts, so it is vital to ensure that the infrastructure has enough I/O bandwidth to handle the throughput requirements—just as you would for a physical infrastructure.

THE ESSENTIALS AND BEYOND

The growth of data since the beginning of the information age has been exponential and continues to accelerate. Data storage has grown in parallel, moving from kilobytes and megabytes to terabytes to petabytes. In virtualization, ensuring that there is not only enough storage but also enough bandwidth to access the storage is vital to success. Fortunately, many of the best practices for storage deployment and maintenance that were developed in the physical environment translate well to managing a virtual infrastructure. Advanced features, such as thin provisioning and data deduplication, make more efficient use of storage resources, while bandwidth policies allow an administrator to prioritize traffic type or individual virtual machines to guarantee quality of service levels. As with the other main resources, a poorly designed or implemented storage architecture can severely impact the overall performance of a virtual environment.

ADDITIONAL EXERCISES

▶ As an administrator, you are given a single host server configured with four six-core processors, 256 GB of memory, and 1 TB of storage to deploy a number of virtual web servers. You have been told that each virtual machine will require 8 GB of memory, one processor, and 100 GB of disk storage. How many virtual machines will you able to deploy? What is the limiting factor?

▶ After deploying the 10 web servers as virtual machines, you request more storage explaining that you could potentially double the number of web servers. Your request is denied due to budget constraints. After a few weeks of observation, information gathering, and a conversation with the application team, you discover that the web servers actually use only 25 GB of storage. The 100 GB request is a comfort number based on the vendor's generic recommendation. In the physical environment, they actually had 50 GB but never approached 30 GB of disk space. With a little more investigation, you discover that converting thick-provisioned disks to thin-provisioned disks is not a very difficult process. If you decide to reconfigure the existing disks to a thin-provisioned model, and use 30 GB as your amount of used storage plus some emergency space, how many more virtual machines could you add to the host? What is the limiting factor? Are there other ways to increase the number of virtual machines you could add? Would you want to add them?

CHAPTER 10

Managing Networking for a Virtual Machine

Networking, like the circulatory system in your body, is the transport mechanism for moving vital supplies. While blood carries nutrients to the organs, computer networks traffic in information, which is just as crucial to the health and well-being of the applications in a data center. In a virtual environment, networking is a critical component of the architecture, ensuring that data arrives in a timely fashion to all of the virtual machines on a host. Much like storage I/O, network I/O is subject to the same bandwidth issues and constraints that can occur in a physical network environment. Because networks also carry storage traffic, they need to be sized, implemented, and managed properly in order to provide adequate performance to the disk storage systems as well.

▶ **Understanding network virtualization**

▶ **Configuring VM network options**

▶ **Tuning practices for virtual networking**

Understanding Network Virtualization

Even more so than data storage, networking is everywhere in our daily lives. We update our Facebook pages, send email, send text messages, and tweet with smart devices that must be connected through a network to the servers that provide these functions. Telecommunications providers charge money for data plans—and as you use more, you pay more, as you would for any utility such as water or electricity. In our cars, the GPS talks to satellites across networks that give us real-time traffic information. In newer models, our devices connect to the Internet via a Wi-Fi connection in the car. At home, our computers can be connected to a cable modem, DSL, or even a dial-up connection to access the Internet. Newer televisions and multimedia devices allow us to stream movies, on-demand content, music, and even YouTube videos from a growing list of satellite providers, cable providers, and other content providers like Netflix, Hulu.com, and Amazon.com. More and more connectivity provides access to data, and bandwidth controls the speed at which it arrives.

IT departments and data centers have been dealing with these technologies and issues for decades, and networking, though at times a complicated topic, has very well-defined models and practices to follow for good performance. Like the storage practices you learned about in the last chapter, network practices also translate very well to the virtual environment. This explanation of networking is a very basic one, good enough for this discussion of how network traffic flows through a virtual environment, but is not by any means comprehensive. At the most fundamental level, networking allows applications on a virtual machine to connect to services outside of the host on which it resides. As with other resources, the hypervisor is the manager of network traffic in and out of each virtual machine and the host. The application sends a network request to the guest operating system, which passes the request through the virtual NIC driver. The hypervisor takes the request from the network emulator and sends it through a physical NIC card out into the network. When the response arrives, it follows the reverse path back to the application. Figure 10.1 shows a simplified view of this transaction.

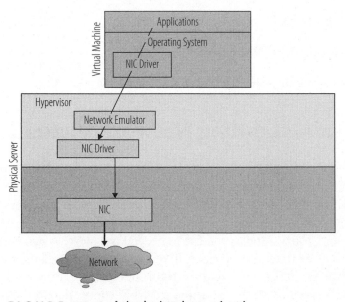

FIGURE 10.1 A simple virtual network path

Virtualization adds a number of wrinkles to the networking environment. One of these is that a virtual network needs to provide a method to connect to other virtual machines on the same host. In order to make this connection, the hypervisor has to have the capability to create internal networks. Just as a physical network uses a hardware switch to create a network to isolate traffic among a set of computers, a virtual switch can create a network inside a host for the virtual machines to use. The hypervisor manages the virtual switches along with managing and maintaining the virtual networks. Figure 10.2 shows a diagram of a simple virtual network inside of a VMware vSphere host. The hypervisor has two virtual switches, one connected to a physical NIC, which is connected to the outside physical network. The other virtual switch has no connections to a NIC or any physical communications port.

The virtual machine on the left has two virtual NICs, one connected to each virtual switch and by extension, each of the virtual networks. Requests through the virtual NIC connected to the external virtual switch will be passed through the physical host's physical NIC out to the physical network and the outside world. Responses to that request follow the route in reverse, through the physical NIC, through the external virtual switch, and back to the VM's virtual NIC. Requests through the internal virtual switch have no path to the outside world and can only go to other virtual machines attached to the internal virtual switch. The right-hand virtual machine can make requests only through the internal virtual switch and, in this simple diagram, can communicate only with the other virtual machine. This is a common strategy in a virtual environment to secure applications and servers from unwanted attacks. Without a connection to a physical NIC, the right-side virtual machine cannot be seen, much less compromised, from an external source. The left-side virtual machine acts as a firewall and, with reasonable security practices, protects the data contained in the other VM.

An advantage of this virtual machine to virtual machine communication utilizing an internal switch is that the traffic never leaves the physical host and takes place entirely in memory. That makes it very fast, much faster than if the data left the host and traveled the physical network, even if it were to a host that was physically adjacent to it in the data center. Very often when applications on separate virtual machines require a great deal of back-and-forth conversation, they are deployed on the same host in a virtual environment to effect the shortest network latency. Another byproduct of this internal-switch-only traffic is that standard network tools cannot see it. In a physical environment, when there are application performance issues, network tools can monitor the type and flow of data to help determine where the issue might be. In this case, the traffic never leaves the host, and standard network monitoring tools are useless because the data never hits the physical network. There are other tools specific to virtual environments to solve these problems, and we will examine them in more detail in Chapter 14, "Understanding Applications in a Virtual Machine," in the context of performance monitoring.

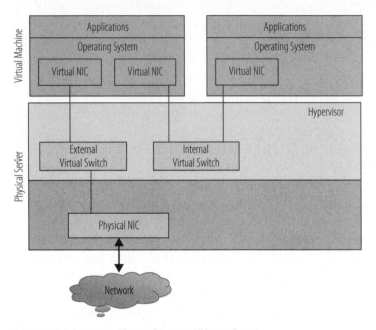

FIGURE 10.2   Networking in a VMware host

In physical networks, switches are used not only to create networks but also to isolate network segments from each other. Often different functional parts of an organization require separate network spaces in which to work. Production is separate from test and development. Payroll applications are set apart from customer services. This architecture helps with performance by reducing traffic on each segment and improves security by restricting access to each area. The technique translates very nicely to virtual networking. In Figure 10.3, a second physical NIC has been added to the host. A second external virtual switch is created that is directly tied to the second NIC. A third virtual machine is added to the host, and it can communicate only to the new external virtual switch. Even though it resides on the same physical host as the other virtual machines, there is no way for it to communicate with them through an internal connection. Unless there is some possible path routed through the physical network, it cannot communicate with them externally either.

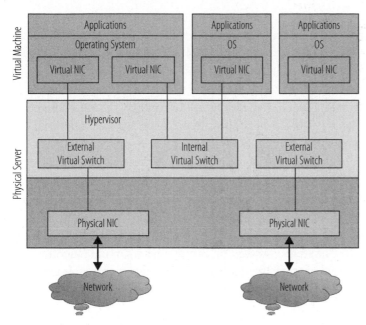

F I G U R E   1 0 . 3   Multiple external switches

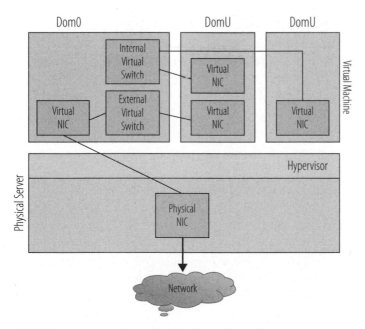

F I G U R E   1 0 . 4   Networking in a Xen or Hyper-V host

As you also saw in the previous chapter, this model is slightly different in the Xen or Microsoft Hyper-V network models. Figure 10.4 highlights the fact that all of the network traffic goes from the user (DomU) or child partitions, through Dom0 or the parent partition. In this model, the virtual switch is in the parent partition. A network request from an application in a child partition is passed through the virtual adapter to the virtual switch in the parent partition. The virtual switch connects to the physical NIC, and the request is passed to the physical network. The second switch shown has no connection to a physical NIC and supports an internal-only network. Virtual machines that connect only to this virtual switch have no way to directly access the external network. Conversely, this virtual machine can be accessed only from another virtual machine that is connected to this virtual switch, and not from an external source. Because in this model the parent partition does directly control the physical NIC, the hypervisor does not manage the network I/O.

Consider that aside from application data transport, the network may need to handle storage data. In Chapter 9, "Managing Storage for a Virtual Machine," you saw that storage can be connected through TCP/IP-based protocols via standard Network Interface Controllers (NICs). Storage data will then traverse the same pathways, physical and virtual, that user network traffic uses. As you architect your virtual connectivity, if you utilize these protocols to access storage, you will need to plan for the appropriate amount of bandwidth and maybe even create dedicated network pathways to those devices. Figure 10.5 shows a virtual switch that is dedicated to storage I/O. Each of the virtual machines has a virtual NIC that is dedicated to storage traffic. The virtual NICs connect to the storage virtual switch. The three switch types (internal, external, and storage) are identical in their construction and operation and have been given different names here only for the sake of differentiating their functions. From the storage virtual switch, you connect to the physical NIC and then out to the network storage device. In this simple model, there is one storage virtual switch connecting to a single storage resource; but as with the network isolation you saw earlier, there can be multiple virtual switches dedicated to storage, each connected to different physical NICs that are each then connected to different storage resources. In this way, you can separate the storage resources from the virtual machines as well as the network access. Whether the virtual NICs are handling user data for the network or data from the storage devices, from inside the virtual machine, everything still looks as it would from inside a physical machine.

Another facet of networking in a virtual environment to be aware of is the concept of live migration or VMotion. *VMotion* is VMware's term for the ability to migrate a virtual machine from one physical host to another while it is still running and without interrupting the user applications that it is servicing. The technology that allows this is essentially a rapid copy of the memory instantiation of the virtual machine to the secondary host fast enough to switch the network connections to the new virtual machine without compromising the virtual machine's data integrity or the user experience. As you might imagine, this operation is bandwidth intensive and requires a dedicated path to guarantee success. This is also a function that is handled by the hypervisor, transparent to the virtual machines. Other vendors have similar live migration capabilities, and we will cover more about them in Chapter 13, "Understanding Availability." This is not a capability we can demonstrate using VMware Workstation Player.

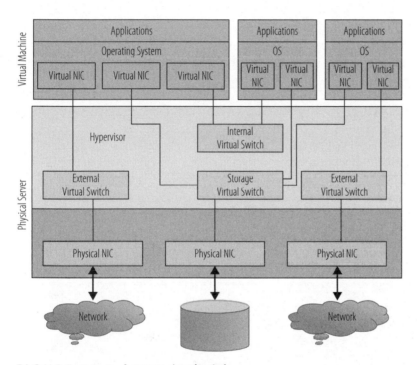

FIGURE 10.5 A storage virtual switch

Virtual switches, like their physical counterparts, can be configured to perform in selected manners. One difference is that you can adjust the number of ports on a virtual switch, without needing to replace it as you would a physical switch. Other properties that can be adjusted fall under the broad category of policies. Policies cover how the switch is to work under certain circumstances, usually dealing with security, availability, or performance-related issues. Because VMware Workstation Player does not afford us the ability to actually create and manipulate virtual switches, we will follow this thread no further.

Another networking area to briefly investigate is system addresses. Every device connected to a network has a unique address that allows the requests it makes of network resources to be returned to the correct place. Virtual machines need addresses just like any other device, and if there are multiple NICs in the configuration, the virtual machine will need an address for each one. A system address can be acquired in numerous ways. A network administrator can assign an address to a physical or virtual server, and it will be assigned for its lifetime. There are also devices that will assign an address to a device for some period of use. Dynamic Host Configuration Protocol (DHCP) is a process that allows a server to assign an IP address to a computer or other device that requests one. If you have spent any time at all setting up, or even utilizing, a Wi-Fi network, your devices are probably getting their network addresses via DHCP. The bottom line is that virtual machines need addresses. Using your Windows 10 virtual machine, you can see what address the virtual machine has been assigned.

1. In the virtual machine, enter **cmd** into the Search text box. Select the cmd icon. When the command-line window opens, enter the command **ipconfig** and press Enter.

   As shown in Figure 10.6, you can see your system IP address in the traditional dot and decimal format, the four octets next to the IPv4 Address label. If there were multiple NICs in this virtual machine, there would be additional entries with additional IP addresses.

2. Close the Command window.

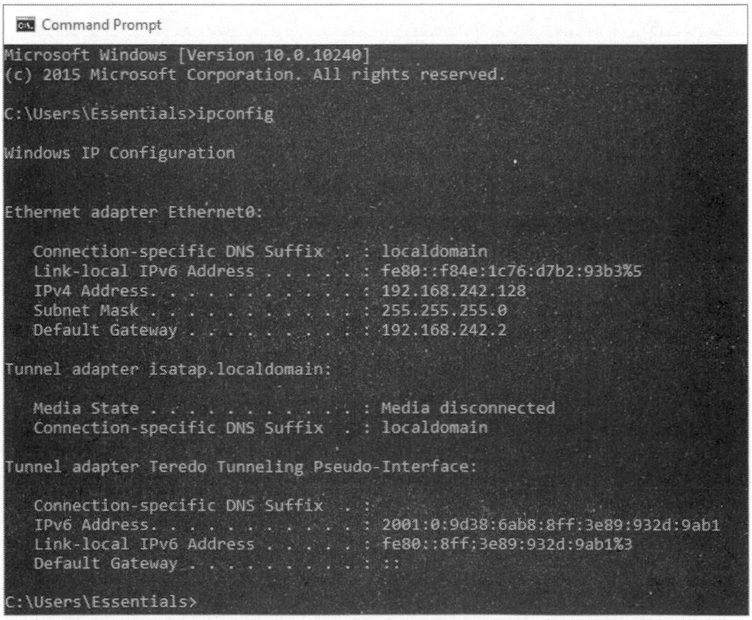

FIGURE 10.6 Determining an IP address

Now let's examine the virtual NIC from a number of perspectives.

1. Again, in the virtual machine, enter **device** into the Search text box. Select the Device Manager icon. When the Device Manager utility opens, select the triangle to the left of the Network Adapters icon to display the adapters.

2. Right-click on the revealed network adapter and choose Properties. Select the Driver tab, as shown in Figure 10.7.

   You can see a standard Intel network adapter with a standard Microsoft driver. From the virtual machine's point of view, the virtual network adapter is identical to a physical network adapter.

3. Select Cancel to close the Properties window. Exit the Device Manager.

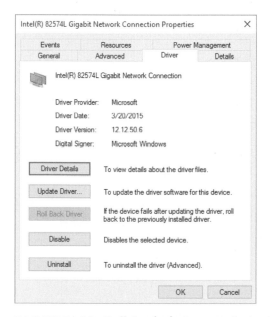

FIGURE 10.7 Network adapter properties in a VM

Let's examine the network adapters from the perspective of the host system.

1. Not in the virtual machine, but from the host Windows operating system, enter **device** into the Search text box. Select the Device Manager icon. When the Device Manager utility opens, select the triangle to the left of the Network Adapters icon to display the adapters. In addition to the two physical network adapters for wired and wireless connections, two others are labeled VMware Virtual Adapters.

2. Right-click on either of the VMware adapters and choose Properties. Select the Driver tab, as shown in Figure 10.8.

You can see that this adapter is a VMware virtual adapter; in other words, it is a software construct that represents an adapter with which the virtual machines can connect. In the case of VMware Workstation Player, this virtual adapter is analogous to the virtual switches that the Type 1 hypervisors utilize. There are two different adapters here, and each has a different function, along with a third that you will see shortly.

3. Select Cancel to close the Properties window. Exit the Device Manager.

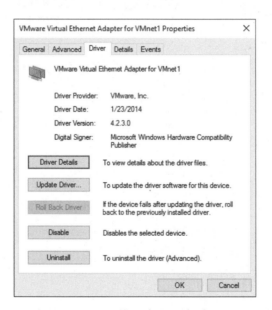

FIGURE 10.8 Virtual network adapter properties

Now we will examine the various connection types you can select when creating a network connection.

1. Back in VMware Workstation Player, under the Player pull-down menu, from the Manage option, select Virtual Machine Settings. Highlight the network adapter. Figure 10.9 shows the network connection choices.

We will focus on three connection types in the next section. They are bridged, NAT, and host-only.

We are going to skip LAN Segments and the Advanced features as outside of the scope of this text. LAN Segments gives you the ability to create a private network to share between virtual machines, and you can learn more by checking the user documentation.

The Custom option, as it states in the window, allows you to choose a specific virtual network. Care should be taken if you opt to use this route because certain virtual networks within VMware Workstation Player are preconfigured for certain connection types. Don't use these for a Custom network. Again, the user documentation provides the pertinent details.

2. Select OK to close the Virtual Machine Settings

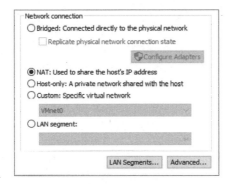

FIGURE 10.9   Virtual machine network-adapter connection types

Configuring VM Network Options

Each of the three connection types is associated with one of the default virtual adapters on the host system. Virtual machines that are configured with a host-only network connection are tied to the VMnet1 virtual adapter. Virtual machines that are configured with a NAT connection are tied to the VMnet8 virtual adapter. Virtual machines with bridged connections are tied to the VMnet0 virtual adapter. You've seen both the VMnet1 and VMnet8 adapters, but not the VMnet0 adapter. The reason is that VMware Workstation Player exposes only a subset of its abilities through the application interface, and not all of the capabilities are accessible by default. In order to investigate virtual networking more closely, you will need to use another utility that is no longer packaged as part of VMware Workstation player.

As of Release 12, the Virtual Network Editor is no longer included as part of the Workstation Player installation package, but it is still part of the Workstation Pro installation. In order to use the utility, if you aren't using Workstation already, you will need to download and install it as an evaluation. Workstation Pro is found on the VMware site where Workstation Player was located, and the installation is almost identical. The installation can be completed using the default settings.

1. Open Windows File Explorer and navigate to the directory where VMware Workstation Pro was installed. The default directory is `C:/Program Files (x86)/VMware/VMware Workstation`.

2. Right-click the `vmnetcfg.exe` entry and choose Run As Administrator to open the Virtual Network Editor. Windows will ask for permission to allow the program to execute. Choose Yes to continue.

3. The Virtual Network Editor opens as shown in Figure 10.10, and you can see all three of the virtual adapters, including VMnet0, which was not visible through the other tools. (It wasn't visible because it was not attached to a NIC.)

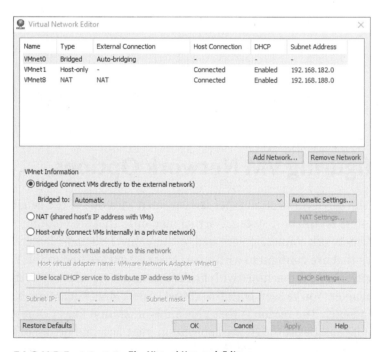

FIGURE 10.10 The Virtual Network Editor

A bridged network allows each virtual machine to have an IP address that is recognized and reachable from outside the host. The virtual adapter, in this case VMnet0, behaves as a virtual switch and merely routes the outbound traffic to its associated physical NIC and out to the physical network. When inbound traffic appears through the NIC, VMnet0 again acts as a switch and directs the traffic to the correct virtual machine. Figure 10.11 shows a simple illustration of two virtual machines connected to a bridged network configuration. Their IP addresses allow them to be seen by other systems on the local network. Again, because VMware Workstation Player is a Type 2 hypervisor, the virtual adapter construct acts as the virtual switch the Type 1 hypervisors utilize.

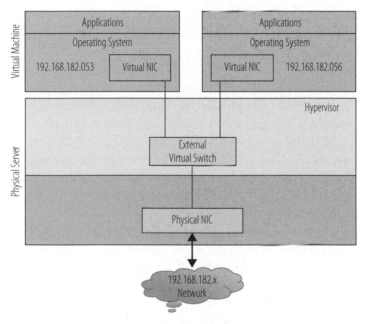

FIGURE 10.11 A simple bridged network

By highlighting VMnet0 in the Virtual Network Editor, you can see the bridged configuration. By default, the external connection is set to Auto-Bridging, meaning it will bind to an adapter that has a physical network connection. If you want to select the physical network connections used for the bridged connection, you can select the pull-down menu next to Bridged to label and change the current Automatic setting to a specific network adapter. You can also modify the Auto-Bridging list, choose Automatic Settings, and, as shown in Figure 10.12, select or deselect the appropriate adapters.

In a bridged network configuration, a VMnet0 adapter is not created like the VMnet1 or VMnet8 adapters. It is a protocol stack that is bound to the physical adapter.

FIGURE 10.12 Automatic bridging settings

A host-only network will create the equivalent of an internal-only network, allowing virtual machines to communicate with other virtual machines on that network, but without an external connection to the physical network. Systems on the physical network would have no awareness of these virtual machines, nor any way to communicate with them. In your installation of VMware Workstation Player, a virtual machine connected to a host-only network would have access to services on the local machine and the local machine could access the services on the virtual machine. By highlighting VMnet1 in the Virtual Network Editor, you can see the configuration settings for the host-only network. As shown in Figure 10.13, there are a number of configuration settings you can adjust. The Subnet IP field allows you to determine the address you will assign to the isolated host-only network. By selecting the Use Local DHCP checkbox, you have the ability to have the local host automatically allocate and assign addresses to the virtual machines connected to this network. If you want to examine or adjust the default DHCP settings, click the DHCP Settings button, and the current parameters for address and lease times will be displayed and available to alter.

NAT stands for Network Address Translation. A NAT network is, in a way, a blending between the host-only and the bridged networks. Virtual machines connected to the NAT network have IP addresses that are isolated from the physical network, but they have access to the network outside of their host. Figure 10.14 shows a simple example of a virtual machine with a NAT connection. Each virtual machine has an IP address that is recognized by other virtual machines on the internal network, but that address is not visible from outside of the host. Each virtual machine, also shares the physical host's IP address for the external network. When the virtual machine sends a network request outside of the host, the hypervisor maintains a table of address translations from the internal to the external networks. When network data arrives, the physical NIC passes it to the hypervisor to retranslate the address and route the information to the correct virtual machine.

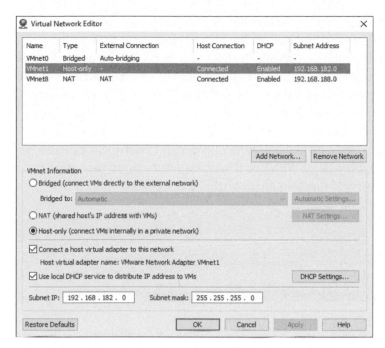

FIGURE 10.13 Host-only network settings

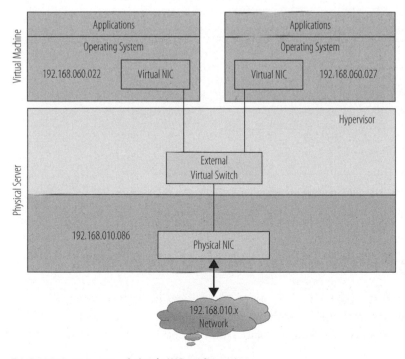

FIGURE 10.14 A simple NAT configuration

In the Virtual Network Editor, by highlighting VMnet8, you can see the NAT configuration as illustrated in Figure 10.15. Like the host-only network, you can create the private subnet. Also like the host-only network, you can have the DHCP service automatically provide IP addresses for the virtual machines connected to the NAT network. In VMware Workstation Player, NAT is the default setting when you create a virtual machine. For one thing, it will protect the newly created operating system from the outside world until you have time to install and configure security and antivirus software. NAT networks can also protect your network topology. With one IP address presented to the external network, the number and function of any virtual machines are hidden from unwanted investigation.

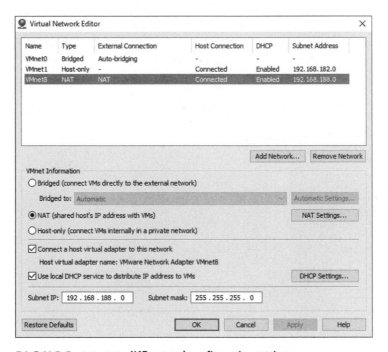

FIGURE 10.15 NAT network configuration settings

Tuning Practices for Virtual Networks

As you saw with storage virtualization, good practices in a physical network architecture work just as well in a virtual network environment. Physical networks use switches to isolate traffic for performance and security considerations. Those same practices carry through into virtual networks. Virtual switches tied to physical NICs can continue the physical segmentation into the virtual networking. A virtual network can be made just as complex and sophisticated as a physical network. One advantage that virtual networking maintains over physical networking from a cost and maintenance standpoint is the lack of cabling, or at least a tremendous reduction.

As you saw with memory and CPU virtualization, network virtualization is also very sensitive to performance impacts due to throughput pressure. As you consolidate ten individual servers onto a single virtualization host, you must plan for that host to carry the aggregated throughput. In the early days of virtualization, hosts might have eight, or ten, or more NICs in order to support the necessary bandwidth to provide adequate throughput and performance. This provided additional network processing capability by adding more processors with each NIC, and it provided physically separate pathways for the data to travel through, rather than relying on software to keep the data flow separate. Experience also recommended not mixing certain traffic types together at the expense of performance. Today, though, we are in a transitional period in which more data is traveling through fewer devices.

In the first *Ghostbusters* movie, Harold Ramis's character, Egon Spengler, tells his fellows, "Don't cross the streams," when he is prepping them on using their proton packs. When asked why, he responds, "It would be bad." This is how mixing traffic types on a single NIC was treated until recently. Now there are new NICs, converged network adapters, or CNAs, which handle greater bandwidth and sometimes multiple protocols. This helps reduce the number of network cards in the servers, but the issue of bandwidth contention still remains. As you saw in managing storage I/O, there are software features in the hypervisor to do the same in network I/O control. VMware's hypervisor has the ability to flag various network traffic types—data, storage, etc.—and assign bandwidth priorities to each type when network contention occurs. This control can be as granular as an individual virtual machine, a group of virtual machines that comprise an important application, or traffic from a particular set of addresses. At the moment, VMware's ESXi is the only hypervisor with this solution. Similar capabilities exist in some form in certain vendors' CNAs. With these technologies, you can have multiple network traffic types share the same bandwidth. Of course, at the end of *Ghostbusters,* they do mix the streams and everything works out just fine. It does here as well.

One of the downsides of consolidation is that multiple virtual machines are on a single host. They communicate across a virtual network in that host through virtual switches that are also inside the host. When a virtual machine sends information to another virtual machine on the same host, the external network never sees the transaction. This is good for performance, but bad for overall network management and debugging. If an application user complains of poor performance, the traditional network tools cannot see inside of the host. In the past, networking teams often surrendered the network configuration and management of the virtual network to the virtualization teams. The network teams had no experience or knowledge of the virtual environment's management tools, while the virtualization team was leery of having the network team work inside the virtualization host. As solutions have evolved, there are now tools that allow a network team to see inside a host and monitor the virtual network. Cisco has developed virtual switches that plug into a hypervisor and replace the vendor's virtual switch. The Cisco virtual switch is built on a Cisco switch operating system and uses all of the interfaces and tools of the physical Cisco switches. This means the network team does not need to learn new technology and the virtualization team can return the network responsibilities without concern.

Another challenge facing a virtualization administrator is that the standard virtual switches managed by the hypervisor are tied to the hosts on which they reside. When a switch needs to be configured, the administrator connects to the host and does that configuration. When a new host is added to the virtual cluster, the virtual switches need to be configured as part of setting up the host. When wider changes need to be applied to the network infrastructure, each of the virtual switches needs to be individually managed. This might not be an issue in a smaller environment, but in one that contains hundreds or even thousands of hosts, the work can become onerous, mind-numbing, and prone to error. Of course, these types of changes can be automated via scripting or other tools, but those items also need to be managed and maintained. Fortunately, as solutions in the virtual environment have matured, a solution has developed to help with these problems.

Each switch, physical and virtual, has two categories of work that it performs. The first group handles the data as it flows through the switch in whatever manner it was configured to do. Another name for this class of functions is the data plane. The second group handles all of the management capabilities that define what the data plane can and should do. A virtual distributed switch splits the work that switches perform into two parts. The data plane functionality remains with the virtual switches on the individual hosts, which makes logical sense. The management capabilities, however, are abstracted from the individual hosts and aggregated into a single management point. Instead of needing to adjust many virtual switches when a change needs to occur, an administrator now has a single place to make that change, and the same change is propagated out to all appropriate switches on the virtualization hosts. VMware's Distributed Switch, Hyper-V Virtual Switch, Cisco's Nexus 1000V (for VMware, KVM, and

Hyper-V), and Open vSwitch (see openvswitch.org) are all examples of this. This is an oversimplification of a sophisticated and complex topic, but this is another example that the technologies are still evolving.

Finally, concluding this discussion of networking and evolution is the emergence of software-defined networks. Just as computing and its resources have been abstracted from server hardware through the development of hypervisors, a similar transformation is underway in the network area. Solutions have been developed that move network configuration and management away from specialized hardware where it has traditionally been. Not just switching and routing of data, but other functions such as firewalls, load balancing, and virtual private network (VPN) can now be deployed as virtual appliances—prebuilt virtual machines that are already loaded with everything they need to run their specific application or service. Virtual appliances are covered in more detail in Chapter 14, "Understanding Applications in a Virtual Machine." Just as most server deployment and operation now takes place in virtual environments, the same is likely to be true for networking in the near future. This is a crucial building block in creating software-defined data centers, entities that are wholly defined in software and are deployed rapidly and repeatedly on many types of nondifferentiated hardware stacks of compute, storage, and network resources. Today, virtual machines can be migrated from one environment to another or from a data center to the cloud. As network virtualization matures, entire virtual data centers will follow.

THE ESSENTIALS AND BEYOND

Networks are the plumbing in the virtual infrastructure providing applications with data. Many of the traditional network best practices are applicable in a virtual environment. Consolidation packs many virtual machines on a single host, so bandwidth constraints must be strongly considered when you're designing network architecture in a virtual environment. Because much of the storage traffic travels across a shared or dedicated network, ample bandwidth must be allocated for that as well, or performance issues will occur. Virtual switches provide segmentation and isolation for network traffic inside of host servers, ensuring security and data integrity. Hypervisors also have varying capabilities to control network traffic to facilitate performance or to enhance security. Similar to compute virtualization, network functions are being abstracted away from specialized hardware, allowing networks to be defined entirely in software.

ADDITIONAL EXERCISES

▶ Add a second network adapter with a bridged connection type. After you reboot your virtual machine, make sure the second virtual adapter is available and has an IP address. What is the result when you ping them both from the host?

CHAPTER 11

Copying a Virtual Machine

Virtual machines are composed of disk files that make certain maintenance operations more timely and less cumbersome than working with their physical counterparts. Creating a new virtual machine is often no more complicated than making a file copy and some configuration changes. Deploying a new virtual machine may take a matter of minutes instead of the days or weeks it takes for physical servers to be ordered, staged, provisioned, and deployed. Templates allow system administrators to create standard images of virtual machines that can be stamped out at will. Even the system administrator's long-time bane, backup and recovery, can be simpler in the virtual environment. Aside from the same back-up solutions and strategies employed with physical servers, you can back up an entire server configuration and data with a data copy. In the event of a problem, you can restore the virtual machine the same way. Snapshots allow a developer to test software or operating system updates against an existing environment, and then instantly roll back to a specific point in time, instead of needing to rebuild the server to retest.

▶ **Cloning a virtual machine**

▶ **Working with templates**

▶ **Saving a virtual machine state**

Cloning a Virtual Machine

Backing up information was a necessary process even before the advent of computers. As you have seen, the amount of data that systems handle today is immense and continues to grow. Protecting that information is a function that needs to be simple, efficient, and reliable. There have been many solutions to back up the data on a system, from the earliest days when computer disks were written out to magnetic tape. If you periodically back up your personal computer, you might use a similar method, a simple utility, or the most basic file copy to move data files to other media, like CDs, DVDs, or USB disk drives. More recent solutions, such as Mozy, Dropbox, and Carbonite, track and copy file changes from the local system to an off-site repository via the Internet. Smart phones, tablets, and other devices also are now either synced with a trusted computer or with a cloud repository, all to prevent data loss in case of a system failure.

Because a virtual machine's actual physical format is a set of data files, it is easy for us to back up that virtual machine simply by periodically copying those files to another place. Because those files contain the application programs, user data, operating system, and the configuration of the virtual machine itself, a backup is created and a fully functional virtual machine that can be instantiated on a hypervisor is created, too. The process to copy a virtual machine is so simple that administrators sometimes use this technique to quickly create a new virtual machine. They merely create a set of file copies with a few configuration adjustments to ensure that there is a unique system name and network address—and it's done! It is faster than the process you went through to create the virtual machine, and much faster than the path of obtaining, provisioning, and deploying a physical server. One other advantage that helps accelerate virtual provisioning is that the virtual hardware presented is consistent from VM to VM and from host to host, removing many possible areas where physical discrepancies, such as firmware incompatibilities, might arise. To see how simple and quick creating a new virtual machine from an existing copy is, let's build one.

THIS IS NOT THE RECOMMENDED PRACTICE FOR CREATING A NEW VIRTUAL MACHINE

In Chapter 4, "Creating a Virtual Machine," you learned that virtual hardware adjustments are not usually made by editing the configuration file. For this example, we will do so for a number of reasons. First, because this is not a production virtual machine and if anything terrible happens, you can merely delete the files and start anew. Second, you might find yourself in a position where this type of work might be necessary and you will have already had experience working with the configuration file. Third, VMware Workstation Player does not have the ability to clone a virtual machine, so though the functionality is limited, that shouldn't obstruct your efforts. We will have the opportunity to create a clone using VirtualBox later in this chapter.

1. To begin, open Windows Explorer and locate the directory where the existing virtual machines reside. If you are not sure where it is, you can start VMware Workstation Player, pick any virtual machine, edit the hardware settings, and select the Options tab. The Working directory is displayed in the right panel. The default is C:\Users\<username>\ Documents\Virtual Machines. Once there, you should see folders for each of the virtual machines that are already created. As shown in Figure 11.1, create a new directory called VM Copy.

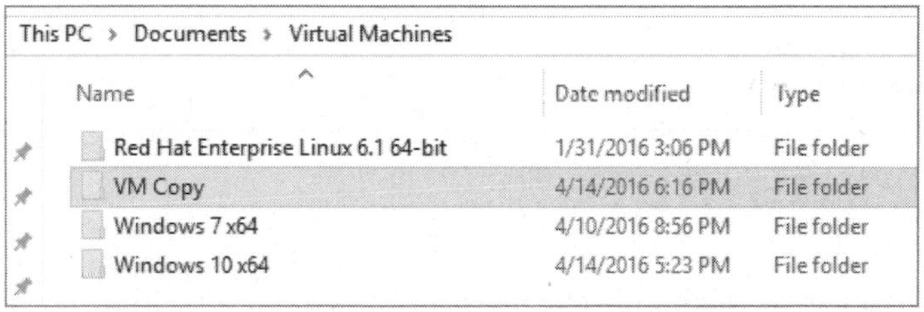

This PC › Documents › Virtual Machines		
Name	Date modified	Type
Red Hat Enterprise Linux 6.1 64-bit	1/31/2016 3:06 PM	File folder
VM Copy	4/14/2016 6:16 PM	File folder
Windows 7 x64	4/10/2016 8:56 PM	File folder
Windows 10 x64	4/14/2016 5:23 PM	File folder

FIGURE 11.1 The VM Copy **directory**

2. Go to the directory where the Windows virtual machine resides, as shown in Figure 11.2. There are a number of files and a cache directory that represent the virtual machine. To copy a virtual machine, you need only a few of these. The others will be created anew the first time you power on the virtual machine. The critical files for this task are the configuration file (.vmx) and the virtual disk files (.vmdk).

   If your file extensions are not visible, you will need to enable them. In Windows 10, you can do this by choosing View from the Windows Explorer tab and selecting Preview pane. Be sure that the File name extensions box is checked. The extensions will now be visible. Copy these files into the VM Copy directory. There should be two virtual disk files if you added a second drive in Chapter 9, "Managing Storage for a Virtual Machine." The copy should take about five minutes, depending on your hardware.

3. In the VM Copy directory, highlight the configuration file and open it with the Windows Notepad utility. Windows Explorer has Notepad as an option in the Open With VMware Workstation Player pull-down menu above the file window. If Notepad is not an option in the list, right-click on the .vmx file and select Open With ➤ Choose another app. If Notepad is not an initial option, select More apps and scroll down until you can select it. Figure 11.3 shows a portion of the configuration file.

This PC > Documents > Virtual Machines > Windows 10 x64			
Name ^	Date modified	Type	Size
caches	2/8/2016 10:18 PM	File folder	
vmware.log	4/14/2016 6:42 PM	Text Document	334 KB
vmware-0.log	4/14/2016 6:36 PM	Text Document	310 KB
vmware-1.log	4/14/2016 6:35 PM	Text Document	322 KB
vmware-2.log	4/14/2016 6:26 PM	Text Document	366 KB
Windows 10 x64.nvram	4/14/2016 6:42 PM	NVRAM File	9 KB
Windows 10 x64.vmdk	4/14/2016 6:42 PM	Virtual Machine Disk Format	13,201,920 KB
Windows 10 x64.vmsd	2/8/2016 9:39 PM	VMSD File	0 KB
Windows 10 x64.vmx	4/14/2016 6:42 PM	VMware virtual machine conf...	4 KB
Windows 10 x64.vmxf	2/8/2016 10:20 PM	VMXF File	4 KB
Windows 10 x64-0.vmdk	4/14/2016 6:42 PM	Virtual Machine Disk Format	11,968 KB

FIGURE 11.2 A virtual machine's files

4. You want to change the name of the virtual machine, so each iteration of the current name needs to be altered. In the example shown, the entry for Windows 10 x64 will be changed to VM Copy. You can make these changes by hand, or use the Notepad Replace feature under the Edit menu. If you do this by hand, do not change the guestOS entry.

5. Save the configuration file and then close it.

FIGURE 11.3 Editing the configuration file

6. Back in the VM Copy directory, rename the three files from their existing name to **VM Copy** as well. Make sure the second disk drive is correctly named VM Copy-0, as shown in Figure 11.4.

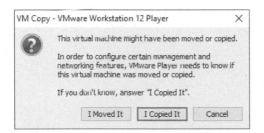

This PC > Documents > Virtual Machines > VM Copy

Name	Date modificd	Type	Size
VM Copy.vmdk	4/14/2016 6:42 PM	Virtual Machine Di...	13,201,920 ...
VM Copy.vmx	4/14/2016 6:59 PM	VMware virtual m...	4 KB
VM Copy-0.vmdk	4/14/2016 6:42 PM	Virtual Machine Di...	11,968 KB

FIGURE 11.4 Renamed virtual machine files

7. Start the virtual machine by double-clicking the configuration file. VMware Workstation Player will start up and boot the virtual machine. If it doesn't automatically boot, you can power it on manually. It will notice that something is different and, as shown in Figure 11.5, ask if you moved or copied the virtual machine. To continue, select I Copied It.

VM Copy - VMware Workstation 12 Player   ×

This virtual machine might have been moved or copied.

In order to configure certain management and networking features, VMware Player needs to know if this virtual machine was moved or copied.

If you don't know, answer "I Copied It".

    [I Moved It] [I Copied It] [Cancel]

FIGURE 11.5 Moved or copied notice

If your virtual machine does not boot up successfully, it means that your changes to the configuration file were incorrect, or they did not match the files names of the virtual disks.vmdk files. Double-check your changes, or recopy the original configuration file and try again. One possible error could be that you missed a critical step in Chapter 4, "Creating a Virtual Machine," when specifying the Disk Capacity. If you did not choose to store your virtual disk as a single file, you now have more than two .vmdk files that need to be copied. In addition to copying the files, there is another configuration step. One of the .vmdk files is much smaller than the others and contains pointers to the multiple parts of the virtual disk. You will need to open it with Notepad and rename the pointers from the original name to VM Copy and save your work for the virtual machine to power on successfully.

Let's examine our cloned virtual machine and see if it is identical to the original.

1. Windows boots and prompts for the same username and password as on the original virtual machine. Enter the password to log in.

2. Congratulations! You have copied a virtual machine. Open a command-line window by entering **cmd** into the Search text box. Select the cmd icon to open the command-line utility.

3. As shown in Figure 11.6, enter **ipconfig** to examine the network setting of the virtual machine. It should look similar, if not identical, to the original virtual machine. There should be the same number and type of adapters and connections. There were two Ethernet adapters previously.

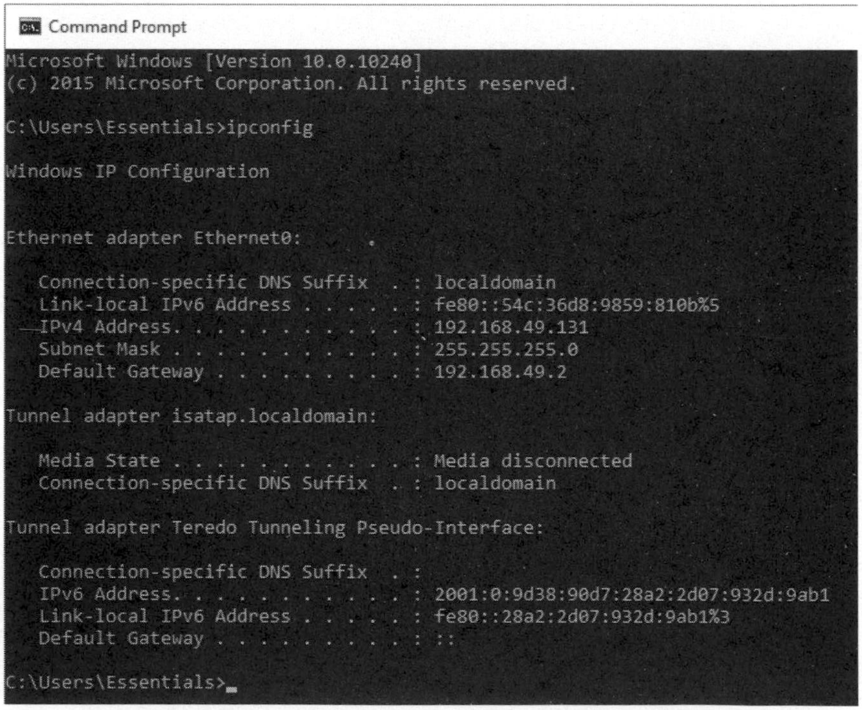

```
Command Prompt

Microsoft Windows [Version 10.0.10240]
(c) 2015 Microsoft Corporation. All rights reserved.

C:\Users\Essentials>ipconfig

Windows IP Configuration


Ethernet adapter Ethernet0:

   Connection-specific DNS Suffix  . : localdomain
   Link-local IPv6 Address . . . . . : fe80::54c:36d8:9859:810b%5
   IPv4 Address. . . . . . . . . . . : 192.168.49.131
   Subnet Mask . . . . . . . . . . . : 255.255.255.0
   Default Gateway . . . . . . . . . : 192.168.49.2

Tunnel adapter isatap.localdomain:

   Media State . . . . . . . . . . . : Media disconnected
   Connection-specific DNS Suffix  . : localdomain

Tunnel adapter Teredo Tunneling Pseudo-Interface:

   Connection-specific DNS Suffix  . :
   IPv6 Address. . . . . . . . . . . : 2001:0:9d38:90d7:28a2:2d07:932d:9ab1
   Link-local IPv6 Address . . . . . : fe80::28a2:2d07:932d:9ab1%3
   Default Gateway . . . . . . . . . : ::

C:\Users\Essentials>_
```

FIGURE 11.6 Examining the network configuration

What might not be the same are the IP addresses. You learned in Chapter 10, "Managing Networking for a Virtual Machine," that systems can automatically get their IP addresses from a DHCP server. When you responded to VMware Workstation Player and verified that you copied the virtual machine, it created a new unique machine ID for the virtual machine. If you had answered I Moved It, the unique identifier would not have been changed. If the IP address was hard-coded into the virtual machine, you would need to change it to a new address by hand or risk network problems with two identically referenced systems.

4. Close the command-line window.

5. Enter **Control** into the Search text box and open the Control Panel. Select System and Security ➢ System. Everything that you can see about this copied virtual machine is identical to the original. Even the computer name is the same, which in any real environment would be a problem. You could alter the system name here, but doing so is not necessary to complete the exercise.

6. You can explore the copied virtual machine further. When you are done, power off the virtual machine. Open the Player menu and choose Shut Down Guest. Notice that the VM Copy has been entered into the top of virtual machine library.

7. You are done with this virtual machine. You can delete it by right-clicking on the virtual machine and choosing Delete VM From Disk. A warning box will appear. Select Yes, and all the files will be removed. Close VMware Workstation Player.

The simple copy scenario works here because it is dealing with a single virtual machine. Even if you were to create a dozen virtual machines over the course of a year, the process would not be a hardship because the effort would still be minimal. But what would happen if you needed to deploy a hundred virtual machines? Or five hundred? That would be a considerably larger effort from a manual-labor perspective and with more opportunities for errors to occur. Fortunately, there are many ways to automate this process. One method is scripting. System administrators build scripts that duplicate the steps you just executed and even more, making sure that the cloned virtual machine has unique system information and network addresses inside the guest operating system and outside. Another method is through the use of automation tools that provide a standard repeatable process but are all front-ended with a user-friendly interface. These tools are either part of the vendor hypervisor management set or available from third-party providers.

Now let's use the vendor tool to clone a virtual machine. We'll use Oracle VM VirtualBox since the VMware Workstation Player doesn't offer this capability.

1. Open Oracle VM Virtual Box. Highlight the virtual machine you want to clone. As shown in Figure 11.7, you can right-click on the virtual machine to get the Machine menu or select Machine from the menu bar at the top.

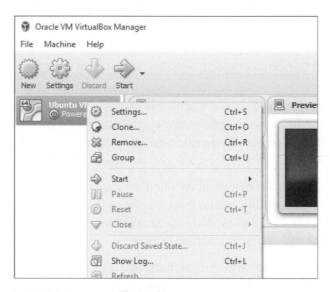

FIGURE 11.7 The Machine menu

2. Select Clone and the New Machine Name screen appears, as illustrated in Figure 11.8. As we needed to do for the manual method of cloning, the new virtual machine will need a unique name. Enter a unique name in the text box. Also select the checkbox that will reinitialize the MAC addresses of the virtual network cards. This is another place of differentiation. Select Next to continue.

3. The Clone Type window is shown. The two clone types are explained. Full clones are entirely separate replicas, while linked clones require being tied to the original machine, though they do require less storage space. Leave the default choice of Full clone. Select Clone to clone the virtual machine.

4. A progress window appears, displaying the time remaining and Dolly the Sheep. The amount of time needed to complete the clones depends on the size of the storage. When it is done, the new virtual machine is added to the list, as shown in Figure 11.9.

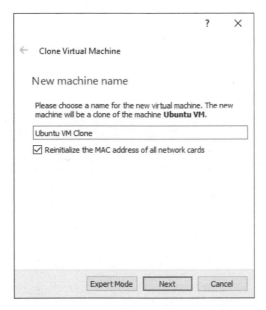

FIGURE 11.8 The New Machine Name screen

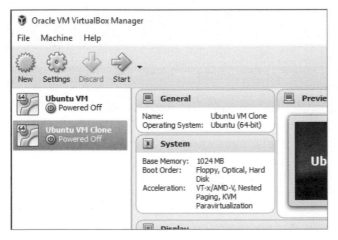

FIGURE 11.9 The completed virtual machine clone

5. Select the virtual machine clone from the list and power it on by selecting Start at the top of the screen using the green arrow icon. When the login screen appears, enter the password that you created for the original virtual machine. Figure 11.10 shows that the virtual machine is now ready for use. You can investigate further by validating that the clone has unique properties by comparing items such as system name and MAC addresses. When you are done, you can shut down the virtual machine.

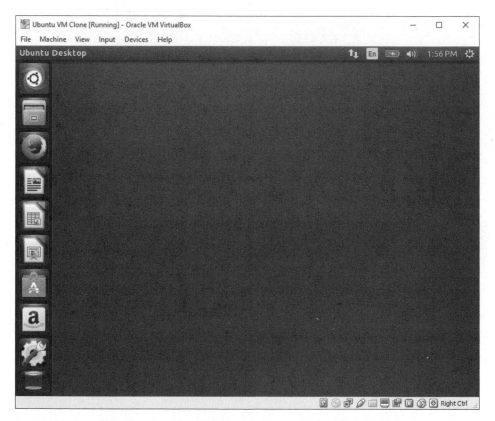

FIGURE 11.10 The virtual machine clone

What Is Sysprep?

As you clone Windows virtual machines, one thing to keep in mind is to be sure that each new cloned virtual machine is unique. Microsoft provides a tool, Sysprep, that is usually part of this process. Sysprep is a Windows-specific utility that allows administrators to customize each installation of Windows from a standard image into a unique copy of the operating system. In addition to injecting unique identification information, Sysprep can add new device drivers and applications to a new image. Each version of Windows—7, 8, 10, etc.—has its own version of Sysprep that needs to be used. Large deployments are outside the scope of these examples, so working with Sysprep will not be included.

Working with Templates

Creating new virtual machines from an existing virtual machine saves a great deal of time and effort in a virtual environment and is one of the largest reasons that system administrators enjoy the change from a physical environment. Cloning requires that you have something to clone from, a standard image that serves as a mold from which to create the new virtual machines. To do that, admins employ an idea called templates, which developed from the provisioning physical servers. A *template* is a golden image—a prebuilt, tested image that contains approved corporate-standard software. Administrators build an operating system deployment with some set of applications and tools. Once the most current patches are applied, the image is written to some media, such as a DVD. When new servers arrive, the image can be rapidly applied without needing to redo all of the various installations that helped define the image. Having the image in a read-only format also prevents unintended changes. Virtual environments also use this technique to great advantage.

The image from which you create new virtual machines contains not just a large bundle of software including an operating system, but the hardware configuration as well. There is also a slight difference between cloning a virtual machine and creating one from a template. In cloning, a virtual machine rather than a template is the source, although that is not necessarily a hard and fast rule. A template is usually a virtual machine image that cannot be powered on—in other words, it is nothing more than a mold for other virtual machines. Templates are created by building a clean, pristine virtual machine deployment and then having a hypervisor management feature, or other tool, do the conversion. For example, Figure 11.11 shows the menu when you highlight and select a virtual machine using VMware vCenter, the interface for managing a VMware ESX infrastructure. When you choose Clone, you can see three options, the first being to clone the selected virtual machine as we've done already, the second to convert the new clone into a template, and the third to convert the new clone into a template and place it into a designated library. If you wanted to convert the selected virtual machine into a template, selecting the Template option would offer that choice.

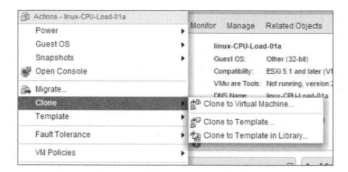

FIGURE 11.11 Template creation choices

The following example will show a new virtual machine cloned from a template. Because VMware Workstation Player does not allow this functionality, VMware Workstation Pro will be used instead. Two steps were made to the Windows virtual machine to create the template. The first was to check the Enable Template mode checkbox in the Advanced Options of the Virtual Machine Settings. The second was to create a snapshot of the virtual machine to be used as the template. We will cover snapshots later in this chapter. Figure 11.12 shows the menu used to clone the virtual machine.

The Clone Virtual Machine Wizard is shown in Figure 11.13. When the initial screen appears, it displays a reminder to enable the template mode in the Virtual Machine Settings.

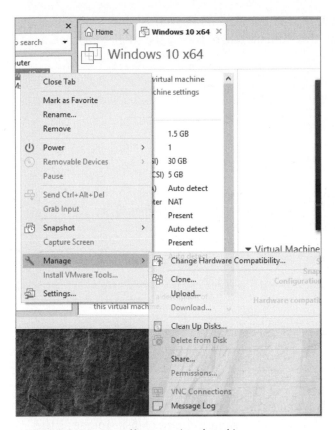

FIGURE 11.12 Manage a virtual machine.

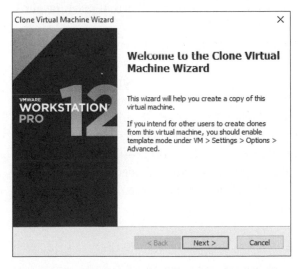

FIGURE 11.13 The Clone Virtual Machine Wizard

Because the virtual machine is in template mode, you need to select a snapshot to use as the clone. In this example, there is only the single snapshot, as shown in Figure 11.14.

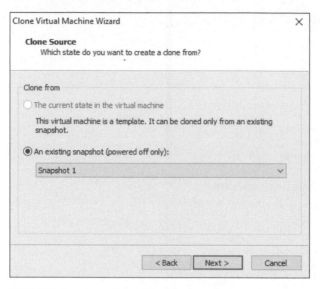

FIGURE 11.14   The Clone Source screen

Figure 11.15 shows that two different types of clones can be created. A *full* clone is a complete copy and requires the same amount of disk storage as the original to deploy successfully. A *linked* clone uses the original as a reference and stores any changes in a much smaller amount of disk storage. Because it is not a full copy, the linked clone needs to have the original virtual machine available. For this example, a full clone will be created.

The final step is to name the new virtual machine, as shown in Figure 11.16. The wizard provides a short list of steps and a progress bar as it performs the cloning process. When it is completed, the new virtual machine appears in the virtual machine list and can be started. A brief examination shows that it is identical in configuration to the template from which it came. By using the available tools, you can see that the process is much quicker and much less error prone than the earlier manual procedure. It is also possible to simultaneously clone a number of virtual machines, though that operation would be heavily dependent on the storage I/O bandwidth because the major portion of a cloning process involves copying data.

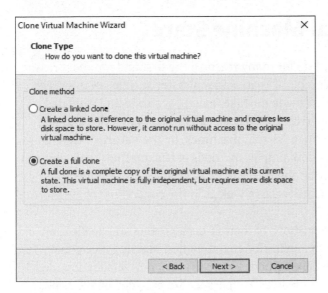

FIGURE 11.15 The Clone Type screen

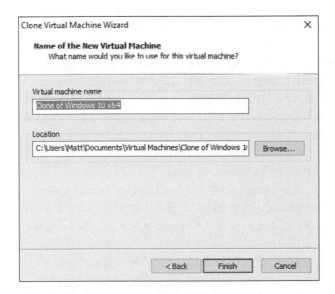

FIGURE 11.16 Naming the clone

Saving a Virtual Machine State

Virtual machines are backed up for many reasons; the first and foremost reason is disaster preparedness. Whether it is an actual disaster such as an unexpected violent act of nature or a man-made mistake, having accurate and validated application data available for retrieval has been a long-term practice and it is crucial for business continuance. Virtual machines, by the nature of their composition as data files, often allow simpler methods of backup than their physical counterparts. We'll cover more about this topic in Chapter 13, "Understanding Availability," but there is one use case to look at in the context of copying virtual machines.

Many companies dedicate portions of their IT departments and application groups to the various types of application maintenance. Maintenance could entail anything from actual development and creation of new application models, to testing existing application modules as upgrades are provided by the application's vendor, to routine testing of an application in the face of new operating system patches, or even major operating system upgrades. Prior to virtualization, IT departments would need to provision a physical server with the exact operating system, patches, and application suite that was running in the production environment, so they could then apply the new changes, whether that was an application or operating system update, and then do the testing necessary to satisfy an acceptance or denial to deploy the changes into the production environment. The hardware used for the test could then be reprovisioned for the next set of tests. It was not unusual for this process to be a bottleneck in a company's ability to deploy new application modules or stay up-to-date with operating system improvements. In larger companies with hundreds of applications, the size of the test environment is often three to five times larger than the production environments, consuming valuable budget dollars as well as data center space and resources. Even as companies transition to using cloud services for some of this development work, the need in this area is still relevant and will be for quite some time.

Virtual machines bring immediate relief to this scenario. By maintaining a template of an application's server configuration, it is a matter of minutes to create a duplicate of the image deployed in production. New patches can be applied and evaluated. At the end of a test, if the results are positive, that updated virtual machine can be converted into the new template that can also be used to update the production system. If no template exists, you can clone the production virtual machine, again guaranteeing that the testing is performed on a duplicate of the production configuration from the application, to the operating system, to the (virtual) hardware configuration. Hypervisor management tools make it simple to create templates, clone virtual machines, and deploy them to a virtual environment for these types of tests. They also add another capability to an administrator's arsenal in the form of snapshots.

Just from its name, *snapshot* tells you most of what you need to know about this capability. It is a method to capture a virtual machine's hardware and software configuration like the copy mechanisms cloning and templating, but it also preserves the virtual machine's processing state. Snapshots allow you preserve a virtual machine at a particular point in time that you can return to again, and again, and again, if need be, making it particularly useful in test and development environments. In a sense, snapshots provide an Undo button for the virtual server. Snapshots are not designed to be a backup solution for virtual machines. In fact, by using them that way, the virtual machine can be subject to poor performance and the entire virtual environment may suffer from a storage performance and usage standpoint. All of the major hypervisors support snapshotting technology. The following description of how snapshots are deployed and managed is specific to VMware, but the overview is similar in other solutions.

When you take a snapshot of a virtual machine, a few new files are created. There is a file that contains all the relevant information about the snapshot. In VMware that file has a .vmsd file extension. One file contains the memory state of the virtual machine, and it has a .vmem file extension. The virtual machine snapshot file (.vmsn) stores the state of the virtual machine at the time of the snapshot. Also created are a number of child disks with the familiar .vmdk extension. The created child disk is what is a termed a *sparse disk,* a storage optimization method to prevent the need for an entire clone for a snapshot. Sparse disks use a copy-on-write strategy where the only data written to it are data blocks that have changed from the original disk. The active virtual machine snapshot reads from the child disk and the original parent disk for current data, but will only write to the child disk. Figure 11.17 shows a simple example of a snapshot. The parent disk at the bottom is locked to writing, and any data-block changes are written to the sparse child disk.

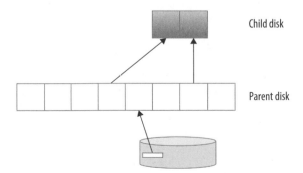

Child disk

Parent disk

FIGURE 11.17 A first snapshot

Figure 11.18 illustrates what occurs when a second snapshot is taken. A second child disk is created, also in the sparse format. As data-block changes are made again, whether in the original disk or the first child disk, those data blocks are written to the second child disk. The first child disk, as the original disk, is locked to writing and is used only as a read-only reference for the current information. You can see that using too many snapshots or changing large amounts of data can consume significant quantities of disk storage. In addition, with many snapshots, the paths to find the most current data blocks can become cumbersome and impact the performance of the virtual machine.

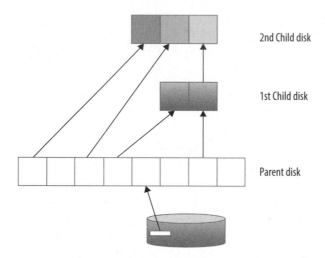

FIGURE 11.18 A second snapshot

Creating a Snapshot

These examples will show a snapshot being created and then rolling back to the original. Because VMware Workstation Player does not allow this functionality, VMware Workstation Pro will be used instead. Using the clone of the Windows virtual machine, it is powered on and logged into. A snapshot is taken to acquire a base state. The snapshot is taken by clicking a Workstation icon or selecting a menu item. The Snapshot Wizard asks for a name to call the snapshot. In the example, the name is Snapshot v1. A progress bar appears while the snapshot is taken and the appropriate files are created. Figure 11.19 shows the data files that now comprise the virtual machine with the snapshot. Note the memory state file (.vmem), the snapshot configuration file (.vmsd), the virtual machine state (.vmsn), and the child disks. Notice that because our original virtual machine had two disks, a child disk has been created for each. Each child disk is designated with a snapshot iteration number, in this case 000001.

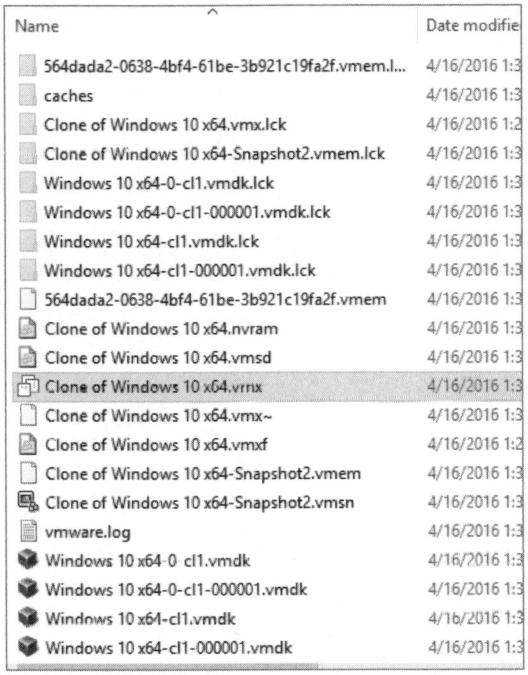

Name	Date modifie
564dada2-0638-4bf4-61be-3b921c19fa2f.vmem.l...	4/16/2016 1:3
caches	4/16/2016 1:3
Clone of Windows 10 x64.vmx.lck	4/16/2016 1:2
Clone of Windows 10 x64-Snapshot2.vmem.lck	4/16/2016 1:3
Windows 10 x64-0-cl1.vmdk.lck	4/16/2016 1:3
Windows 10 x64-0-cl1-000001.vmdk.lck	4/16/2016 1:3
Windows 10 x64-cl1.vmdk.lck	4/16/2016 1:3
Windows 10 x64-cl1-000001.vmdk.lck	4/16/2016 1:3
564dada2-0638-4bf4-61be-3b921c19fa2f.vmem	4/16/2016 1:3
Clone of Windows 10 x64.nvram	4/16/2016 1:3
Clone of Windows 10 x64.vmsd	4/16/2016 1:3
Clone of Windows 10 x64.vmx	4/16/2016 1:3
Clone of Windows 10 x64.vmx~	4/16/2016 1:3
Clone of Windows 10 x64.vmxf	4/16/2016 1:2
Clone of Windows 10 x64-Snapshot2.vmem	4/16/2016 1:3
Clone of Windows 10 x64-Snapshot2.vmsn	4/16/2016 1:3
vmware.log	4/16/2016 1:3
Windows 10 x64-0-cl1.vmdk	4/16/2016 1:3
Windows 10 x64-0-cl1-000001.vmdk	4/16/2016 1:3
Windows 10 x64-cl1.vmdk	4/16/2016 1:3
Windows 10 x64-cl1-000001.vmdk	4/16/2016 1:3

FIGURE 11.19 Physical files of a snapshot

In addition to the new files in the host file system, Workstation Pro has a map to use in the Snapshot Manager. Figure 11.20 shows the simple map created so far. The snapshot is merely an initial stake in the sand as you make some changes to the virtual machine.

Even if no alterations are made to the virtual machine, changes still occur. As time passes, operating system logs and monitoring tool logs are filled with time-stamped entries. These changes add data blocks to the child disks. As illustrated in Figure 11.21, creating a Notepad document and saving it to the desktop adds changes.

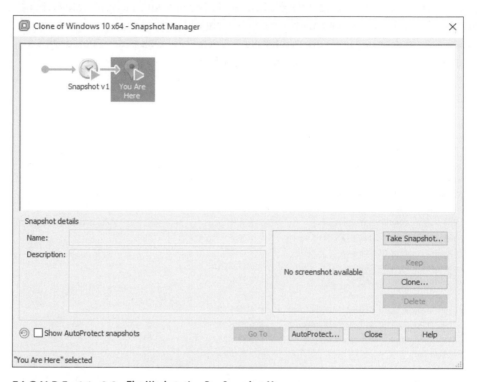

FIGURE 11.20 The Workstation Pro Snapshot Manager

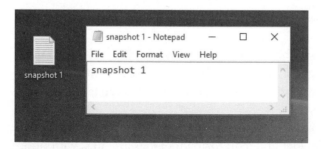

FIGURE 11.21 Changing the virtual machine

A second snapshot is taken at this point. As with the first, it is named in this iteration, Snapshot v2. The contents of the Notepad document are also changed and saved to the disk. The virtual machine's physical files are shown again in

Figure 11.22. There is now a second set of child disks along with a second memory state and system state file.

Clone of Windows 10 x64.vmxf	4/16/2016 1:22
Clone of Windows 10 x64-Snapshot2.vmem	4/16/2016 1:36
Clone of Windows 10 x64-Snapshot2.vmsn	4/16/2016 1:36
Clone of Windows 10 x64-Snapshot3.vmem	4/16/2016 1:44
Clone of Windows 10 x64-Snapshot3.vmsn	4/16/2016 1:44
vmware.log	4/16/2016 1:31
Windows 10 x64-0-cl1.vmdk	4/16/2016 1:35
Windows 10 x64-0-cl1-000001.vmdk	4/16/2016 1:35
Windows 10 x64-0-cl1-000002.vmdk	4/16/2016 1:44
Windows 10 x64-cl1.vmdk	4/16/2016 1:35
Windows 10 x64-cl1-000001.vmdk	4/16/2016 1:44
Windows 10 x64-cl1-000002.vmdk	4/16/2016 1:44

FIGURE 11.22 Physical files of a second snapshot

The Workstation Pro Snapshot Manager, shown in Figure 11.23, now has a second point in time in the snapshot chain to which the virtual machine can be restored. From here there are a number of choices. Adding more snapshots will create additional snapshot files and provide more places to roll back to, but eventually at the expense of performance and data storage. Not only can snapshots be added sequentially in the line that has been shown, but you can also use snapshots to construct very large branched maps to handle sophisticated testing models. By reverting back to the first snapshot, making changes, and creating a third snapshot, there would be two branches from the first snapshot. If the tests that were performed on the snapshotted virtual machine proved valuable, you could merge the snapshots into the original virtual machine, in effect, updating that original virtual machine. You will walk through that example in a moment. Finally, and probably most frequently, you will want to revert to a previous snapshot.

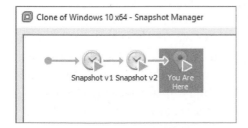

FIGURE 11.23 A second snapshot

As with creating a snapshot, you can revert to a previous snapshot from a Workstation icon, a menu selection, or from the Workstation Pro Snapshot

Manager. Reverting to Snapshot v2 is quick, as shown in Figure 11.24. You right-click on the snapshot you want to revert to and select Go To Snapshot from the menu. Workstation Pro provides a helpful message that all work done in the virtual machine since the snapshot was taken will be lost. A progress bar is shown during the rollback. Once the rollback is complete, the Notepad file with the original data is restored to the desktop.

If you reverted to the first snapshot, the same process would occur, but you would be presented with the virtual machine at the time of that snapshot. There would be no Notepad document at all. You could continue various tests and revert back to this virtual machine's point-in-time state as often as needed.

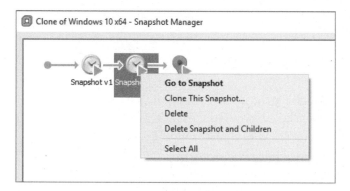

FIGURE 11.24 Reverting to a previous snapshot

Merging Snapshots

Suppose your tests necessitate an update to your original virtual machine. You discover that the operating system patches were not detrimental to the application environment and want to include them as part of the system. The process to do that involves collapsing the snapshots back into the original virtual machine. In Workstation, by deleting the snapshots in the chain, you can apply the snapshot changes to the original virtual machine. The first step, as shown in Figure 11.25, shows that the data in the second child disk was merged with the data in the first disk. The first child disk is now unlocked for writes so that it can be updated. Data blocks unique to the second child disk are added to the first child disk. Data blocks in the first child disk that were altered and also in the second child disk can be updated with those changes in the first child disk.

The next step is to collapse the first snapshot's child disk, now including the second child disk's additions, into the unlocked parent disk. This is illustrated in Figure 11.26. Note that this process doesn't increase the size of the original disk at all. As a last step, all of the associated snapshot files are physically deleted from the disk. All of the changes have been merged into the original virtual machine. Because each child disk can potentially grow to the size of the parent disk, without periodically collapsing or deleting snapshots, large swaths of disk storage can be consumed and performance on the virtual machine can degrade. Again, snapshots are for testing, not for backup.

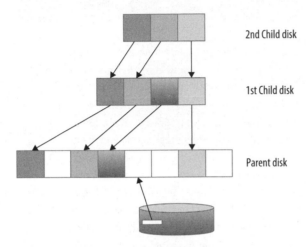

FIGURE 11.25 Deleting the second snapshot

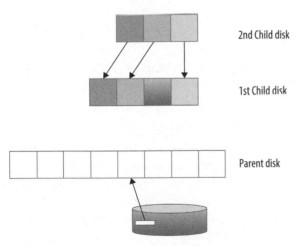

FIGURE 11.26 Deleting the first snapshot

Although the VMware terminology is a bit confusing regarding deleting snapshots, you can actually remove snapshots that you no longer need and don't want to merge into the original machine. When you do, the snapshot files are removed from the physical disk, the snapshot entries are cleared from the Snapshot Manager, and the parent disk is again unlocked for writes.

THE ESSENTIALS AND BEYOND

Virtual machines, because they are data files that contain the entire hardware and software configuration of a server, lend themselves to simpler methods of backup and recovery than their physical counterparts. Cloning a server becomes not much more than making a file copy with some identity configuration, which means the deployment of new servers is a faster and more reliable process than creating new instances for each server. Templates allow the creation of standard images, providing a clean model as a baseline for all of a company's new servers. Both of these capabilities have made virtual server provisioning and deployment so fast and simple that there is a condition known as *virtual sprawl*, in which too many virtual servers have been deployed, without the accompanying life-cycle management procedures that would limit this undisciplined, resource-consuming growth. Snapshots allow the creation of a point-in-time virtual machine that can be rolled forward or back to a specified state. These snapshots can be used to great effect for testing potential changes to an application environment, such as adding new operating system patches or new application code. All of these capabilities—cloning, templating, and snapshots—allow the rapid creation, deployment, and reuse of accurate test environments with minimum effort and far fewer resources than are required in a similar physical configuration.

ADDITIONAL EXERCISES

▶ Open the .vmx file of the original virtual machine side by side with the cloned virtual machine. Look for the uuid.location entries. Are they the same? If not, why not?

▶ What other identifiers would you need to alter in a cloned virtual machine to be sure it was unique? What might happen if these changes are not done?

▶ Using the cloned virtual machine created in Oracle VirtualBox, create a snapshot of the machine state while it is running. Make some changes on the virtual machine. They can be anything as simple as creating the new file illustrated in the chapter, adding bookmarks to a browser, or installing a new application. Create a few additional snapshots between each of the changes. Now revert to the original snapshot. What happens to your changes? Revert to a different snapshot. Now what has happened?

CHAPTER 12

Managing Additional Devices in Virtual Machines

Server virtualization focuses most of the attention on the CPU, memory, disk storage, and networking—the four main resources responsible for providing a superior user experience in a virtual environment. This makes perfect sense, but these four are not the only devices that users and applications need to work with in a virtual machine. Hypervisors support a wide selection of device types and connections to allow everything from serial and parallel device connections up to the latest USB devices and advanced graphical displays. Vendors handle optimization of devices in many ways, usually with the installation of a software suite that can provide a number of enhancements to the guest.

▶ **Using virtual machine tools**

▶ **Understanding virtual devices**

▶ **Configuring a CD/DVD drive**

▶ **Configuring a floppy drive**

▶ **Configuring a sound card**

▶ **Configuring USB devices**

▶ **Configuring graphic displays**

▶ **Configuring other devices**

Using Virtual Machine Tools

In Chapter 5, "Installing Windows on a Virtual Machine," you installed the VMware Tools as part of preparing a virtual machine for use. VMware Tools is a suite of utilities that not only improves the performance of a virtual machine, but also improves the user experience by providing capabilities that are not available without them. Without these tools installed, the guest operating system works, just not as smoothly as it does with the tools. VMware Tools is actually deployed as three separate parts: an operating system service, a set of enhanced device drivers, and a user process for a better user experience. In a Windows operating system, VMware Tools Service is deployed as the Windows service vmtoolssd.exe. On Linux systems, it is the daemon vmtoolsd. Both start when the virtual machine is powered on. They provide a range of services including:

- ► Cursor handling (Windows)
- ► Time synchronization between the guest and the host
- ► Heartbeat for availability
- ► Enhanced Hypervisor to Virtual Machine communications
- ► Display synchronization (Windows)
- ► Executing commands (Windows) or scripts (Linux) to help cleanly shut down or start a virtual machine OS

VMware Tools also provides a suite of enhanced device drivers for:

- ► Mice
- ► SCSI devices (BusLogic)
- ► SVGA graphical display for improved performance and higher resolutions
- ► Networking (vmxnet and vmxnet3)
- ► Audio
- ► Shared folders
- ► Virtual printing (Windows)
- ► Automatic backups
- ► Memory control

The VMware Tools user process is deployed as part of the `vmtoolssd.exe` service on Windows. On Linux systems, it is the program `vmware-user` and is started when you begin an X11 session. The user process provides:

- ▶ Display synchronization (Linux)

- ▶ Cursor handling (Linux)

- ▶ Text copying and pasting between a virtual machine and various other places

- ▶ Other product-specific user enhancements

VMware is not the only solution that uses this methodology to help improve virtual machine performance. In Chapter 6, "Installing Linux on a Virtual Machine," you used Oracle VirtualBox as the hypervisor platform. As part of preparing that virtual machine, you installed the VirtualBox Guest Additions. A similar suite of functionality is provided when the Guest Additions are installed:

- ▶ Time synchronization between the guest and the host

- ▶ Improved video support

- ▶ Shared folders

- ▶ Improved mouse/pointer integration

- ▶ A shared Clipboard between the guest and the host

- ▶ Additional guest/host user experience capabilities

A similar suite is used for Citrix XenServer implementations. Citrix Tools for Virtual Machines is also installed in the operating system and replaces the native network and SCSI device drivers with an optimized version that provides enhanced throughput between the virtual machine and the hypervisor. Without these drivers, performance will be degraded and some capabilities, such as live migration, will not work. These tools also allow the XenCenter management suite to see the performance metrics in a Windows virtual machine.

Microsoft Hyper-V employs an additional package called Integration Services. The installation modifies the operating system kernel and adds new virtual device drivers to optimize virtual-machine-to-hardware communications. In addition to the device drivers, enhancements are made to improve:

- ▶ Time synchronization

- ▶ Virtual machine heartbeat

▶ Operating system shutdown

▶ Data exchange

All of these solutions help provide an optimized virtual machine, an improved user experience, and, most importantly for this context, enhanced device drivers for the best device performance.

Understanding Virtual Devices

When you created a virtual machine, it was already preconfigured with a base set of virtual resources (compute, memory, storage, and network) without additional customization. Once the VM was created, the resources could be configured further to provide more flexibility. Beyond these four main areas, additional devices are available. If you consider a personal computer, there are USB devices like keyboards or mice. Printers can be connected in a variety of ways. Other sensory interfaces, such as graphical displays and sound cards, are used as well. All of these are available.

1. To examine the various virtual hardware devices, in VMware Workstation Player, open the Virtual Machine Settings on the Windows virtual machine. The Hardware tab should be selected by default, displaying the devices in the virtual machine. In the following example, the virtual machine is powered off.

2. As a quick review, you can adjust the amount of virtual memory up or down. You can also add or subtract from the number of virtual processors. You can add network adapters and configure them for various uses and network connection types. You can add hard disks of various sizes and configure properties as well.

Configuring a CD/DVD Drive

The CD/DVD drive is one of the standard devices initially configured for a virtual machine, and the reason is obvious. To load many software applications and operating systems, CDs and DVDs are still the preferred transfer media. Today, if you accept electronic delivery of software, often it will be downloaded in the ISO format, which is a standard format for a CD or DVD. As you saw when you loaded both the Windows and Linux operating systems, you can boot a system from an ISO image.

Highlight the CD/DVD drive. As shown in Figure 12.1, the physical CD/DVD device is the specified connection, rather than the ISO image file that you used earlier. Under the Device Status, note that it shows the device is connected and that it will automatically connect at power on. While this is fine for the simple configuration we are using here, in a normal environment with many virtual machines on a single host, this choice would be troublesome. If each virtual machine on the system tried to connect to the device, only the first one booted would be successful and it would retain control of the device until it was either shut down or an administrator disconnected it through the Settings Panel. For that reason, this device would not normally be set to Connect at power on.

The drop-down menu in the Connection box will display all of the CD/DVD devices available on the physical server. If there is more than one, you can select a preferred device. The Advanced button allows you to select a specific address for the device, but this needs to be done with the virtual machine in a powered off state.

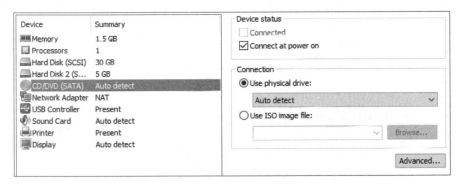

FIGURE 12.1 The CD/DVD device configuration

Configuring a Floppy Disk Drive

While CDs and DVDs are still being used for both commercial and consumer purposes, floppy disks are barely around. The original floppy disks were made of a round piece of magnetic media sealed in a thin, square, usually black plastic envelope. Both the disk and the envelope were fairly flexible and, well, floppy, hence the name. They were one of the first methods of portable storage for moving data files from one system to another. With the spread of personal computers, they were the transportable media of choice. The first floppies, developed during the 1970s, were 8-inches square and could hold 1.2 MB of data. As technology improved, they shrank to 5¼ inches square with roughly the same capacity. By the end of the 1980s, they had shrunk again to 3½ inches, could hold 1.44 MB of data, but had a harder plastic case and could no longer flop. Today, they have been replaced by smaller, denser, and faster storage devices such as USB flash drives, SD memory cards, and removable hard drives.

So why still support an almost extinct mode of storage? There are a number of good reasons. One reason that consolidation and virtual environments are attractive to companies is because of the continued support of older operating systems and the hardware devices on which they rely. A Windows NT server that uses a floppy disk image to receive information can still do so in a virtual environment. A virtual floppy disk image can still be used to transfer data from one system to another, though these days it would probably be sent by a network or hand-carried on one of the newer devices mentioned earlier—not necessarily a realistic solution, but still possible.

Notice that no floppy drive is present in the Virtual Machine Settings. Mirroring the trend in the physical world, a floppy drive is no longer included as a default device in a new virtual machine, but you can add one.

1. Select Add at the bottom of the Hardware tab. If the Windows User Account Control asks for permission to make changes on the PC, respond Yes. The Add Hardware Wizard appears. Select Floppy Drive and then click Next to continue.

2. On the Floppy Media Type screen, choose Create A Blank Floppy Image. The other choices require connecting to a physical floppy disk or an existing floppy disk image file. Click Next to continue.

3. Enter a name for your floppy image file. Unless you explicitly place the file elsewhere with the Browse function, the file is by default in the same directory as the other files that comprise this virtual machine. Uncheck the Connect At Power On checkbox and select Finish. Notice that the file extension for the virtual floppy disk is `.flp`.

Highlight the Floppy drive. Figure 12.2 shows the configuration options for the virtual floppy disk drive. The Device Status and the Connection options are the same as the CD/DVD device with a few exceptions. The first is the Read-Only checkbox. Physical floppy disks had a write-protect tab that could be flipped to prevent additional changes to the data on the disk. This option serves the same function and will prevent accidental erasure or rewriting of the disk. The second option is the Create button. You can create a virtual floppy disk and copy files to it as you would a physical floppy disk. In the case of VMware Workstation Player, the floppy disk is actually a file in the host file system. After you create the virtual floppy disk, it will need to be formatted for use.

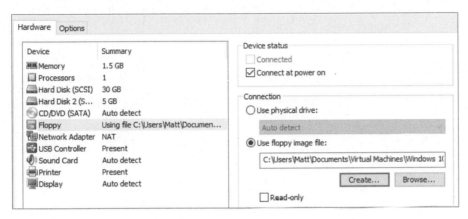

FIGURE 12.2 **Floppy disk configuration**

1. If your virtual machine is powered off, close the Virtual Machine Settings window and power the virtual machine on now. Log in to it. At the top of the VMware Workstation Player window is a Device Panel that displays the virtual devices available to the virtual machine. The Floppy icon ( ) is now present but grayed out. To connect the floppy drive, right-click on the Floppy icon and select Connect. The other choice, Settings, will open the Virtual Machine Settings.

2. Note the Floppy Drive icon ( ) is now active and, like the other available and mounted devices, has a virtual green LED to display I/O activity.

3. In the virtual machine, open the File Explorer and select This PC. The floppy disk drive is now available and mounted, but not quite

usable. Right-click on the Floppy Disk Drive, as shown in Figure 12.3. Choose Format from the menu. When the Disk Format menu appears, accept the default selections and click Start to begin the initialization of the virtual floppy disk.

4. A warning appears that you will be erasing the new floppy disk. Click OK to continue. A moment later, the Format Complete message appears. Click OK to dismiss the message. Choose Close to exit the Format screen.

F I G U R E 1 2 . 3   **Floppy disk management options**

5. Double-click on the Floppy Disk Drive, and it opens into a Windows directory. You can now copy a file there as you would to any other disk. When you are done, close the Computer window.

6. In your host, open Windows File Explorer and navigate to the directory where the virtual machine files reside. As shown in Figure 12.4, you can see that the floppy disk image you created, Essentials.flp, is there and it is the 1.44 MB size that a physical floppy disk would be. You could open this file on another virtual machine by attaching to it in the Virtual Machine Settings and using the Use Floppy Image File option.

7. Close Windows Explorer and reopen the Virtual Machine Settings.

Name	Date modified	Ty
caches	2/8/2016 10:18 PM	Fi
Essentials.flp	4/20/2016 5:09 PM	FL
vmware.log	4/20/2016 5:09 PM	Te
vmware-0.log	4/20/2016 4:43 PM	Te
vmware-1.log	4/19/2016 10:26 PM	Te
vmware-2.log	4/17/2016 6:26 PM	Te
Windows 10 x64.nvram	4/20/2016 5:09 PM	VI
Windows 10 x64.vmdk	4/20/2016 5:09 PM	Vi
Windows 10 x64.vmsd	4/15/2016 6:53 PM	VI
Windows 10 x64.vmx	4/20/2016 5:09 PM	VI
Windows 10 x64.vmxf	2/8/2016 10:20 PM	VI
Windows 10 x64-0.vmdk	4/20/2016 5:09 PM	Vi

(This PC > Documents > Virtual Machines > Windows 10 x64)

FIGURE 12.4 The floppy disk image file

Configuring a Sound Card

Sound is not usually considered mandatory for virtual machines, because most business applications don't rely on audio to provide data to their users. However, that is rapidly changing. From the spread of virtual desktops, to social media applications, to educational and informational audio and video clips, sound is becoming an integral part of how computer services are being delivered. This change is accelerating as the line between consumer services and corporate services continues to blur, forcing each side to adopt characteristics and expectations of the other. Fortunately, hypervisors already have the ability to deliver a virtualized sound card. The virtual sound card actually passes control back to the local sound card that the virtual machine's guest operating system can then utilize. A desktop virtual machine that is running Windows 10 on a host server in the data center uses the physical sound card of the client device from which the user accesses the virtual machine. Most hypervisors have this ability and are architected similarly.

An icon (🔊) at the top of the VMware Workstation Player window shows whether sound is available and active. Because the sound card is one of the default devices added when the virtual machine was created, the icon is not grayed out. Highlighting the Sound Card will show the device options, as illustrated in Figure 12.5. Like the floppy and CD/DVD drives shown earlier, the Device Status Settings will automatically connect the device to the virtual machine when it is powered on. The virtual sound card can be configured after the virtual machine is created. The Connection area offers two options. The first is to Use Default Host Sound Card. If you select Specify Host Sound Card, you can examine the pull-down menu that will allow you to change the default if your system has more than one sound option.

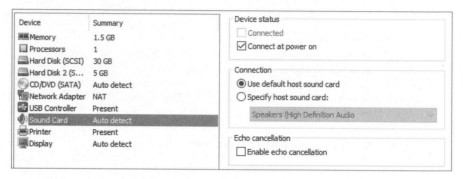

F I G U R E   1 2 . 5   Sound card options

Configuring USB Devices

PCs and other computers in the 1980s had many ways to connect storage and interface devices. Printers were initially connected through parallel ports. Serial ports connected modems for communications. Other connectors were available for keyboards and mice. There was even a special port for a joystick to play games. None of them were compatible with each other in form or often function. In 1994, a number of PC-related companies including IBM, Microsoft, and Intel began to work on a unified way to connect these external devices. Two years later, the result was the *Universal Serial Bus (USB)* standard. USB created one common connection, enabled greater throughput speeds, and provided a way to supply power for the devices. Taking the place of many first-generation connections for computer peripherals, USB is now the de facto standard for device connection.

Floppy disks soon gave way to thumb drives for easy, portable storage. You probably have personal experience with USB devices and their plug-and-play ease of use. Today we connect digital cameras, MP3 players, and even speakers, in addition to mice, keyboards, and printers via the USB port. Since the standard's first release, there have been two major updates. USB 2.0 was released in

2000, with the largest change being a quadrupling of the speed to 60 MB per second. Interim enhancements provided portable-electronics consumers two of the most common capabilities they use: synchronizing and recharging mobile devices by connecting them to a computer through the USB port. Bluetooth and Wi-Fi are creeping into the synchronization space, but until broadcast power is available, recharging will still depend on the wired connection. USB 3.0 was released at the end of 2008. Capable of delivering 625 MB per second, ten times greater than USB 2.0, it provided a large improvement in throughput speed. In 2015, USB 3.1 was released providing twice the throughput of USB 3.0. Also, the first new cable changes, USB-C, are appearing to accommodate the greater data speed and power demands that the new specification offers. With additional improvements and enhancements on the roadmap, it appears that the USB standard will be around for quite a while.

More companies are involved with the USB standard today than the original seven. Find out more about what is coming, including Wireless USB, at `http://www.usb.org`.

1. Figure 12.6 illustrates the few options that are available to manage the USB connection for a virtual machine. The Connections box has three checkbox items. The USB Compatibility pull-down menu allows you to choose which version of the USB standard the virtual machine should support.

2. The Automatically Connect New USB Devices option will allow the virtual machine to access newly connected devices.

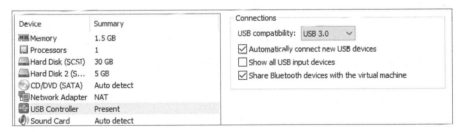

FIGURE 12.6 USB management options

3. The Show All USB Input Devices option will display the connected USB devices at the top of the VMware Workstation Player window. If the device is already connected to the host, it will appear but be grayed out. You can right-click the icon, as shown in Figure 12.7, and connect the device to the virtual machine. Because a USB device can be connected to only one computer at a time, it will be disconnected from the host system before being connected to the guest.

4. The Share Bluetooth Devices With The Virtual Machine option does as its name suggests; it allows devices connected to the host by Bluetooth to be connected to the guest.

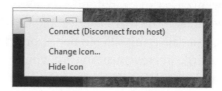

FIGURE 12.7   Connecting a USB device from a host

Type 2 hypervisors initially had superior support for USB devices because they could leverage the host operating system underneath the hypervisor. In this way, solutions like VMware Workstation Player offer certain capabilities that are not available in Type 1 hypervisors, such as the Bluetooth connectivity. This is not usually an issue with enterprise environments. Initial Type 1 hypervisor releases did not have USB support at all, one reason being the live-motion capabilities. You will learn more about moving a running virtual machine from one physical host to another in Chapter 13, "Understanding Availability." If a USB device were connected to the first physical server, when the virtual machine was relocated, it would no longer be available on the second physical host. Newer releases, however, do support some level of this functionality.

Configuring Graphic Displays

Like a physical machine, a virtual machine supports a graphical display or monitor. In practice—much like a mouse, a keyboard, or other human interface devices (HIDs)—a virtual machine does not have its own dedicated monitor. Instead, the user connects to the virtual machine with a common set of basic peripherals for the duration of a session. Even though this is the norm, many applications and situations now require a wider set of more specialized configurations. Software developers typically use multiple screens for additional desktop space. Newer operating systems have higher visual performance requirements than the classic 640×480 screen resolution. The blending of higher quality video into many application experiences also necessitates support of this kind. Again, hypervisors handle these devices by leveraging the hardware of the display itself.

For the next few devices, you will need to have the virtual machine powered off. If it is running, shut down the VM, reopen VMware Workstation Player, and edit the Virtual Machine Settings of the Windows 10 VM. By highlighting the Display device, as shown in Figure 12.8, you can see the checkbox option for accelerated 3D graphics, specifically for Windows DirectX support. In the Monitors area, the Use Host Setting For Monitors option uses the settings of the host machine. This is for VMware Workstation Player, where there is a host operating system underneath to access.

The Specify Monitor Settings option can be used to set the number of monitors the virtual machine can access, as well as the configuration for those monitors. In this way, a virtual machine can have multiple, high-performance graphical displays.

There is a pull-down menu where the amount of guest memory can be allocated specifically for video graphics memory. A recommended value is provided based on the operating system installed in the VM.

The final checkbox automatically scales the virtual machine's display.

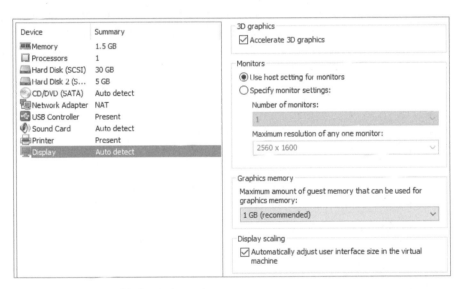

FIGURE 12.8 Display device options

Configuring Other Devices

Other device connection types that are not part of the initial default virtual machine creation can be configured. Often, they are not included because the devices, which once were connected by legacy methods, are now connected by other means such as USB. Serial and parallel port devices are two of these devices.

Serial ports pass information through them serially, or one bit at a time; and in early computers, serial ports were frequently reserved for pre-Internet communications via an external modem. Today, PC modems are typically part of a PC's motherboard connected to the external world by an RJ11 phone jack, if they are there at all.

Parallel ports can pass many bits of data simultaneously, depending on the actual cable configuration. Originally designed as a high-bandwidth connection for printers, parallel connections soon found their way onto other external peripherals such as tape drives and disk drives. Today, they have been superseded by USB devices and are rarely included on most computer hardware. In both cases, parallel and serial ports, there are times when the virtual machine may need to use or emulate them.

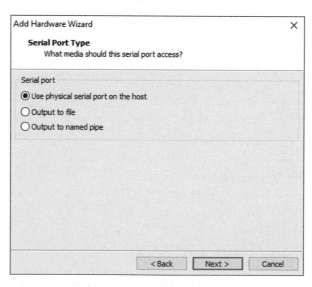

Microsoft Windows 64-bit operating systems no longer provide native legacy parallel port support.

1. Normally, the virtual machine needs to be powered off for this process, but because you are not actually adding a serial port, it will not be necessary. Click the Add button at the bottom of the Virtual Machine Settings window to add a hardware device. Select the Serial Port option and click Next to continue. As shown in Figure 12.9, there are three serial port types from which to choose.

FIGURE 12.9 The Serial Port Type screen

2. The Use Physical Serial Port On Host option is similar to the other devices discussed earlier. Click Next to continue. The default setting is Auto detect, but if you have a serial port on your system you could examine the pull-down menu to select it. There is also the familiar checkbox to automatically connect the port to the virtual machine when it is powered on. Click Back to return to serial port types.

3. Select the Output To File option and then click Next. On this screen, you can browse for an existing file to connect to as a port, or you can create one to which to stream information. This capability can be used for simulations. Click Back to return to the Serial Port Type screen.

4. Select the Output To Named Pipe option and then click Next. Named pipes are used for inter-process communications in a single system, or they can be used to pass data from virtual machine to virtual machine.

5. Click Cancel to close the window.

Now let's examine the parallel port. As before, the virtual machine normally needs to be powered off for this process, but because you are not actually adding a parallel port, it will not be necessary.

1. Click the Add button at the bottom of the Virtual Machine Settings window to add a hardware device. Select the Parallel Port option and click Next to continue. As shown in Figure 12.10, there are two parallel port types from which to choose.

2. The Use Physical Parallel Port On The Host option is also similar to the other devices discussed earlier. Click Next to continue. The default setting is Auto detect, but if you have a parallel port on your system you could examine the pull-down menu to select it. Beneath the Device Status heading is the checkbox to automatically connect the port to the virtual machine when it is powered on. Click Back to return to the Serial Port Type screen.

3. Select the Output To File option and then click Next. On this screen, you can browse for an existing file to connect to as a port, or you can create one to stream information. This capability can be used for simulations.

4. Click Cancel to close the window.

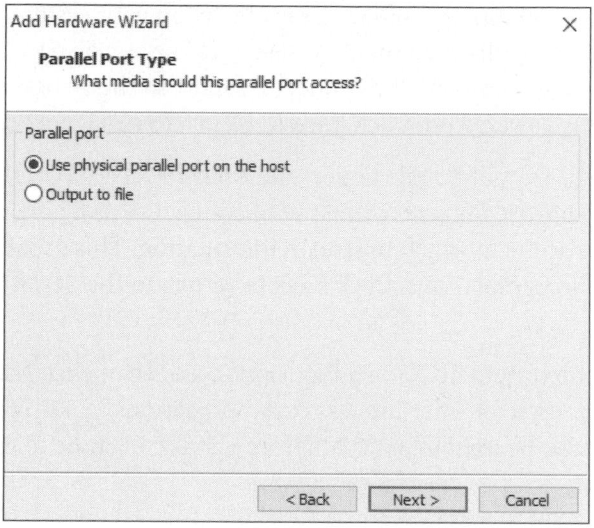

FIGURE 12.10 The Parallel Port Type screen

Finally, let's examine a generic SCSI device.

1. Click the Add button at the bottom of the Virtual Machine Settings window to add a hardware device. Select the Generic SCSI device and click Next to continue. Figure 12.11 illustrates the SCSI device options. The connection pull-down menu allows you to choose a CD drive or a hard disk. As with the other devices, the Connect At Power On checkbox will connect the device when the virtual machine is powered on.

2. Click Cancel to close the window.

Not all devices can be used in a virtual environment. Certain specialized PC boards such as fax modems have no virtual analogies. Industry-specific hardware (telephony systems, for example) cannot be virtualized. Aside from a few scattered examples, the bulk of peripherals in use today can be connected and optimized for use with a virtual machine. As technology and hypervisors continue to mature and evolve, the number of devices that cannot be virtualized should diminish to virtually zero.

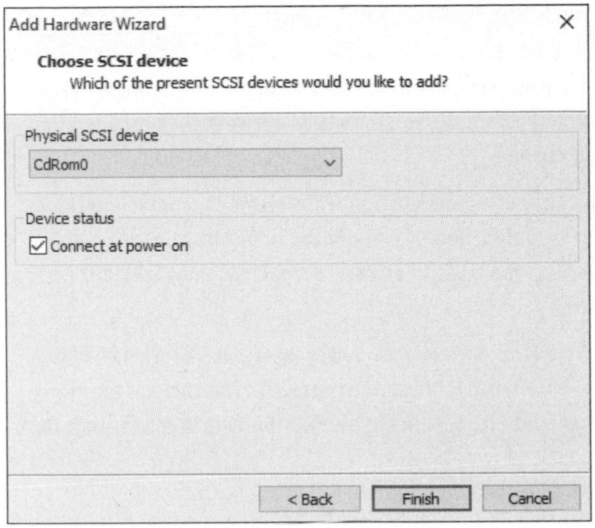

FIGURE 12.11   Generic SCSI device options

THE ESSENTIALS AND BEYOND

Beyond the CPU, memory, disks, and networking, virtual machines use other peripheral devices for their operation. Everything from a mouse and keyboard, to a CD/DVD drive and the sound card for stereo speakers also need to be efficiently virtualized for applications to run correctly and provide a good user experience. To optimize these additional devices, a combination of optimized device drivers and additional guest operating-system processes are added to the virtual machine as a software installation. One of the strengths of virtualization is support for older device technologies to extend the life of an application after the original hardware has become obsolete. As peripherals have evolved over time, hypervisors have also matured and are now capable of handling the outdated, current, and emerging devices and their connection methods.

ADDITIONAL EXERCISES

▶ Add another USB controller in the Virtual Machine Settings. What happens? Add a second sound card. Add another printer. Why did they react the same way as the USB hardware device?

(Continues)

THE ESSENTIALS AND BEYOND *(Continued)*

▶ Connect a USB device to your virtual machine. Use a thumb drive or a similar storage device. How difficult is the process? Can you easily transfer information between the host operating system and the guest operating system?

▶ Copy a file to the virtual floppy disk. Unmount the floppy disk from the virtual machine. Add a floppy drive to a different virtual machine. Remount the floppy disk onto the second virtual machine. What happens? Can you do this between virtual machines with different operating systems?

▶ Many consumer devices, such as keyboards, headphones, and speakers, now provide Bluetooth connectivity. If you have such a device, try to connect it to your virtual machine. Is the device actually connected to the virtual machine, or is the hypervisor making it appear that the device is connected?

CHAPTER 13

Understanding Availability

The information age has altered our expectations regarding services. The Internet provides round-the-clock service and gives us access to everything from the latest news to our latest bank statements. The servers and data centers that deliver information need to be available as close to 100 percent of the time as possible. This requirement also holds true in a virtual environment. By using traditional availability solutions, a single virtual machine can be as reliable as a physical one. With capabilities physical servers cannot easily replicate, virtual machines can be more available than physical servers. By stacking multiple virtual machines on a single host, new techniques are available to ensure that a host failure does not severely impact the group. Finally, virtualization allows less expensive and more flexible options to protect an entire data center from an interruption due to a large-scale disaster.

▶ **Increasing availability**

▶ **Protecting a virtual machine**

▶ **Protecting multiple virtual machines**

▶ **Protecting data centers**

Increasing Availability

Recent history has numerous examples of new technologies becoming vital resources in our everyday existence. Thomas Edison built the first power plant in 1882, but it took almost another 70 years to provide electricity to just about everyone in the United States. Refrigeration, appliances, heat, and light all fail when the power is off. Energy companies have employed sophisticated power grids to prevent such occurrences, but they still inconvenience us with regularity. Telephone service followed a similar path. Invented in the mid-1850s and brought to market 20 years later, there were almost 6 million telephones by

1910 in AT&T's system. Fifty years later the number jumped to 80 million phones, and when the first cellular phones appeared in the early 1990s, over 200 million telephones were in use. As the communication service provided by the telephone became indispensable, keeping the service available became vital. Because of the relative simplicity of the system, telephony engineers were able to achieve upward of 99.999 percent availability, or having less than six minutes of downtime per year. This level of service is what many companies strive for, so it is often referred to as dial-tone availability. How many times in your life have you picked up a (non-cellular) telephone and not heard a dial tone?

We now rely on these basic services as crucial necessities and can't imagine living without them even for a few hours. While instant communications and electricity do perform potentially life-sustaining functions, there are services we use that are not so critical. The first ATM was introduced in the United States in 1969, and today there are over 400,000 across the country. Before the advent of ATMs, you needed to visit a branch during banking hours and interact with a human bank teller. When was the last time you saw a bank teller? Today the expectation is that we can perform transactions at any time. Checking account balances, money transfers, and even paying monthly bills can be done from a home computer. Mobile devices add another dimension to financial transactions with digital wallets, which are already widely used in Japan. But if the ATM is not available, how crucial is it? The truth is, an offline ATM or a bank website closed for service is inconvenient, but not as critical as a power outage. The expectation, though, has become the same.

This demand for availability is not limited to ATMs, and it touches just about everything fueling our information-driven age. Just as we are not content to manage financial transactions only during banking hours, we are increasingly insistent that all services, both corporate and commercial, be available on a 24-hours-a-day, 7-days-a-week, 365-days-a-year schedule. And companies are providing services on those terms. You can get music from Apple's iTunes store, Skype with a foreign friend, stream a movie from Amazon.com, buy insurance for your car, download a book to your e-reader, Google anything, post an update on Facebook, or attend an online college class any time of the day or night. In 2015 it was estimated that there were 4.5 billion smartphones in use and about another 1 billion tablets. These ubiquitous devices that we now depend on for communication also give us constant access to all of these services via specialized applications (apps). This constancy only increases the expectation of always-on availability. The providers of these services have huge data centers to supply what is being demanded, and their goal is to deliver their products with dial-tone availability. Table 13.1 shows some different availability percentages to compare against that goal.

TABLE 13.1 Availability Percentages

Availability (%)	Downtime per Year
99	3.65 days
99.9	8.8 hours
99.99	53 minutes
99.999 ("five nines")	5.3 minutes

Like an ATM outage, a service outage from one of the prior examples is inconvenient but not a disaster. Or is it? If a company's data center suffers a catastrophic failure due to a natural disaster, it might be the end of the company. You'll learn more about this possibility at the end of the chapter. But what about a shorter term failure? As another real-world example, consider email and the Blackberry. In every year from 2007 through 2011, users of Research In Motion's Blackberry Internet-based email services suffered through major outages that in some cases spanned a number of days. Each time the event was either national or international news. Having no email is inconvenient, especially if you are a business, but the larger impact here is that RIM began to lose customers based on the outages. In the early part of this century, they had over 40 percent of the smartphone market but as of 2015 were down to just over 1 percent. While availability was not the only reason for this precipitous drop, it was a large contributor. Loss of service equates to lost income, and studies have shown that an average business can lose $100,000 per hour as a result of downtime. Long outages for larger companies can put a lot at risk. Internally, system downtime equates to lost productivity, adding to the losses. When companies who support these services evaluate virtualization benefits, increased availability is near the top of the list. As virtualized data centers transform into the engines that will drive cloud computing, availability will become even more important.

Here are two additional thoughts about downtime. The first is that there are two types of downtime: planned and unplanned. Planned downtime is scheduled time to bring systems offline for maintenance. It could be for software updates or hardware upgrades, but whatever the reason, the system is unavailable and not servicing the users. Unplanned downtime is when disaster strikes.

CIO surveys concerning the business drivers of moving to a virtual environment have consistently shown increased availability, along with consolidation and business agility, to be among the top three reasons to move.

A study commissioned in the mid-1990s by Stratus Computer, a manufacturer of fault-tolerant hardware, revealed that the number one reason for system outages was human error.

Application miscues, hardware failures, wrong buttons pressed, or power cords tripped over—these are sudden and costly events that might take hours or longer to resolve. The second thought is that you don't get to choose when unplanned outages occur. Even 99.9 percent uptime means there will still be almost nine hours of downtime in an average year. If you are a retailer and Murphy's Law dictates the outage occurs the Friday after the Thanksgiving holiday, it could result in millions of dollars in lost revenue.

Protecting a Virtual Machine

Let's examine availability in a virtual environment. There are three layers to consider: a single virtual machine, a host or groups of hosts, and the entire data center. In addition to the virtual machines and their hosts, there is also the additional infrastructure such as the network and storage systems, not to mention the environmental factors such as electrical power and air conditioning. All of the aforementioned areas have their own methods to improve availability, and they will not be covered here except in a virtualization context. Beginning with the individual virtual machine, you will learn how, in many ways, workloads in a virtual environment are actually often more available than those on physical servers. At first, this may seem counter-intuitive. If a single physical server goes offline, for whatever reason, only a single workload is impacted, whereas when a virtual host fails, multiple virtual machines would be affected. Virtual infrastructures have capabilities that will automatically protect and recover all of the workloads with greater speed than most physical infrastructures.

As with other areas in virtualization, many availability strategies utilized with physical servers translate well to the virtual environment. There is still no replacement for good backup and recovery practices. Though not covered in detail here, application files can still be backed up and recovered using the same tools that are used on a physical server. This is not always the best choice in a virtual environment because it is a very resource-intensive operation, and attempting to simultaneously back up multiple virtual machines can quickly choke a host's processing and network bandwidth. You learned earlier in Chapter 11, "Copying a Virtual Machine," that because a VM is actually a set of files, you could protect not just the applications files but also the entire server, including the operating system and the virtual hardware configuration, by backing up those virtual machine files. Numerous applications are available from virtualization vendors, storage providers, and third parties that work by backing up on the storage level, which minimally impacts the virtual machines and the hypervisor.

The first line of defense is to protect the individual workload, and here the focus will be on managing or recovering from a failure. There are other aspects that can be considered as part of the larger discussion: antivirus and other security measures to prevent malicious intent, proper VM sizing, architecture, and capacity management to handle performance spikes and growth, and good life-cycle management practices to prevent virtual server sprawl, virtual zombie servers, and wasted resources. These are important areas to consider, but more advanced than this discussion will cover. The following features and solutions are offered in VMware's hypervisor offering, but are not necessarily exclusive to VMware. Each release from VMware adds new features and functionality, and each release from Microsoft and Citrix does as well. Because VMware offers the greatest depth and breadth of features, and owns more than 70 percent of the market, it makes sense to focus there.

SOME ADVANCED TOPICS

The ease and speed of creating virtual machines provides huge benefits to IT departments, but as the Sorcerer's Apprentice discovered, ease and speed are not always the blessing you think they are. Without adding additional business processes along with the technology, companies found that they were soon drowning in virtual machines. A developer could request a test environment and an hour later it would be there. Next week, he could get another. Eventually, dozens of virtual machines were in the environment that had no associated decommission date, and the resources for business-critical workloads were being consumed far ahead of schedule. This is *server sprawl*. Many of these short-time-use but long-time-deployed virtual machines are not shut down. These server zombies run in the environment using minimal resources but actually perform no useful work, having been abandoned by their requesters—or saved "just in case." A wealth of information is available concerning security in virtual environments, covering topics that overlap with physical environments—for example, PCI (credit card processing standards) and other types of compliance and environment hardening, securing systems against unwanted intrusions, and antivirus solutions. Each vendor has specific recommendations and best practices. You can see them at the following sites:

VMware:

  `http://www.vmware.com/security/`

(Continues)

SOME ADVANCED TOPICS   *(Continued)*

Microsoft:

https://technet.microsoft.com/en-us/library/dn741280
.aspx

Citrix:

https://www.citrix.com/about/legal/security-
compliance.html

As a result of these virtual infrastructures, a number of ways to attack these problems have been developed. In the antivirus space, for example, the traditional solution to load an antivirus engine on each guest doesn't scale. Imagine all of them downloading updates and then doing system scans at the same time. VMware has developed a virtual appliance that monitors an entire host and works with third parties to manage the virus definitions and guest scanning, which is much more efficient and scalable than the old method.

Cloud computing is becoming another alternative to providing some of this capacity. For certain use cases like development, virtual environments can be rapidly created, maintained for the duration of the project, and purchased on a pay-as-you-go program to help manage costs. This still doesn't prevent issues like server sprawl or security breaches, and it may even present new issues, but for many companies it is a viable method for quickly acquiring affordable infrastructure resources.

Virtual architectures use a number of strategies to help prevent hardware failures from bringing down a virtual machine. Many of these techniques were developed and deployed in physical environments. In Chapter 9, "Managing Storage for a Virtual Machine," you learned about RAID technologies, in which greater availability is afforded to data stored on disks by combinations of disk mirroring, disk striping, and other techniques to prevent data loss in case of a disk drive failure. All of these standard practices are transparent to the operating systems that access the data on the protected disks. Because they are transparent, they work just as well in a virtual environment as they do in the physical world. Often, storage arrays that provide disk space to systems support both physical and virtual servers. In addition to higher availability in the disk storage, the path from the storage to the host system, and by extension the virtual machine, can also be protected against a failure. This *multipathing* is accomplished by having more than one path from the host to the storage array. The physical path is duplicated through the environment traversing two controllers in the storage array, separate network switches, and two physical NICs in the host server. If any of the components fail, a path still remains for the operating system on the virtual machine to use, and this capability is transparent to the operating system and any applications that depend on it. Multipathing provides additional performance benefits by load balancing the data across the two paths.

NIC *teaming,* shown in Figure 13.1, bundles together two or more physical network adapters into a group. This group can load balance traffic across all of the physical devices for higher throughput, but more importantly, can continue to service the network if one of the adapters were to fail. All of the physical NICs in a NIC team need to be associated with the same virtual switch.

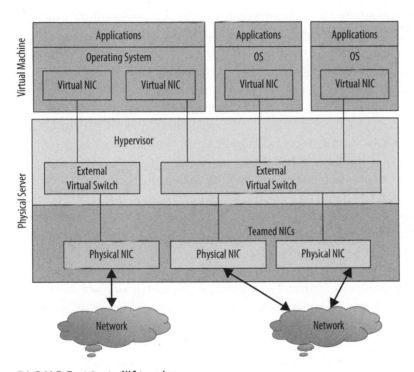

FIGURE 13.1 NIC teaming

Inside the virtual machine, VMware Tools provides a heartbeat between the guest operating system and the hypervisor. If the guest fails due to an operating system crash, or due to an application failure that causes an operating system crash, the hypervisor can then reboot that guest. To prevent an endless loop of reboots, user-configurable parameters determine how many times the attempt to restart a guest will be performed before discontinuing. The event can be configured to trigger a notification process for an administrator to be alerted.

There are also third-party tools that can monitor applications. If the application fails, but the operating system does not, the application can be automatically restarted without human intervention.

All of these techniques, features, and solutions can help increase the uptime of a single virtual machine and the workload it supports. But the virtual machine and the hypervisor still rely on the server hardware beneath them. What happens when the virtualization host server fails?

Protecting Multiple Virtual Machines

There are various solutions to minimize the chances of a server failure. Since the 1980s, there have been commercially available fault-tolerant solutions that relied on software and then hardware to prevent server outages. Fault-tolerant hardware uses redundant systems, down to the fans that cool the systems, the power supplies, and sometimes with the duplicate power cords plugged into separate electrical grids. With such designs, a single component failure won't bring down a server or the application it supports. These systems were originally aimed at organizations that needed extraordinary uptime such as emergency services or flight control systems. Soon businesses that had critical transactional windows began using them as well—financial service companies where downtime during the trading day might cost millions of dollars an hour, public transportation services where downtime resulted in rider delays, and even home shopping channels where an hour of missed orders translates into a sizable financial loss. These systems still exist, but have fallen out of favor as commercial servers have become more reliable, and other solutions have appeared.

One of these solutions is *clustering*. By linking together two or more servers with a physical network, shared storage resources, and clustering software, a simple cluster allows an application to quickly recover from a server outage. When the primary server fails, for whatever reason, the cluster software routes the application traffic to the secondary server and processing can continue. The cluster software makes the multiple servers appear to be a single resource, but it is often complex to manage, sometimes requiring application changes and specialized knowledge. Some examples of these are Microsoft Cluster Service (MSCS), Symantec Cluster Server, and Oracle Real Applications Clusters (Oracle RAC). As with other solutions you've seen, these can also be used inside of the virtual environment, but again there are some new capabilities that virtualization offers. Not only can you cluster from one virtual machine to another, but you can cluster from a physical machine to a virtual machine as well. Some companies that are experienced with clustering, but not yet comfortable with virtualization, often deploy the latter configurations. But that is just one application in one server, physical or virtual. What happens in a virtualization host?

Virtualization solutions have some degree of high availability (HA) architected into them through clustering as well. A simple virtual cluster, shown in Figure 13.2, is composed of two or more physical servers, a shared storage resource, and appropriate networking resources. Hypervisors are on each host, and virtual machines are staged on each hypervisor. When a virtualization host fails, all of the virtual machines dependent on it also fail. Because of the shared storage, HA has access to the virtual machine files and can restart all of the failed virtual machines on other hosts in the cluster, and a few minutes later they are all running again. Performance algorithms ensure that there is enough spare capacity on the hosts before adding these virtual machines. When you're planning for the configuration of a virtual environment, consider spare capacity for HA as one of the constraints. While this process is still a recovery, there is a great deal of benefit to this architecture. In a physical environment, this functionality requires specialized software and additional hardware, and typically protects a single application. In a virtual environment, this functionality is designed into the architecture, protects all of the virtual machines on the host, and is transparent to the guest operating systems and their applications. Application workloads that in the past could not be protected due to cost constraints can now partake of increased availability just by virtue of being on the virtual infrastructure. Ultimately, though, a failed host server means crashed virtual machines, and there is only one exception to this.

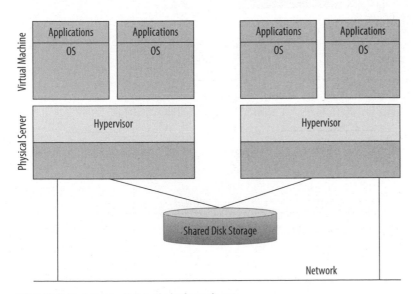

FIGURE 13.2 A virtual platform cluster

Similar to clustering software, but providing greater availability, is *fault tolerance (FT)*. A fault-tolerant virtual machine is able to withstand the failure of a virtualization host without incurring any downtime or impact on the user application. Figure 13.3 shows a simple illustration of a fault-tolerant virtual machine. When fault tolerance is enabled, a second virtual machine is instantiated on a different host than the primary. It rapidly duplicates the state of the primary; and as changes occur on the primary, they are duplicated in lockstep on the secondary. The two virtual machines monitor each other's heartbeat; and in the event of the primary host's failure, the secondary immediately takes over as the primary. A new secondary is created on a different host, and the virtual machine is protected again. No transactions are lost, and users are not impacted. When you're planning capacity resources, remember that a fault-tolerant virtual machine consumes double the resources because two copies are executing in the infrastructure. Additional network resources are also required to convey the continuous virtual machine changes. As with HA, no specialized software is required; the capability is built into the hypervisor and is enabled with a checkbox selection. Because of the extra resource consumption, only mission-critical workloads are selected to be fault tolerant. As of this writing, only VMware provides this ability.

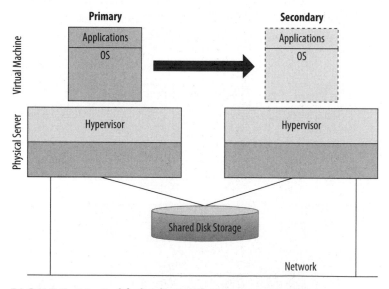

FIGURE 13.3 A fault-tolerant VM

You learned earlier about live migration capabilities, where a virtual machine can be moved from one virtualization host to another without downtime or impacting application performance. While this is an amazing feature, if a physical server fails, it will be too late to move the virtual machines. Where this does impact availability is during planned downtime. In a physical environment when a server needs maintenance, or even replacement, the application needs to go offline until the maintenance or the upgrade is complete. The exception to this would be a system protected by a cluster solution where the application could be failed over to the secondary server for the duration of the maintenance. In a virtual environment, when the server needs to go offline, all of the virtual machines are migrated to other hosts in the cluster. Figure 13.4 illustrates this process. When the host maintenance is complete, the server is added to the cluster again and repopulated with virtual machines. No application downtime is needed and no users are impacted. Hosts can be transparently replaced in the cluster; and maintenance work, since it no longer impacts individual virtual machines, can be done at any time, instead of being scheduled for off hours. This is the type of flexibility that cloud computing services will need to provide to succeed.

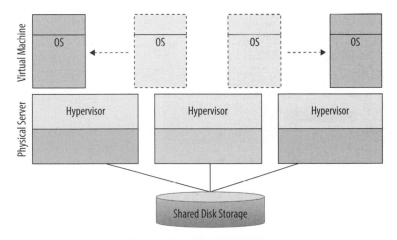

FIGURE 13.4 VM migration during maintenance

Live migration can provide availability to virtual machines during virtualization host maintenance, but that is only part of the infrastructure. There are times when storage arrays also need to be taken offline for maintenance or replacement. Fortunately, a similar technology exists for the storage element of a virtual machine. Figure 13.5 shows a simple illustration of storage migration. While live migration transfers the running virtual machine, in essence the memory structures, from one host to another, storage migration moves the physical files from one disk to another, again while the virtual machine is running, without downtime, and without impacting the application. This ability can help during storage array replacements, moving the virtual machine files from the old array to the new array without downtime. This capacity can also help with performance issues. If a disk is suffering degraded performance due to an uneven distribution of data, storage migration can allow an administrator to rebalance the virtual machine files for a more even performance profile. The latest versions of storage migration can execute this operation in an automated manner, proactively resolving performance problems due to I/O contention.

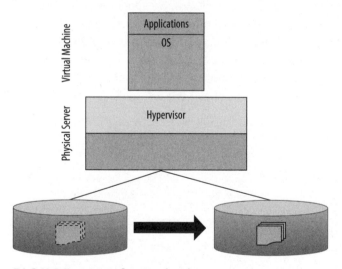

FIGURE 13.5 Storage migration

One last scenario involves a partial host failure. In the event that a network path or a storage path is lost from a particular host, the virtual machines would still be running but unable to access their data or communicate with the users. The virtualization host would also still be running. Newer versions of VMware ESX can determine if the path is still available from other hosts in the cluster. If it is, the HA functionality will fail over the affected virtual machines to the hosts that still have visibility of the network or the storage resource. If the path is not available, or there are not enough resources available to support the HA event, then nothing will happen.

Protecting Data Centers

Even by protecting the infrastructure, there are still events that cannot be con-trolled. Natural and man-made disasters strike without warning, and there is little that can be done for a data center affected by such an event. The results of the event can be even more catastrophic for the company. Unlike the nega-tive publicity short-term outages generate, the loss of a data center often costs the company its existence. According to the National Archives and Records Administration, 93 percent of companies that lost their data centers for 10 days were bankrupt within the year. Even short lapses are devastating. Gartner reported that companies who lose access to their information for more than 24 hours due to a disaster have a 40 percent chance of failing. How do compa-nies mitigate these terrible risks?

Many companies have disaster recovery (DR) plans already in place in case of these scenarios. They either have a secondary data center already in place or have contracted with a service provider who can provide them with an infra-structure to stage the minimum functions critical to the business until they can return to their own data center. This practice applies to both physical and virtual environments, though virtualization adds a few interesting twists. A common practice is to have a portion of the IT staff travel to the DR site with a set of system backups to annually test the plan. This test requires the staff to create a functional duplicate of the application; they will test and measure the effort involved to restore a working environment. Often duplicate hardware needs to be available with matching peripheral infrastructure down to the firm-ware patches on the NIC cards. Another downside is that such exercises frequently test only a fragment of the infrastructure that would be required in the case of an actual emergency. Most successful DR tests restore less than 10 percent of the necessary infrastructure, take three to five business days to execute, and do very limited application testing. The monetary considerations are usually considerable when you factor the travel costs for the team and their time away from their regular job.

Virtualization, even if you change nothing else, allows a team to restore the infrastructure in a manner that is identical to the original. Because the hypervisor abstracts the physical hardware from the guests, you can restore onto any hardware server platform without worry. The setup is merely a hypervisor install, if the hosting provider doesn't already have a virtual environment in place, and then you copy the virtual machine files from the backup media to the disk storage. It isn't quite that simple, but it is close. Vendors have developed many solutions to protect data centers, or at least the critical systems. Application solutions involve different degrees of data replication, near-time or real-time transfers of information to a second site. Storage vendors also leverage replication, shipping data block changes from the storage array in one site to the storage array in a DR site. These often have the advantage of being application agnostic and don't add processing to the CPU because it is all managed and run through the storage array. Virtualization vendors leverage these existing channels to prevent data loss in the event of a disaster. Illustrated in Figure 13.6, VMware's Site Recovery Manager leverages either storage or processor replication to copy a virtual machine's files to the DR site and keep them up-to-date. In the event of a disaster, all of the virtual machines are already at the DR site, ready to be powered on. DR tests are then comprehensive, guaranteeing that all of the necessary virtual machines are available and their data is current. Another advantage of this solution is that a company's DR site can be a local or remote hosting provider with a virtual infrastructure. The company does not necessarily need to build and maintain a private DR site. There are other solutions that provide similar capabilities.

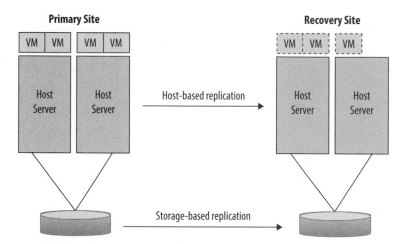

FIGURE 13.6 Site Recovery Manager

New solutions are emerging. In 2015, VMware introduced Cross-Cloud VMotion, where a virtual machine can be migrated from an on-premise virtual infrastructure to an off-premise cloud-based infrastructure without interruption. Another fairly new ability is Long Distance VMotion, the ability to move a virtual machine across a cross-continental distance, again without disrupting the application. Certain infrastructure criteria need to be met for this to be possible, but coupled with advances in virtualized networking and virtualized storage, an entire data center could be moved without interruption. This software-defined data center is setting the stage for a time when workloads might travel the globe to the places where the users are, or to where the resources are, all transparent to their operation. In the context of disaster recovery, by moving the data center out of harm's way before an event, assuming there is time, there might be no need for recovery. These capabilities had been demonstrated in the past; but for wider use, it required much greater network bandwidth than was generally available until recently.

This capability of dynamically shifting a workload without service interruption will be crucial to the deployment of cloud computing. While we are still in the first stages of providing services in this manner, we can already see the need and the higher expectations of companies utilizing these architectures and services. In 2011, Amazon's EC2 (Elastic Compute Cloud) service suffered two sizable outages, and at least one was caused by natural events. Microsoft, who has been transitioning certain online services such as Office365 and Hotmail to their cloud services, also had availability issues throughout the year due to the same natural events as well as some networking issues. A memory management issue prevented millions of Google Docs users from accessing their cloud-based documents. In 2015, through more than fifty outages, Amazon Web Services suffered through only a little more than two and half hours of downtime. Microsoft's Azure platform experienced close to eleven hours of service interruptions across seventy outages, while Google experienced roughly the same downtime with more than double the outages. Clearly, the industry is improving in the handling of cloud-scale architecture, and you can be sure that virtualization will be a large part of providing enterprise-level availability, flexibility, and agility to cloud service infrastructures.

THE ESSENTIALS AND BEYOND

Application availability is crucial to business operations and customer satisfaction. Because the information age we live in offers more services through technology channels, protecting the platforms that support those channels from outages is a top focus. Virtualization combines existing availability solutions that were developed and proven in the physical world with new capabilities possible only with virtual machines. From single virtual machines, to groups of virtual machines on a cluster of hosts, to entire data centers, the virtual infrastructure offers multiple levels of availability. Many workloads, that with a physical server did not merit an HA solution, now can easily have that level of availability, increasing the overall data center uptime. As more businesses embrace cloud computing to deliver services to their external and internal customers and this convenience turns to necessity, the raised expectations to have those services always accessible will drive businesses to employ many of these solutions.

ADDITIONAL EXERCISES

▶ Your company's data center has suffered a recent power outage, and corporate applications were unavailable for two days. You have been asked to craft a strategy to quickly continue operations in the event of another outage. What type of availability (HA/DR/FT) would you recommend and why?

▶ You are asked to provide availability for an application that has been deemed to be critical to the daily operations. Any downtime will potentially cost the company hundreds of thousands of dollars per hour. What type of availability (HA/DR/FT) would you recommend and why?

▶ How would you convince an owner of a business-critical application to move to a virtual environment? Her major concern is sharing a server with other virtual machines that might impact availability.

Understanding Applications in a Virtual Machine

Virtualization and all of its accompanying benefits are changing the way infrastructures are designed and deployed, but the underlying reasons are all about the applications. Applications are the programs that run a company's business, provide them with a competitive advantage, and ultimately deliver the revenue that allows a company to survive and grow. With the corporate lifeblood at risk, application owners are reluctant to change from the existing models of how they have deployed applications to a virtual infrastructure. Once they understand how a virtual environment can help mitigate their risk in the areas of performance, security, and availability, they are usually willing to make the leap. Hypervisors leverage the physical infrastructure to ensure performance resources. Multiple virtual machines can be grouped together for faster and more reliable deployments. As both corporate and commercial services begin to shift to cloud computing models, ensuring that the applications supported on the virtual platforms are reliable, scalable, and secure is vital to a viable application environment.

▶ **Examining virtual infrastructure performance capabilities**

▶ **Deploying applications in a virtual environment**

▶ **Understanding virtual appliances and vApps**

Examining Virtual Infrastructure Performance Capabilities

Our efforts so far have focused on virtual machines and the virtual environment that supports them. While this is valuable, the result has to be that the applications deployed on physical servers can be migrated to these virtual environments and benefit from properties you have already investigated. Applications are groups of programs that deliver services and information to their users. These services and information provide income for their companies. Fearful that the service will be compromised, the groups responsible for the applications (the application owners) are often reluctant to make changes to their environments. Application owners are unwilling to risk application changes that might impact the application's availability, scalability, and security. In Chapter 13, "Understanding Availability," you saw some of the ways a virtual environment can increase the uptime of an application. The ease of altering a virtual machine's configuration to add additional resources can make virtual machines more scalable than their physical counterparts. Other virtualization capabilities, such as live migration or storage migration, bring greater flexibility and agility to applications in a virtual environment. Another area where virtualization provides great benefits is the creation and manageability of the virtual machines through templates and clones, which can significantly reduce application deployment time and configuration errors, both areas that impact a company's bottom line. All of these are important, but probably most crucial is application performance.

Applications that perform poorly are usually short lived because they impact a business on many levels. Aside from the obvious factor that they extend the time it takes to accomplish a task and drive down efficiency, slow applications frustrate users, both internal and external to a company, and could potentially cost revenue. Again, it raises the topic of increased user expectations. Think about your own experiences with online services. Would you continue to purchase goods from a website where the checkout process took 20 minutes, or would you find another vendor where it would be less cumbersome? This is one reason why application owners are hesitant about virtualization—they are unsure about sharing resources in a virtualization host when their current application platform is dedicated entirely to their needs, even though it might be costly and inefficient.

Virtualization has a number of technologies that allow a business-critical application to get the resources it requires to operate quickly and efficiently, even at the expense of less critical virtual machines. The model used here is from VMware's ESXi solution. While these features are not in every vendor's virtualization solution, as products evolve, they will probably appear in some future release. The first of these is resource settings. Each virtual machine has three settings that can be adjusted to affect the amount of CPU and memory resources that it can receive. Figure 14.1 illustrates the options for these virtual machine settings (Shares, Reservations, and Limit). The first setting is Shares, and it is used to measure against the *shares* that other virtual machines have been allocated to determine precedence. If a virtual machine has half the CPU shares of another virtual machine, it will be entitled to only half of the resources. In times of CPU contention, a virtual machine with more shares will be entitled to more scheduled CPU time. A *reservation* is the guaranteed minimum that a virtual machine will always have, even when resources are scarce. If there are not enough resources on a virtualization host to meet the reservation, the virtual machine cannot be powered on, and the virtual machine will be powered on in another host in the cluster. The *limit* is the greatest amount of resources that can be allocated to a virtual machine. This is normally not used because the resource configured for the virtual machine, the memory amount or number of processors, is the upper limit.

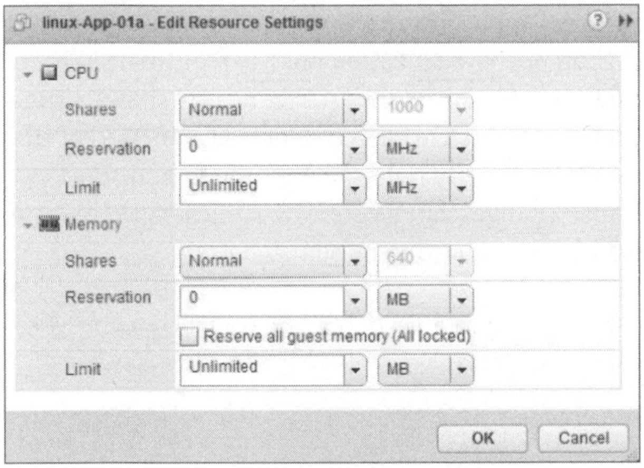

FIGURE 14.1 Virtual machine resource settings

On a single virtualization host, the hypervisor uses these settings to prioritize how memory and CPU resources should be rationed. If there is no resource contention, then all the virtual machines receive all of the resources they require, as they need them. This is the optimal scenario. In situations where virtual machines begin to request more resources than the physical host can provide, the hypervisor will allocate the resources using the resource settings as the governing rules. When these settings are configured correctly, virtual machines that contain critical applications can be assured of receiving enough resources to maintain their performance. Less critical applications may suffer performance degradation, but that should not impact the business.

This model is simple enough for a single virtualization host, but what happens in the case of a virtualization cluster? Here *resource pools* are used. The name is an accurate description of its function: a pool of resources. Resource pools can be applied on a single virtualization host, or across multiple hosts in a cluster, and they aggregate the CPU cycles and memory to be shared out among the virtual machines, groups of virtual machines, or other entities such as departments. Resource pools can be further subdivided into smaller child resource pools, enabling an administrator to have more granular control of the resource allocation. The options for managing a resource pool are similar to the individual virtual machine settings and involve defining resource shares, reservations, and limits. The difference is that you then assign multiple virtual machines to each of these pools, and that resource pool can span one or more virtualization hosts. Again, a critical application composed of multiple virtual machines, spread across more than one virtualization host, can be assured that enough resources will always be available for its needs. Figure 14.2 shows a simple example of two resource pools on a cluster. Each is allocated a portion of the aggregate resources with some extra capacity put aside for growth and short-term performance spikes. Because changes can be done dynamically, there is no performance impact when resource pools need to be adjusted.

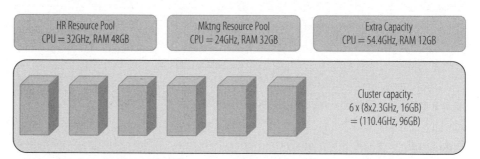

| HR Resource Pool | Mktng Resource Pool | Extra Capacity |
| CPU = 32GHz, RAM 48GB | CPU = 24GHz, RAM 32GB | CPU = 54.4GHz, RAM 12GB |

Cluster capacity:
6 x (8x2.3GHz, 16GB)
= (110.4GHz, 96GB)

FIGURE 14.2 Resource pools

Another feature that aids good application performance in a virtual environment is live migration. If an application in a physical server runs out of resources, the application needs to be taken offline to add additional resources to the server, or to replace the server entirely with a larger machine. You saw earlier that virtual machines are nimbler because in the same circumstance adding resources would require minimal downtime, if any, depending on the operating system hot-add capability. But what happens in a virtualization server where most of the physical resources are already being consumed by the multiple virtual machines being hosted, and more resources are being demanded by a VM? In this case, one or more virtual machines can be live migrated to other virtualization hosts in the cluster, freeing up resources for the hungry virtual machine. When the resource demand has been satisfied, and the overall requirement on the virtualization host recedes to previous levels, virtual machines can be migrated back. Obviously, resources need to be available on the other hosts in order to migrate the guests there. If there are no more available resources in the cluster, it is time to add more hosts to the cluster. Does this mean a virtualization infrastructure administrator needs to constantly monitor the performance characteristics of the cluster in order to actively migrate virtual machines? Fortunately, that level of involvement is not necessarily required. Virtual infrastructure solutions have automated load-balancing capabilities as part of the architecture. When, from a resource-utilization standpoint, a cluster becomes unbalanced, virtual machines can automatically be migrated from one virtualization host to another, providing an optimal and even allocation of the available resources.

This is a simple description of a sophisticated performance load-balancing mechanism. There are levels of automation that can be configured allowing administrators to oversee the process or permitting a fully automated migration strategy. Complex application rules, such as *VM-affinity,* can be applied that guarantee certain virtual machines always run together on the same physical server, ensuring that if one virtual machine is migrated, the other goes with it. One reason for this might be that the two virtual machines are constantly exchanging high amounts of data. On the same virtualization host, that traffic occurs at high speed on the virtual network, rather than having to traverse a slower physical wire between physical hosts. An additional benefit of this situation is that the whole of the network data volume between these two VMs has been removed from the physical network, freeing that capacity for other work and extending the network bandwidth.

The converse, *anti-affinity,* can be configured as well, guaranteeing that if necessary, two selected virtual machines won't ever be permitted to be guests on the same virtualization host. This case might be used where a critical application service provided by redundant virtual machines would still be available in the event of a virtualization host failure. In Chapter 13, "Understanding Availability," you learned about storage migration. Like live migration, storage migration can also be automated, allowing virtual infrastructures to communicate with storage arrays to automatically resolve disk performance issues without needing a storage administrator to discover, diagnose, and resolve the issue.

Though you saw mention of them earlier, it is worth a brief second look at two other features. In Chapter 9, "Managing Storage for a Virtual Machine," one of the tuning features discussed was Storage I/O Control, a quality of service capability that can moderate storage throughput on a per virtual machine basis. By assigning higher priorities to the virtual machines of a critical application, you can ensure that disk I/O contention will not be a bottleneck for that application. That is, of course, assuming that there are enough physical resources to accommodate the need. Priorities are administered with shares and limits as you saw with the resource pools. Similarly, in Chapter 10, "Managing Networking for a Virtual Machine," you learned that there is a capability to prioritize network throughput as well. Also administered with shares and limits, Network I/O Control can be applied to traffic types, groups of virtual machines, and individual virtual machines. Both of these technologies can ensure good performance for critical applications, even in situations that might otherwise be subject to resource pressure. As a secondary effect, they improve efficiency by reducing the time and effort an application administrator needs to monitor and manage these types of performance issues.

These are not all of the things that can be applied to ensure good performance for applications staged in virtual machines. You have seen before that good configuration and architecture practices in the various infrastructure areas—CPU, memory, network, and storage—all offer similar benefits when translated from physical to virtual systems. The same applies here as well. The use of more and faster disks will provide better response time from storage devices. More bandwidth accommodates less network contention. Virtualization features contribute to greater availability, flexibility, and better performance, but they are not the sole reasons.

Deploying Applications in a Virtual Environment

The best way to be sure that an application performs well is to understand the resource needs of the application, but more importantly, to measure that resource usage regularly. Once you understand the requirements, you can begin to plan for deploying an application in a virtual environment. There are some things that you can always count on. A poorly architected application in a physical environment is not necessarily going to improve when moved to a virtual environment. An application that is starved for resources will perform poorly as well. The best way to be sure an application will perform correctly is to allocate the virtual machine enough resources to prevent contention. Let's look at a simple example.

Many applications are delivered in a three-tier architecture, as shown in Figure 14.3. The configuration parameters in the figure are merely sample numbers. There is a database server where the information that drives the application is stored and managed. Usually, this will be Oracle, Microsoft SQL Server, or maybe the open-source-solution MySQL. This server is typically the largest one of the three tiers with multiple processors and a large amount of memory for the database to cache information in for rapid response to queries. Database servers are resource hungry for memory, CPU, and especially storage I/O throughput. The next tier is the application server that runs the application code—the business processes that define the application. Often that is a Java-oriented solution, IBM Websphere, Oracle (BEA) WebLogic, or open-source Tomcat. In a Microsoft environment, this might be the .NET framework with C#, but there are many frameworks and many application languages from which to choose. Application servers usually need ample CPU resources, have little if any storage interaction, and have average memory resources. Finally, there is the web server. Web servers are the interface between users and the application server, presenting the application's face to the world as HTML pages. Some examples of web servers are Microsoft IIS and the open-source Apache HTTP server. Web servers are usually memory dependent because they cache pages for faster response time. Swapping from disk adds latency to the response time and might induce users to reload the page.

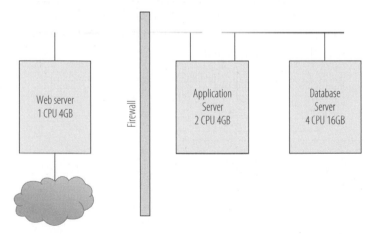

FIGURE 14.3 Three-tier architecture—physical

When you visit a website, the web server presents you with the HTML pages to interact. As you select functions on the page, perhaps updating your account information or adding items to a shopping cart, the information is passed to the application server that performs the processing. Information that is needed to populate the web pages, such as your contact information or the current inventory status of items you are looking to purchase, is requested from the database server. When the request is satisfied, the information is sent back through the application server, packaged in HTML, and presented to you as a web page. In a physical environment, the division of labor and the division of resources is very definite because each tier has its own server hardware and resources to utilize. The virtual environment is different.

Figure 14.4 shows one possible architecture for this model. Here, all of the tiers live on the same virtual host. In practice, that is probably not the case, but for a small site it is definitely possible. The first consideration is that the virtualization host now needs to be configured with enough CPU and memory for the entire application, and each virtual machine needs to have enough resources carved out of that host configuration to perform adequately. The virtual machine resource parameters discussed earlier—shares, limits, and reservations—can all be used to refine the resource sharing. Note that while in the physical model, all of the network communications occurred on the network wire; here, it all takes place at machine speeds across the virtual network in the virtualization host. Here also, the firewall separating the web server in the DMZ from the application server can be part of the virtual network. Even though the application server and the database server are physically in the same host as the web server, they are protected from external threats because access to them would need to breach the firewall, the same as in a physical environment. Because they do not have direct access to an external network, through the firewall is the only way they can be reached.

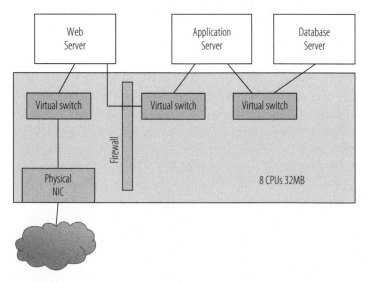

FIGURE 14.4 Three-tier architecture—virtual

As the application performance requirements change, the model can easily adjust. Applications that need to support many users run multiple copies of the web server and the application server tiers. In a physical deployment, it would not be unusual to have dozens of blade servers supporting this type of application. Load balancers are placed between the tiers to equalize traffic flow and redirect it in the event of a web server or application server failure. In a virtual environment, the same can be true when deploying load balancers as virtual machines. One large difference is that as new web servers or application servers are needed to handle an increasing load, in a virtual environment, new virtual machines can be quickly cloned from an existing template, deployed in the environment, and used immediately. When there are numerous cloned virtual machines on a host running the same application on the same operating system, page sharing is a huge asset for conserving memory resources. When resource contention occurs in a virtualization cluster, virtual machines can be automatically migrated, assuring best use of all of the physical resources. Live migration also removes the necessity of taking down the application for physical maintenance. Finally, in the event of a server failure, additional copies of the web server and application server on other virtualization hosts keep the application available, and high availability will restore the downed virtual machines somewhere else in the cluster.

With all of the different layers and possible contention points, how do you know what is happening in an application? There are tools that will monitor the activity in a system and log the information so it will be available for later analysis and historical comparison. This information can be used to detect growth trends for capacity modeling exercises, allowing the timely purchase of additional hardware, and prevent a sudden lack of resources. Virtualization vendors supply basic performance management and trending tools as part of their default management suites. Additional functionality is offered as add-on solutions for purchase. There is also a healthy third-party market of tools that supports multiple hypervisor solutions. As always, there are many tools developed as shareware or freeware and easily available as a download. All of these can be viable options, depending on your particular use case. The point is that measuring performance, and understanding how an application is functioning in any environment, should be a mandatory part of an organization's ongoing application management process.

1. For a quick look at observing performance in a virtual machine, power on the Linux virtual machine you created in Chapter 6, "Installing Linux on a Virtual Machine."

2. Log in to the virtual machine.

3. Open a browser and navigate to the website `http://dacapobench` `.org/`. DaCapo is a benchmark suite that you will use to generate load on the Linux virtual machine.

4. Select the Download link on the left side of the page. On the Download page, click on the first hyperlink, which will download the dacapo `jar` file. A new tab will open on another site where the download is staged. Documentation is available on the DaCapo site. Navigate into the `9.12-bach` folder and download the dacapo `jar` file. When the Download window appears, as shown in Figure 14.5, choose Save File and select OK. The download is large (~160 MB) and will take a few minutes, depending on your network connection. Close both the Download window and the browser when it completes.

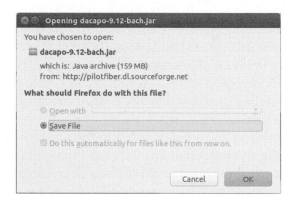

F I G U R E   1 4 . 5   Saving the `jar` file

5. Open a Terminal window, which you can find by selecting the top icon in the left panel known as the Dash. If Terminal is not displayed as one of the Application offerings, enter **terminal** in the search bar, and then open a Terminal window. Navigate to the directory where you downloaded the `jar` (Java Archive) file. The default download directory is the Downloads directory and it is located at `/home/<user>/Downloads`.

6. Execute the benchmark by entering **java -jar dacapo-9.12-bach .jar h2**. This is an in-memory benchmark test that will stress the virtual machine. It will run through the benchmark test and finish

by displaying metrics about the test, as shown in Figure 14.6. If you receive an error message stating that java isn't available, select one of the offered packages and follow the suggested command to install it.

```
essentials@essentials-VirtualBox:~/Downloads$ java -jar dacapo
-9.12-bach.jar h2
Using scaled threading model. 1 processors detected, 1 threads
 used to drive the workload, in a possible range of [1,4000]
===== DaCapo 9.12 h2 starting =====
....
Completed 4000 transactions
        Stock level ............   155 ( 3.9%)
        Order status by name ....  108 ( 2.7%)
        Order status by ID ......   65 ( 1.6%)
        Payment by name ........  1050 (26.2%)
        Payment by ID ...........  661 (16.5%)
        Delivery schedule .......  167 ( 4.2%)
        New order ..............  1774 (44.4%)
        New order rollback ......   20 ( 0.5%)
Resetting database to initial state
===== DaCapo 9.12 h2 PASSED in 12048 msec =====
essentials@essentials-VirtualBox:~/Downloads$
```

FIGURE 14.6 Executing the benchmark test

7. You might be underwhelmed by that last step because there is not that much to see. Monitoring the resources of the virtual machine will show how the benchmark application affects the system. Select the top icon in the left panel, also known as the Dash. If you hover over the icon, it will display "Search your computer and online sources." In the text bar, enter system. A number of choices, both utilities in your virtual machine and other things the extended search system has found, are displayed. Select System Monitor. Select the Resources tab, as shown on Figure 14.7.

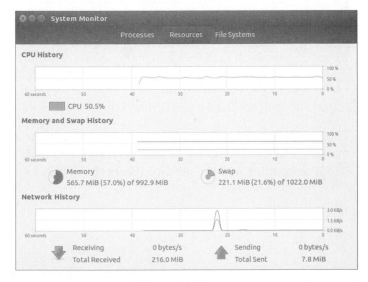

FIGURE 14.7 The System Monitor

8. The screen displays the last 60 seconds of activity for CPU utilization, memory and swap usage, and network I/O. Because the benchmark is memory based, you should see activity in the first two areas. Move the Terminal window so you can enter commands and see the System Monitor.

9. Execute the benchmark test again and watch the effect. As illustrated in Figure 14.8, you can see an instant rise in CPU utilization spiking to the 100 percent mark where it remains for the duration of the test. Although memory rises, it never goes above 50 percent utilization, so it seems the 2 GB of memory allocated for this virtual machine is more than adequate. Swapping and network I/O are not affected.

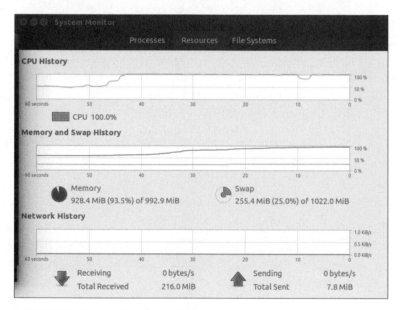

FIGURE 14.8 Benchmark effects

10. This is only half the picture—the view from inside of the virtual machine and the resources that have been allocated to it. The next step is to examine how this activity affects the virtualization host.

Resize the Virtual Machine window on your desktop so you have space for another window.

11. On the Windows toolbar, enter **perf** into the Search The Web And Windows text box. Select the Performance Monitor program to open it. Position it so you can see both the Performance Monitor and the virtual machine, as shown in Figure 14.9.

12. In the Performance Monitor, open the Monitoring Tools folder and highlight the Performance Monitor icon. The default display is the CPU performance, and you can observe the CPU utilization. You can clear the Monitor window by right-clicking on the performance chart and selecting Clear from the menu.

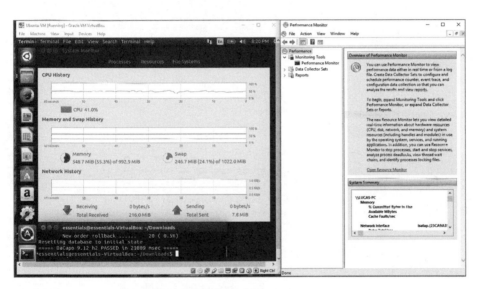

FIGURE 14.9 Examining the virtualization host

13. In the Linux virtual machine, restart the benchmark test. In the Linux System Monitor, everything occurs as it did in previous iterations. The CPU activity spikes to 100 percent for the duration of the

test. In the Performance Monitor, as shown in Figure 14.10, the CPU utilization spikes as well, but far short of the top. In an actual application environment, this might indicate that you need to add one or more vCPUs to the virtual machine for improved performance.

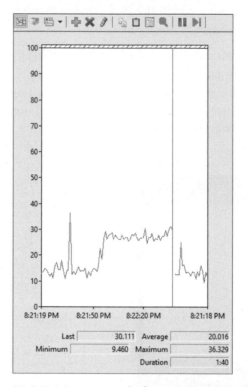

FIGURE 14.10 Performance Monitor on the host

These are obviously simple tools and simple tests but even in large multi-tier and multiple-system application deployments, the same principles apply. In a virtual environment, performance measurements need to be done from inside the virtual machine to understand where resources are constrained and affecting application performance. Measurements also need to be done on the virtualization host and at the overall cluster layer to have a full picture of the performance environment. Many organizations undergo constant performance monitoring of their critical applications, allowing them to regularly review how their environment is behaving. With this information, they can be proactive about preventing resource constraints, instead of waiting for issues to occur and managing them in the midst of application problems.

Understanding Virtual Appliances and vApps

The three-tier application discussed earlier was probably created by a number of people in the IT department, although in smaller shops one person can wear all of the hats. A virtualization administrator created the original virtual machines and configured them according to some basic parameters. An operating system engineer provisioned the operating systems on each one and then updated it with the latest patches. Any corporate standard tools were added at this time. The application developer or specialist then installed and configured the application components—web server, application server, application code, and database. Integration tests were run to validate and stress the virtual machines as an application unit. Once all the testing was complete and any resulting changes had been applied, they were converted into templates, the gold images to produce the production virtual machines. You learned earlier that virtual machines can speed this provisioning procedure by orders of magnitude, but it is still a transfer of the physical server provisioning process to a virtual infrastructure without fundamental operational changes. Virtual appliances change this model.

Virtual appliances are prebuilt virtual machines that already contain everything needed to deploy an application. Often the operating system is an open-source deployment or a specially developed thin OS, also called JeOS (pronounced "juice," for Just Enough Operating System) that only has what the application requires and no more. Because of this, virtual appliances require none of the patching and maintenance of a traditional operating-system-based installation. When a new version is available, the entire virtual machine is replaced, minimizing the time needed to deploy a new release. In many cases a virtual appliance installation consists of a download, unpacking the virtual machine on a virtualization host, powering it on, and performing some minimal configuration steps to connect it to the desired network and storage. Virtual appliances are often delivered in OVF format so they can be quickly deployed on any hypervisor solution.

WHERE CAN YOU GET A VIRTUAL APPLIANCE?

Software application providers are beginning to offer their solutions as virtual appliances. It makes the acquisition and deployment of the solution much simpler than traditional methods. There are repositories of virtual appliances available at:

VMware

`http://www.vmware.com/appliances/directory/`

JumpBox

`http://www.jumpbox.com/library`

Oracle

`http://www.oracle.com/technetwork/community/developer-vm/index.html?ssSourceSiteId=ocomen`

Vagrant

`https://atlas.hashicorp.com/boxes/search?page=0`

They are also available from thousands of other software providers that an Internet search will return. Some, as in the case of Oracle, are only in a proprietary format, while many others are offered as OVFs. As antivirus and security models change in the virtual environment, vendors such as Trend Micro are offering their solutions as virtual appliances. There is also a profusion of open-source tools now being offered as virtual appliances. Some examples of these are StressLinux (`http://www.stresslinux.org/`) and Apache CouchDB (`http://wiki.apache.org/couchdb/FrontPage`).

The next step is to package one or more virtual machines that comprise an application into a container. This container, called a *vApp,* might contain the three virtual machines described earlier that made up the three-tier application. Like a virtual appliance, a vApp is stored in the OVF format making it easily transportable. A vApp also packages information about the application's networking, availability, and security requirements. Think of a shipping container on a cargo transport ship. When the ship docks, thousands of these containers are offloaded and sent in a thousand different directions quickly and efficiently. Dockyard workers use technology to read the barcodes on each container, which can supply all the inventory, customs, ownership, and routing information. vApps have all of the deployment information as part of their container. When deployed in a virtual environment, a vApp packaged application can be provisioned in the cluster and provide the desired level of availability, security, and the proper network configuration, all without an administrator's assistance or intervention.

This functionality (the ability to rapidly clone, deploy, and move applications while maintaining service levels around application availability, scalability, security, and manageability) is at the heart of the promise of cloud computing. Delivering new services more rapidly and more efficiently—and providing them in a secure, scalable, and highly available manner—will fuel this next evolution of computing. It will not be long before new cloud computing models provide entire data centers with the same capabilities you have seen for virtual machines. The foundation of this new model is virtualization.

Open Stack and Containers

New methods of deploying applications are rapidly appearing. Where virtualization was a disruptive technology a decade ago, new models are now beginning to disrupt virtualization.

One of these is *containers*. Containers provide a technology to package applications and everything those applications need to run into a standard unit that can then be rapidly and repeatedly deployed in many environments. This may sound identical to what virtualization provides, and in many ways the benefits that containers provide mirror what you saw earlier in this text. The differences are where companies make decisions about deployments. For example, one large difference between the two models is that the container engine sits above an operating system and shares the kernel among the containers. Each container has its own files—code, executables, system libraries—just like a virtual machine, except by sharing the kernel code for efficiency, each container must run the same single version of an operating system. As you have seen, each virtual machine can have its own copy of an operating system and VMs on a single host can all run different operating systems without difficulty. If the deployment model only requires a single operating system across of the workloads, then containers might be a possible option. Containers are widely used for development environments because they allow a very rapid instantiation of one or more environments and are easy to share among a team of people. Other use cases involve companies that entirely control their applications from start to finish. Google and eBay are examples of companies that deploy many of their applications and services in a containerized environment. You can learn more about containers at https://www.docker.com/ or http://kubernetes.io/.

OpenStack is an open-source project that is designed to manage pools of compute, network, and storage resources, both in traditional data centers and in cloud computing architectures. It is a framework that includes the compute virtualization we have focused on, adds network and storage services, and provides additional capabilities like orchestration for automation, telemetry for metering, and containers to include engines like Docker or Kubernetes in the framework. Similarly, virtualization engines like VMware ESXi and Red Hat KVM can also be employed as part of an OpenStack infrastructure. As the area of compute virtualization has matured, the complementary and supporting infrastructures have also matured. There are many third-party solutions that provide virtualized storage or virtual networking. More robust solutions include these capabilities and offer integrated performance monitoring, capacity planning, application catalogs, automation and orchestration services, security, compliance, and more. OpenStack is the open-source community version of this effort, allowing anyone to download and use the solution at no cost. Like other open-source projects, developers around the globe contribute code to the project, helping to incrementally add stability and functionality to the whole. Similar to how Red Hat provides enterprise-level support for Linux at a cost, there are companies that provide support for OpenStack as well. You can discover more about the OpenStack project at `https://www.openstack.org/`.

THE ESSENTIALS AND BEYOND

The benefits of virtualization encompass many parts of the data center, but the largest recipients are the applications that run in virtual machines. Critical applications need to be in a secure and available environment, or a company can be put at risk. Features such as live migration, rapid provisioning through the use of templates, and high availability all provide applications with that flexible infrastructure and many advantages they could not leverage as physical deployments. Application performance in a virtual machine is the most common reason for application owners to hesitate before adopting virtual deployments. Proper configuration through the use of monitoring tools can ensure performance that equals or exceeds a physical deployment. Applications can be delivered as preloaded virtual appliances, reducing costs and deployment times even further. As cloud computing continues to expand, applications will be deployed in virtual data centers and resource pools will be carved out of large physical infrastructures. These models are supporting an ever-increasing number of the services we consume, and virtualization is the technology that supports it all.

(Continues)

THE ESSENTIALS AND BEYOND *(Continued)*

ADDITIONAL EXERCISES

▶ Download a virtual appliance from one of the repositories and power it on. Was it an easier process than what you did earlier when you created a virtual machine and installed the operating system? For a simple appliance, you might try one of the many MySQL appliances available. This will provide not just the virtual machine and operating system, but an application as well.

▶ Add a second processor to the Linux virtual machine and rerun the DaCapo h2 benchmark. Are there any performance changes? Is CPU utilization still at 100 percent? If so, what does that tell you about the benchmark? CPU was the bottleneck during the single vCPU tests. Has another bottleneck been uncovered? How are resources affected on the physical host?

▶ Vagrant provides a standardized way for developers to quickly instantiate a virtual machine without managing a library of virtual machines. Since you already have VirtualBox and VMware Workstation installed, spend a few minutes investigating Vagrant at https://www.vagrantup.com/docs/. Download and install the Vagrant package. Then install a Vagrant box. Compare this process with the one in the first exercise and with creating a virtual machine with an operating system by hand.

Answers to Additional Exercises

Chapter 1

- In the 16 years that have passed since the year 2000, processors' speeds have doubled roughly every 18 months, or quadrupled every three years, for an aggregate gain of roughly 2,000 times. If the trend continues, over the next 10 years they will be roughly another 250 times faster than today's processors.

- At the present time, there are more than a dozen different offerings for server virtualization. Of those, the top three cover 95 percent of the commercial market deployments. Two architectures are being deployed in the mainstream, although a few others exist in niche solutions. Cloud-based solutions are also appearing.

- There is no minimum number of servers where virtualization is viable, although at smaller numbers the time for a return on investment (ROI) will be longer. The replacement savings for every physical server removed from an infrastructure go directly to a company's bottom line, aside from virtualization investment, for every year after the initial investment. Environmental savings, such as power and data center square footage, also affect the bottom line. Increased flexibility, greater availability, improved security, and faster, more agile provisioning capabilities easily outweigh any process changes that are implemented. Even if the initial investment costs outweigh the initial savings, the benefits will continue to pay dividends.

Chapter 2

▶ Many Type 2, or hosted, hypervisors are available. A small sample includes VMware Workstation Player, VMware Workstation Pro, VMware Fusion, Microsoft Virtual Server, Oracle VirtualBox, and Parallels Desktop. At a high level, any and all of these do the same thing: they allow users to run one or more virtual machines on their systems. The differences are where users would choose one over another. Some of the solutions are freeware; so if cost is an issue, you might lean toward those. Others, such as VMware Fusion and Parallels Desktop, run on a particular operating system, in this case Mac OSX. Application developers who are more sophisticated users with complex needs might lean to Oracle VirtualBox or Workstation Pro.

▶ The bulk of this effort is currently in server virtualization, but various branches appear in smart devices. Cell phones and tablets are capable of running multiple personalities in the form of guests. A mobile device owned by an employee can easily have a second corporate personality loaded onto it. This workspace can be entirely contained and managed by the company. It wouldn't mix with the personal side of the device, so rogue apps could not affect corporate infrastructure. Other devices, such as smart TVs or even cars, could host multiple personalities that could be preloaded but separate from each other to enable custom personalization for the device, but not overlap the various users.

▶ Like the first exercise, the answer to this question is usually determined by the core need. The more expensive, fuller-featured solution might provide capabilities that will give the business competitive differentiation or improve availability that might be critical to the business. Conversely, the business might not require the extra capabilities of that solution, and a less expensive solution would provide all of the necessary functionality. In this case, the business could save some of its budget for another project. Many vendors also offer different editions of their product from bare bones to all the bells and whistles—think economy car versus luxury sedan. Often, you can begin at the basic tier and upgrade to include advanced features as the company's needs mature.

Chapter 3

▶ There are few remaining reasons not to use virtual machines. The cost savings alone are enough to justify the move from a physical environment to a virtual one. Many of the availability and manageability advantages only add to the move toward virtualization. The few exceptions at this point fall into three main areas. The first are machines that still cannot be virtualized due to their sheer size and resource requirements. At this writing, VMware can support 128 virtual CPUs in a single virtual machine and up to 4 terabytes of memory. Both are more than large enough to support more than 99.9 percent of the physical x86 servers that are currently in use. Second are systems that have physical devices that are part of the server and cannot be virtualized. *Faxboards* are one example of this. Other servers require a physical server because of application licensing requirements that check for certain physical components. Over time, many of these devices and checks are being added to the virtual environment as well. Lastly, some organizations feel that certain minimum server quantity thresholds need to be reached before virtualizing their environments is worth it. There is no correct minimum value that indicates virtualization would be beneficial to an organization. Even organizations with a handful of servers can accrue both operational and capital advantages by moving to a virtual environment.

▶ As of this writing, there are dozens of different places to find and download the thousands of virtual appliances that are available. They are not all available in the OVF format, although many are. Some application providers supply their appliances only in a format that is targeted for a specific hypervisor. This might be due to partnerships or alliances they maintain with the virtualization company, or sometimes it is just due to lack of the resources needed to maintain support for multiple virtualization platforms.

▶ The requirements for an OVF package are fairly simple. At a minimum, it requires an OVF *descriptor*, which is an XML document that describes the package and its contents. Additional material is optional. That additional material, though, would take the form of the virtual machine files—both the configuration files and the virtual disk files. An OVF package can also contain more than one virtual machine. The package can also be stored or transported as a single file using the TAR format to bundle the package contents.

Chapter 4

▶ The minimum value is based on the guest operating system selected and what the operating system vendor recommends. The maximum value is based on the total available physical memory minus the overhead for VMware Workstation Player and the host operating system. On a 32-bit host, the maximum amount of memory a single VM can be assigned is 8 GB. On a 64-bit host, the maximum amount of memory a single VM can be assigned is 64 GB. This is considerably less than what is possible with the Type 1 hypervisor solution but usually more than enough for the work done on the Type 2 hypervisor solution.

▶ The virtual machine that was created is close to the bare minimum as far as hardware devices go. You could still remove the sound card and printer without affecting the system. Leaving them in will have little effect. Across many virtual machines, unnecessary hardware device definitions consume memory and storage resources. There are no missing devices. Additional hardware devices will be added in later chapters.

▶ The .vmx file is a plaintext file that can be examined to determine how a virtual machine is configured outside of the management interface. You can make adjustments to the virtual machine by editing the .vmx file and then restarting the virtual machine. This is usually not a preferred method because errors in the .vmx file can prevent the virtual machine from booting; it can even cause irreversible damage. There are entries in the file for devices or device parameters that are not active.

Chapter 5

▶ There are many solutions to the first part of the question. One possible solution is Microsoft Hyper-V (https://technet.microsoft .com/en-us/library/mt126119.aspx). As of this writing, it supports seven versions of Windows operating systems from Windows 2008 R2 Server SP1 through Windows Server 2016 Technical Preview. There is support for numerous Linux offerings including CentOS Linux, SUSE Linux, Red Hat Enterprise Linux, Oracle Linux, Debian, Ubuntu, and FreeBSD. Also supported are six desktop Windows versions from Vista SP2 through Windows 10. The answer to the second part of the question would be yes. Supporting older operating systems as virtual machines often allows companies to extend the useful lifetime of applications that are still valuable but are either running on deprecated operating systems or running on hardware that is no longer reliable or repairable.

▶ The depth and breadth of what operating systems each virtualization vendor supports varies widely. They all support versions of Microsoft Windows as well as a wide array of the more popular Linux offerings. Citrix XenServer (`http://docs.citrix.com/content/dam/docs/ en-us/xenserver/xenserver-7-0/downloads/xenserver-7-0-vm- users-guide.pdf`) supports 61 versions of nine different operating systems. VMware (`http://partnerweb.vmware.com/GOSIG/home .html`) supports 26 *different operating systems* and over a hundred versions of those, including 18 Windows versions beginning at MS-DOS 6.22 and Windows 3.1. If your application operating system support requirements are more diverse, it will definitely impact your choice of virtualization platform.

Chapter 6

▶ VMware Workstation Player performs an immediate save and restore of the machine state, but a reboot of the operating system does not occur. The System Monitor Utility needs to be closed and reopened for the value to be refreshed, but the memory is added.

▶ For ordinary users, there are few daemons that run on behalf of only that unique user. You would probably see some related to the file system or some of the other utilities as well as the `vmtoolsd` discussed in Chapter 12, "Managing Additional Devices in Virtual Machines." Connected as root, there are quite a few more visible daemons in addition to those you could see earlier. Because root is the superuser account, all of the system daemon processes are run on its behalf.

When ordinary users require these services, the root processes perform for them, but cannot be affected by ordinary users, providing a degree of security.

Chapter 7

▶ With 4 quad-core physical CPUs, you have 16 CPUs as your processing resource. At 18 vCPUs per physical CPU, you could potentially support 288 single vCPU virtual machines. Keeping 20 percent of the resource in reserve would limit that number to 230. Most hosts do not have this many guests, and the reason is that CPU is rarely the gating resource. It is usually memory.

▶ With four 8-core processors, you would have 32 physical CPUs on which to schedule. At 18 vCPUs per physical CPU, you could potentially support 576 single vCPU guests. Reserving 20 percent would reduce that number to 460. The 17 new guests reduce that number by 68, leaving you with the ability to support 392 single vCPU virtual machines.

Chapter 8

▶ 21 (6 GB times 21 machines plus hypervisor overhead of 1 GB).

▶ 28 (4.5 GB times 28 machines plus hypervisor overhead). Each virtual machine is overcommitted for one-fourth of its allocated total, so it is actually counted for 4.5 GB.

▶ 169 (three-fourths times 169 virtual machines plus hypervisor overhead). Each virtual machine is now only counted for three-fourths of a GB or 768 MB. This is more than the 32 you planned to P2V.

▶ 152 (90 percent of 169 VMs). Because the virtual machines are all running the same operating system and application, there is a good chance that the memory overcommit ratio is very conservative. Depending on the application makeup and performance characteristics, this may or may not be a realistic example.

Chapter 9

▶ With a total of 24 cores, you could dedicate a core to up to 24 virtual machines. With 256 GB of memory, and without taking advantage of memory overcommit, you could deploy up to 32 virtual machines. With a terabyte of disk storage, you can thick provision 10 virtual machines. There could potentially be some disk storage needed for the hypervisor, but it would be negligible enough that you could get to 10 virtual machines. The limiting factor here is the amount of storage available.

▶ At 30 GB per virtual machine, you could now provision up to 33 virtual machines, 23 more than the initial deployment. This would be more than your memory model would support, but with page sharing, you could easily meet this mark. Thirty-three virtual machines would also exceed your 24 processors. The limiting factor is now the number of processors. You would need additional information about how the CPU resources are being utilized before you could make a decision about adding more than 14 virtual machines. You might not want to add many more virtual machines to your host for a number of reasons. As a single host, a potential failure would cause a severe outage of your service. You would probably spend some time getting used to the virtual environment and investigate strategies that would increase availability. Also, you would want to be sure that your physical host could handle all of the demands that were made on it throughout a variety of conditions over a reasonable period of time. If you ran out of resources—CPU or memory, for example—contention would occur and cause performance issues and customer dissatisfaction. On a single host, there is a finite amount of resources to go around, so you'd want to be sure it was always enough.

Chapter 10

▶ Using the Edit Virtual Machine Settings, add a second network adapter and choose the Bridged option. Reboot the virtual machine. Windows will add the device on the reboot. Open a command-line window via cmd.exe and run ipconfig. There should now be two Ethernet adapter connections, each with its own IP address. If they are both bridged adapters with unique IP addresses on the same subnet as your host machine, they should both successfully return the pings.

Chapter 11

▶ The UUID entries of the original and the clone virtual machines should be different. The UUID of the clone was altered when the power-on message asking if the virtual machine might have been moved or copied was answered with "I copied it." If the question was answered with "I moved it," or the cloned virtual machine has not yet been powered on, then the UUIDs would still be identical.

▶ Anything that other systems or applications use to identify a virtual machine would need to be changed. These include, but are not exclusive to, the system name, any IP addresses that are associated with the network connections, and any hard-coded system or network address references in user application code. Network directory tables (DNS) would need to have the new virtual machine added so network requests would be routed to the new system. Without these changes, it might be possible that two virtual machines with the same system name or IP address could be simultaneously active, which would wreak havoc with applications and networking.

▶ When you revert to the original snapshot, the state of the machine at the time of that snapshot is presented. Any changes made to the virtual machine since that snapshot will be undone and not seen. If you revert to a different snapshot, the state of the virtual machine at the time of that snapshot is then presented. Any changes made up until that point will still be seen.

Chapter 12

▶ The short answer is that the virtual machine hardware limits how many of each device you can add to the virtual machine's configuration. In some ways, this mirrors a physical server's limitations due to the limited number of slots available for PC interface cards. In the case of the USB device, it will probably never be an issue because you can connect up to 127 USB devices through one port. This, obviously, may not be a realistic case, but it is possible. In the case of the printer, most modern printers can connect via the Ethernet network or the USB port as well.

▶ USB devices are very simple to connect and disconnect from both physical and virtual machines. They are architected through the USB standard to be able to move from different operating systems as well, without undergoing any reformatting. It should be a simple process to move a file from the host operating system to a USB device, attach that device to the guest operating system, and move the file onto the guest file system. VMware Workstation Player has an advanced feature that actually circumvents this procedure by setting up a shared directory between the host and the guest operating systems. Files placed in the shared directory are visible and accessible to both. You can configure this by enabling Shared Folders under the Options tab of the Virtual Machine Settings.

▶ Mounting and unmounting a virtual floppy disk is probably more time-consuming than difficult, but it is conceptually no harder than actually ejecting a physical floppy disk and reinserting it into another machine. A floppy disk can be mounted across operating systems. Depending on where it was formatted, there might restrictions writing to it, but reading from it should be fine.

▶ Like other physical resources, the hypervisor is managing the connection from the virtual machine to the physical Bluetooth device. The actual connection is more complex than managing USB connectivity. You can find additional details at `https://kb.vmware.com/kb/2005315`.

Chapter 13

▶ This type of outage requires a change of venue because the local resources are unavailable. Your recommendation would be to implement a disaster recovery solution and include the application workloads that are critical to the company's operations.

► Because any amount of downtime would be critical, fault tolerance would be the preferred choice. Depending on other factors, including a disaster recovery option might also be applicable.

► A virtual environment is no less available than a physical environment. If this is indeed a critical application, an HA solution might already be in place. This solution could be run in the virtual environment as well. Other options are available to smooth the transition, bridging from a physical to a virtual machine that would be less expensive than having two physical servers. If there is no HA solution in place, you could offer one, or even provide fault tolerance if the application is indeed critical. Because individual virtual machines cannot affect the physical server, sharing the virtualization host would not affect availability.

Chapter 14

► The Turnkey Linux MySQL virtual appliance is available at `http://www.turnkeylinux.org/mysql`. They have many virtual appliances with different development stacks already preloaded and preconfigured for use. The Ubuntu Linux-based virtual machine can be downloaded (~286 MB and 4 minutes) as an `.ova` file. Read the Usage Details & Logging in for Administration section for pertinent details. Navigate down to the directory with the `.ova` file. Right-click on the file and choose to Open With VMware Player. VMware Player will import the VM and prompt you for a name and path. You can accept the defaults. The virtual machine is imported and begins to boot. It prompts for a root operating system password and a MySQL password. You can choose to skip the offer for Hub Services. Install the security updates. I entered the Advanced menu and then Quit. At the Linux login prompt (`mysql login:`), you can log in as root. At the root prompt (`root@mysql ~#`), you can connect to `mysql` with **mysql -u root -h 10.0.0.19 -p**. Enter the password when prompted. You can see the database is running by a simple `status` command or `show databases;` (note the semicolon at the end). To exit, enter **exit**. This process is much simpler and faster than the process you executed to create virtual machines, plus the database application is already installed and configured.

▶ The benchmark shows that a second thread will be used to execute
the test. Watching the Linux System Monitor shows that while the
vCPU utilization does spike up to 100 percent, it doesn't remain
there. A third vCPU might be warranted—or not warranted if the
performance is now acceptable. Memory is being used at the same
rate, and networking is still unaffected with this test, so there are no
new bottlenecks affecting performance. (On the physical host, CPU
spikes are observed to reach almost 80 percent in my system, but
there is still capacity available if necessary.) Keep in mind that on a
sufficiently provisioned host system, the results might vary, whereas
on a constrained host system, this would be more apparent.

▶ Akin to the virtual appliance, Vagrant provides not just the virtual
machines, but a framework to rapidly and repeatedly download and
instantiate virtual machines. By offering a repository that can be
used among team members or the community at large, standardized
environments can be easily shared. Vagrant is often used in development environments where many iterations of testing need to be
performed, and this methodology skips large amounts of installation
time, allowing projects to be completed faster. This process, once
Vagrant is installed, is slightly faster than the one in the first exercise
but also provides that framework for team collaboration.

Glossary

ballooning

A process that allows the hypervisor to reclaim physical memory pages by forcing the virtual machine operating system to flush memory pages to disk.

bandwidth

A measure of network performance defined by the amount of data that can travel through the network over a period of time. Typically given in bits per seconds.

bare-metal

A computer server without any operating system software installed.

BCDR

Business Continuance and Disaster Recovery. An availability topic area that covers how businesses can protect their business-critical processing from disasters, natural and man-made, that would otherwise destroy or significantly interrupt service from the datacenter.

bridged network

A connection type that allows a virtual machine adapter to have a direct connection to the physical network with a unique IP address.

CIFS

Common Internet File System is similar to NFS but focused on Microsoft Windows environments.

clone

An exact copy of a virtual machine. Once cloned, the new virtual machine still needs final customization to ensure a unique identity.

CNA

Converged Network Adapter. A single network adapter that supports multiple network-protocol types, usually at much greater bandwidths than older NICs.

compression

A memory optimization technique that compresses memory pages and stores them in a designated cache in physical memory, rather than swap them from memory to disk storage.

consolidation

The practice of condensing multiple physical servers into one server through the use of virtualization.

consolidation ratio

A measure of consolidation calculated by counting the number of virtual machines on an individual server.

containment

The practice of deploying new applications on virtual machines, rather than buying, provisioning, and deploying new physical server hardware.

core

Microprocessors come in packages that contain one or more processing units. Each individual processing unit is a core.

CPU

Central Processing Unit. The core or brain of a computer where the user and system commands are executed. Today's computers use microprocessor technology, and the term *processor* is often used interchangeably with CPU.

daemon

A UNIX or Linux program that runs as a background process. Daemons typically perform certain system tasks such as cron (crond), the system scheduler, or managing the ftp capabilities (ftpd).

DAS

Direct Attached Storage. The disk drives that are internal to a physical computer.

data center

A large computer room, an entire floor in a building, or a separate building outfitted and dedicated to the health and well-being of a company's computing infrastructure.

deduplication

A storage technology that compresses data and reclaims disk storage space by removing duplicate copies of information. Only one copy is retained and pointers to that copy replace the additional duplicates. Deduplication can be done on a byte, block, or file level.

DHCP

Dynamic Host Configuration Protocol is a widely used standard that allows servers to assign IP addresses to computers and other devices on a network.

DMZ

A network area outside of a company's firewall that connects to the Internet. Few resources, typically web servers, are kept there. They are hardened against malicious attacks, keep little information of value, and connect to the protected network through a firewall.

Fibre-Channel

An industry standard protocol defined for connecting Storage Area Networks to computers.

FT

Fault Tolerance. Hardware and/or software solutions and implementations that allow a server to lose one or more components to a failure without data loss or service interruption.

guest

A virtual machine, or VM. Called a guest because it runs on a host server.

HA

High Availability. Hardware and/or software solutions and implementations that provide greater uptime and resiliency for a computing infrastructure.

HBA

Host Bus Adapter. Also called a host adapter, it is a hardware device that connects a computer to either a network or a storage network. Originally associated with Fibre-Channel connectivity.

HID

Human Interface Device is a broad definition for a class of computer peripheral devices that either receive or deliver information to humans. Examples of these would be, but are not limited to, mice, touchpads, and joysticks. Newer candidates are Wii remotes and Kinect for Xbox.

host

A physical server that supports virtual machines, or guests.

hyper-threading

An Intel microprocessor technology that improves performance by making more efficient use of the processing scheduling —effectively scheduling two threads of work where there was only one in the past.

hypervisor

Originally called a Virtual Machine Manager, it is a layer of software that is installed either between an operating system and the virtual machines or directly onto the hardware, or "bare-metal," and provides the environment in which the virtual machines operate.

IP address

Internet Protocol address. The unique 32-bit number that identifies a computer or other device on a network. Traditional notation breaks the 32 bits into four 8-bit, or 1-byte, segments. Each byte is converted to a decimal number and the four are separated by periods—e.g., `192.168.000.001`.

iSCSI

Internet Small Computer System Interface is the industry standard that defines how storage devices connect and transfer data to computers by sending the SCSI commands over Ethernet networks.

ISO image

A data file in an industry standard format that contains the exact image of an optical disc, like a CD or a DVD. They are used in this context to contain operating system or application files, usually for installation.

Linux

An open-source operating system that is a UNIX derivative. Usually available for low or no cost, Linux runs on a wide variety of hardware, including mainframe computers, servers, desktops, mobile devices, and other commercial appliances such as cable/satellite boxes, and video game consoles.

load balancer

A hardware or software appliance that balances traffic from multiple sources, preventing one pathway from being overloaded. Load balancers can also redirect traffic in the event of a pathway failure.

memory overcommit

The ability of a hypervisor, through the use of memory management optimizations, to allocate more virtual memory to its virtual machines than the amount of physical memory in the host on which it resides.

modem

A device that turns digital signals into analog signals and back again. A modem allows a user on one computer to connect and share data with a second computer by using a telephone line as the transfer medium. The base technology has evolved and is still in wide use today.

multicore

A microprocessor that contains more than one processing unit.

multipathing

Having more than one path available from data storage to a server by having multiple I/O controllers, network switches, and NIC cards.

NAS

Network Attached Storage is usually disk storage that is connected to one or more computers across a network by a file-based protocol, such as CIFS or NFS. As a file-based system, Network Attached Storage has file systems created and is managed external to the computer systems it supports.

NAT

Network Address Translation. A connection type that allows a virtual machine to share an IP address on the physical network with other virtual machines. Each virtual machine has a unique local address that is translated to the shared address for outbound traffic, and back again for inbound traffic for proper data delivery.

network switch

A device that connects computers, printers, file servers, and other devices, allowing them to communicate efficiently with each other. In some ways, switches create and define the networks that they manage.

NFS

Network File System is an open industry protocol standard that is typically used for computers to access Network Attached Storage systems.

NIC

Network Interface Card. A device that allows a computer to connect to a network. Also called a network adapter.

NTP

Network Time Protocol is an open standard that defines and implements a computer's ability to synchronize with Internet time servers, or with other servers.

OVF

Open Virtualization Format. A platform-independent industry standard that defines a format for the packaging and distribution of virtual machines.

P2V

Shorthand for Physical to Virtual. The manual or automated process that transfers the data on a physical server into a virtual machine.

The data includes the operating system, applications files, and all data files.

page sharing

A memory optimization technique in which identical pages in memory are stored only as a single copy and shared between multiple virtual machines. Also works for identical pages in one virtual machine. Similar to disk storage deduplication.

paging

The process that computers use to copy blocks, or pages, of data from disk to memory and back again.

resource pool

An aggregation of resources that permits a virtualization administrator to allocate resources to individual virtual machines, groups of virtual machines, or groups of people.

RHEL

Shorthand for Red Hat Enterprise Linux. Red Hat is one of the leading providers of Linux distributions, and it makes its profit from support rather than license sales. Enterprise Linux is one edition of its offerings.

right-size

The process of configuring a virtual machine to have enough resources for good performance with enough overhead to handle periodic spikes and some growth without vastly over-allocating resources that would be wasted.

SAN

Storage Area Network. A combination of networking resources and disk arrays that provides data storage for computers. Multiple computers will access the SAN, which is external to the physical (or virtual) servers.

SCSI

Small Computer System Interface is the industry standard that defines how storage devices connect and transfer data to computers.

SMP virtualization

Symmetric Multiprocessing. A computer architecture that provides enhanced performance through the concurrent use of multiple processors and shared memory.

snapshot

A snapshot is a set of files that preserve the state of a virtual machine at a given point in time so you can repeatedly revert back to that given state. A virtual machine can have multiple snapshots.

swap space

Disk space reserved for memory pages to be written to in the event that not enough memory is available in the virtual (or physical) machine for the work that needs to be done.

template

A virtual machine that is used as a mold for a commonly used configuration. Once deployed from a template, the virtual machine still needs final customization, such as being given a unique system name and network information.

USB

Universal Service Bus, or USB, is an industry standard for connecting external devices to a computer. The standard defines the physical connections as well as the capabilities for the disparate devices it can support. In addition to data transfer, USB devices can draw electricity from the computer they are connected to for operational power or, in the case of mobile devices, to recharge their internal batteries.

vCPU

A virtual CPU. The virtual representation of a computer processor.

VM-affinity (and anti-affinity)

VM-affinity rules link together two or more virtual machines so they reside on the same virtualization host. Anti-affinity rules ensure that two machines do not reside on the same virtualization host. Live migration, automatic and manual, as well as high-availability recovery, will respect these rules.

VMware tools

A combination of device drivers and processes that enhance the user's experience with the virtual machine, improve virtual machine performance, and help manage the virtual machine. VMware tools are specific to VMware, but other virtualization vendors provide similar suites.

virtualization

The process by which physical servers are abstracted into software constructs that, from their user's standpoint, appear and behave identically to their physical counterparts.

virtual machine, or VM

A container that runs a guest operating system and applications in a software abstraction of a physical server. A powered-off virtual machine is merely a set of files that comprise and describe the virtual hardware and the data that make up the virtual machine.

INDEX